Health Education in Context: An International Perspective on Health Education in Schools and Local Communities

Editors

Neil Taylor, Frances Quinn and Michael Littledyke
University of New England, Armidale, Australia

and

Richard K. Coll
University of Waikato, Hamilton, New Zealand

SENSE PUBLISHERS
ROTTERDAM/BOSTON/TAIPEI

A C.I.P. record for this book is available from the Library of Congress.

ISBN: 978-94-6091-874-2 (paperback)
ISBN: 978-94-6091-875-9 (hardback)
ISBN: 978-94-6091-876-6 (e-book)

Published by: Sense Publishers,
P.O. Box 21858,
3001 AW Rotterdam,
The Netherlands
http://www.sensepublishers.com

Printed on acid-free paper

TABLE OF CONTENTS

NEIL TAYLOR, FRANCES QUINN, MICHAEL LITTLEDYKE AND
RICHARD K. COLL

1. HEALTH EDUCATION IN CONTEXT

An Overview and Some Observations

INTRODUCTION

This book presents a range of international perspectives on the development and
implementation of health education. It is the third in a series that has previously
explored science education and environmental education in largely non-Western
contexts, particularly those in developing countries. The obviously strong links
between science, the environment, and health mean there is considerable overlap in
aspects of education relating to these three areas. Also, because health is
influenced by lifestyles and the environment people live in, and because people's
lifestyles and consumer habits directly affect the environment, health is a key
aspect of sustainable development.

Despite enormous advances in health and medicine in recent times, significant
challenges still exist, especially in developing countries where resources are
often limited. Since the advent and recognition of HIV/AIDS in 1981, the disease
has spread to infect more than 33.3 million people worldwide, with the greatest
incidence of infection occurring in sub-Saharan Africa (United Nations, 2010).
The enormous social and economic toll that this epidemic exacts on countries
means that it tends to receive a high profile in the media. However, HIV/AIDS
sometimes overshadows other important health issues of much longer standing.
For example, more than one billion people are infected with soil-transmitted
helminthes, for example, hookworms, while about 200 million people are
infected with parasitic waterborne worms (schistosomes), which cause the
chronic and debilitating disease known as bilharzias (Focusing Resources on
Effective School Health, 2011). About 225 million cases of malaria occurred
worldwide in 2009, with associated deaths of about 781,000 people, many of
whom were children from sub-Saharan Africa (World Health Organization,
2010a). Much of the disease burden in developing countries is associated
with wider problems, including poor environmental hygiene, poverty, and
inadequately resourced or staffed health services (World Health Organization,
2010b).

Furthermore, the growing middle class in many developing countries is
associated with the emergence of more chronic health issues related to lifestyle
choices. Over the past few decades, diabetes, heart disease, and obesity have
become much more prevalent as individuals move away from traditional

low-energy diets and embrace high-energy convenience foods. This change is often accompanied by an increase in more sedentary lifestyles. These lifestyle changes are also affecting children in these countries, with Southeast Asia, the Pacific Islands, the Middle East, and China facing the most serious threat (Hossain, Kawar, & El Nahas, 2007). Moreover, issues relating to mental health and wellbeing are receiving increasing attention outside of Western contexts.

A considerable body of research highlights the relationship between children's health and their social and educational outcomes. The literature also notes the reciprocal benefits of access to quality education on individual and family health status (see, for example, Basch, 2010). While medical advances can play a significant role in improving health outcomes, education at the school and community level is also crucial in promoting the measures that are so important in preventing and thereby reducing the incidence of many diseases and other health problems.

Against this background, this book explores developments in health education in the formal and non-formal sectors of non-Western countries (loosely interpreted to include countries outside of the English-speaking block of the UK, USA, Canada, Australia, and New Zealand). The intention is to provide the reader with a picture of the developments that are taking place in health education across a range of countries and about which little has been written.

THEORETICAL BASIS OF THE BOOK

As with the previous publications in this series, the theoretical basis to this book is derived from sociocultural theories of learning championed by authors such as Vygotsky (1986) and Wertsch (1991). Sociocultural views of learning place considerable emphasis on the social component within the particular context or situation in which learning occurs. The basic tenet of a sociocultural approach is that human mental functioning is inherently situated in social-interactional, cultural, institutional, and historical contexts. This, to some extent, explains the various taboos associated with many health issues in both Western and non-Western contexts. Beliefs about how diseases are contracted can often be scientifically inaccurate but may be advocated by large sectors of societies and cultures. Furthermore, what is accepted as treatment practice in one context may be rejected in another.

ABOUT THE CONTRIBUTORS

The book draws upon the experiences and research of local experts from an extremely diverse cohort across the world. It is intentionally diverse in its approach to health issues and education. Most authors provide a broad overview of the major health challenges specific to their country or region. Some continue this overview approach by examining the major national developments in formal and non-formal health education, while others focus on specific health education case studies. Some chapters take the form of a story or narrative; others draw from particular research inquiries conducted by authors and their colleagues. Many of the stories contained in this book highlight the interplay between social, political, economic, and environmental matters and the health issues people are experiencing. That they do makes evident the need for policymakers and practitioners to attend to these interlinked aspects of the health context when determining interventions and education aimed at improving health outcomes, and when securing funding for these initiatives.

Between them, the book's authors address many topics. The following list is but a sample: the content of health education (HE) and its integration into national and school curriculums, the impact of formal and non-formal HE programs, the influence of political, cultural, societal, and religious mores on HE, and tensions between government ministries (in particular health and education) for ownership of HE.

We (the book's editors) have made a conscious effort to allow the contributors' own voices to be heard. This book represents their stories, not ours.

REFERENCES

Basch, C. (2010). *Healthier students are better learners: A missing link in school reforms to close the achievement gap* (Equity Matters: Research Review No. 6). New York: Colombia University. Available online at http://www.ashaweb.org/files/HealthierStudentsCB.pdf.

Focusing Resources on Effective School Health (FRESH). *Access to health and nutrition services.* Retrieved from http://www.freshschools.org/Pages/AccesstoHealthandNutritionServices.aspx.

Hossain, P., Kawar, B., & El Nahas, M. (2007). Obesity and diabetes in the developing world—a growing challenge. *The New England Journal of Medicine, 356*(3), 213–215.

United Nations. (2010). *Global report: UNAIDS report on the global AIDS epidemic 2010: Joint United Program on HIV/AIDS (UNAIDS).* Available online at http://issuu.com/unaids/docs/unaids_globalreport_2010.

Vygotsky, L. (1986). *Thought and language* (A. Kozulin, Trans.). Cambridge, MA: MIT Press.

Wertsch, J. V. (1991). A sociocultural approach to socially shared cognition. In L. B. Resnick, J. M. Levine, & S. D. Teasly (Eds.), *Perspectives on socially shared cognition* (pp. 85–100). Washington, DC: American Psychological Association.

World Health Organization (WHO). (2010a). *World malaria report 2010.* Geneva, Switzerland: Author. Available online at http://www.who.int/malaria/publications/atoz/9789241564106/en/index.html.

World Health Organization (WHO). (2010b). *Health systems financing: The path to universal coverage.* Geneva, Switzerland: Author. Available online at http://www.who.int/whr/2010/en/index.html.

Neil Taylor, Frances Quinn and Michael Littledyke
School of Education
University of New England
Armidale
Australia
email: ntaylor6@une.edu.au

Richard K. Coll
Faculty of Science and Engineering
University of Waikato
Hamilton
New Zealand

2. WHOLE SCHOOL APPROACHES TO HEALTH PROMOTION

The Pacific Journey

The Pacific region consists of 22 countries and areas (excluding Australia, New Zealand, and Hawaii). Its total population is approximately nine million people, living on land masses encompassing 551,684 square kilometers and situated within a vast area of ocean. The number of people per country range from around 1,500 in Niue to approximately six million in Papua New Guinea (PNG), which has the largest population in the region.

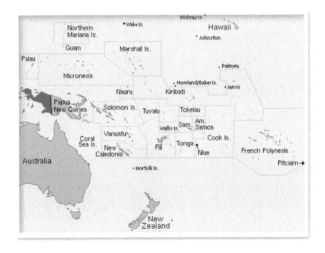

Source: http://www.tropicalresortjobs.com/map

The Pacific is plagued with lifestyle and non-communicable diseases such as obesity, diabetes, heart disease, and cancer, which together are responsible for 75% of all deaths, most occurring prematurely (before people reach age 60). There is a high prevalence of risk factors for these diseases. In some countries, up to 95% of the population in the 25- to 64-year-old age group is overweight, more than 50% smoke cigarettes, and most people do little physical activity (WHO NCD STEPS Survey in the Pacific 2002–2009).

Health and health education in Pacific schools was traditionally left to visiting school clinic nurses and dental teams, who carried out inspection and

N. Taylor, F. Quinn, M. Littledyke and R.K. Coll (eds.), Health Education in Context, 5–16.

monitoring activities, and to classroom teachers, as a curriculum subject. As such, little was done to ensure that the health of students was actively supported and promoted in schools and the wider school community. This situation changed with the introduction of the health promoting schools (HPS) concept to the Pacific in the early 1990s, a concept that gained credibility because of increased understanding that children's health is a major factor affecting their capacity to learn.

The HPS concept is thus seen to offer advantages. One is that health promotion is more effective if it targets children before (hopefully) they have opportunity to develop unhealthy habits. The second is that because schools are a central part of Pacific communities, access to those communities and significant proportions of Pacific Islanders is made relatively easy. Schools in the Pacific typically bring parents, government agencies, school authorities, and key health and education stakeholders together in the interests of the education of their children. Hence, it is not surprising that many Pacific countries chose schools as settings for "healthy islands" within the context of the World Health Organization's (WHO) themes in the late 1990s of *Preparation for Life* and *Protection of Life* (Erben, 1998).

WHO's definition of a health promoting school as "a school that is constantly strengthening its capacity as a healthy setting for living, learning and working" (WHO, 1998, p. 2) positioned schools as a place where all members of the school community could work together to promote and protect health among students, staff, families, and the members of wider societies. The principles and practice of HPS also aligned with application of international declarations such as *Health for All by Year 2000* and *Education for All*, sentiments that Pacific nations embraced.

The HPS concept furthermore supported proactive and preventative measures that many ministries of health in Pacific countries were beginning to welcome. These measures included, amongst others, raising awareness about non-communicable diseases, conducting anti-smoking campaigns, and providing information about HIV/AIDS. However, ownership of these initiatives tended to remain exclusively with the health sectors. Partnerships between ministries of health and ministries of education were the exception rather than the rule. This disjunction has been acknowledged in more recent years, and efforts have been made at regional and national levels to address it.

The focus on health promotion received considerable support from the WHO Regional Office for the Western Pacific (WPRO), which outlined three key strategies for maintaining the initiative over the long term:

- Build supportive policies and links to other health initiatives;
- Collaborate with countries in order to advance the development of HPS; and
- Facilitate training directed at ensuring implementation, monitoring, and evaluation of activities and establishment of HPS-related networks and partnerships, especially with the United Nations and regional organizations.

DEVELOPMENT OF HEALTH PROMOTING SCHOOLS IN THE PACIFIC REGION

At the regional level, the Pacific states are grouped with Asian countries under the WHO Regional Office for the Western Pacific (WPRO) banner. In 1993, the health promotion program for the Pacific region focused on settings through which the program could be supported and implemented. The Pacific states, especially, endorsed schools as settings for this initiative, given that schools are, as noted above, such an integral part of their communities. The policy document *New Horizons in Health*, developed in 1994 by WPRO (WHO, 1995a), assisted member countries to clarify and position health promotion and protection as central features of health programs. A discernible shift in focus from curative to preventative approaches was soon apparent in relation to health initiatives. It may even be fair to say that because of this paradigm shift, every citizen in the region can now find a foothold that will allow him or her to take more responsibility and action with respect to health promotion.

The publication of the *New Horizons in Health* document was followed by a workshop on school health promotion in 1994 in Sydney, Australia (WHO, 1995b). The workshop created urgency and impetus for the development of HPS within the Pacific member states of the region. A similar workshop held soon after in Singapore focused on developing HPS in the northern part of the Western Pacific region. Parallel to and in support of these initiatives, the ministers of health in the Pacific countries expressed their commitment to the Healthy Islands concept via the Yanuca Island Declaration (WHO, 1995c), thereby raising the platform for priority national action in member countries.

Participants at the Sydney workshop welcomed and supported the development of HPS proposed by WHO under the theme *New Horizons in Health, Preparation for Life*. Twenty-seven countries in the Pacific region expressed interest in collaborating to promote school-based health. The outcome of the workshop was an eight-point proposal for guiding further work on the HPS initiative. The following recommendations were put forward:

1. Gain a better understanding of the needs of school students;
2. Engage in effective teaching for health;
3. Foster a healthy school community;
4. Create a supportive school environment;
5. Reorient school health services;
6. Engage families and communities;
7. Develop and implement health-supportive public policy; and
8. Draw on international support and develop networks.

Donor agencies were encouraged to support the implementation of the recommendations, especially in terms of helping build local capacity and expertise, sponsoring country coordinator positions and projects designed to establish HPS, supporting the development of a clearinghouse for health-promotion resource materials, and conducting in-country research.

In October 1995, WHO/Manila and the Institute of Education at the University of the South Pacific (USP) jointly organized and hosted a follow-up workshop, which was held in Suva, Fiji. Twenty-three participants representing health and education ministries from 17 countries in the region attended. The workshop resolved to:

- Develop national HPS committees and identify national focal points;
- Develop a HPS manual to assist in implementing HPS; and
- Establish national networks and a regional network to support HPS.

The workshop participants appointed the University of the South Pacific's Institute of Education as the focal point from which to coordinate the regional HPS network. The Fiji-based steering committee that was subsequently formed included representatives from regional organizations and key stakeholders in health and education in Fiji. Representation on the committee also came from the United Nations Children's Fund (UNICEF), WHO, the Secretariat of the Pacific Community (SPC), the Fiji Ministries of Health and Education, the Fiji Trilateral Health Project, the Fiji National Food and Nutrition Committee, and the South Pacific Action Committee on Human Ecology and the Environment.

New Zealand's Official Development Assistance Programme provided the seed funding necessary to set up the regional support network for HPS and to assist the network implement its planned activities. These activities included in-country workshops and purchase of resources. The network's primary focus was to enhance implementation of HPS in the region. It therefore sought to provide professional and material support to its members.

After a decade of activities across the region, an opportunity to scale up the HPS work occurred when WHO officials were invited to give a presentation at the Forum of Education Ministers meeting in October 2006 in Nadi, Fiji. During this forum, the ministers passed resolutions promoting health as an essential element of growth, learning, and education. More specifically, they endorsed the following initiatives:

- Adoption and implementation of HPS in their respective countries as a mechanism to strengthen the inextricable link between health and education and to take advantage of the considerable opportunity for health and education ministries to work together to meet the common goal of ensuring generations of youth who are healthy and productive;
- Establishment of HPS as a workshop discussion theme during the next Forum of Education Ministers meeting, with this work being conducted in collaboration with the Pacific Regional Initiative on Development of Basic Education (PRIDE), and with WHO personnel acting as facilitators;
- Incorporation of health as an additional benchmark indicator in the educational strategic plans of Pacific countries, with this process being exercised through the PRIDE project;
- Close collaboration and partnership between the ministries of education and health in the participating countries in order to realize national strategies;
- Ongoing advocacy for closer collaboration between education and health agencies at the country level as well as at the regional level in association with

personnel from WHO, the SPC, and the PRIDE project, as well as from other regional agencies;

- Encouraging donors, governments, and non-governmental organizations to work toward operationalizing regional and country-level cooperation.

The sub-regional workshop was conducted at Griffith University in Brisbane, Australia; 15 country representatives from the education and health sectors attended. The workshop resulted in most countries strengthening the partnerships between their respective ministries of health and education. It also led to the establishment of a memorandum of understanding between the two ministries in the Cook Islands, Fiji, the Marshall Islands, the Federated States of Micronesia (FSM), and Nauru. Soon after, increasing numbers of schools from the 15 countries began adopting the HPS concept and creating plans for implementation. Networking was strengthened further through dissemination of regular newsletters and establishment of the Pacific Health Promoting Schools (PacHELPS) website (http://www.pachelps.org/).

HEALTH PROMOTING SCHOOLS MANUAL

The HPS manual (Pacific Network of Health Promoting Schools, 1997) for the Pacific region that was written and distributed after the 1995 workshop provided practical suggestions for getting HPS programs underway at both national and school levels. The manual also provided guidance on actions relating to six key areas identified during earlier HPS work in other regions of the world, namely, school health policies, the physical environment, the social environment, community relationships, personal health skills, and school health services. Some of the procedures featured in the manual follow. The first set of items given here relate to national actions, with ministries and departments of education and health asked to:

1. Jointly endorse the HPS concept and regional guidelines for action;
2. Select a national coordinator (preferably from the education sector);
3. Select a national advisory committee consisting of representatives of the education and health sectors, the unions, WHO, UNICEF, SPC, non-governmental organizations, and other agencies as appropriate;
4. Select schools within which to pilot HPS or invite schools to apply to be a pilot school;
5. Identify goals and objectives for the national committee;
6. Conduct a survey of the national health status of school children;
7. Declare a health day or health week.

This next set of items covers school-based actions. Each participating school was asked to:

1. Have the head teacher/principal, teacher, or national HPS coordinator explain the HPS concept to staff, student representatives, members of the school committee, and parents;
2. Elect a coordinator;

3. Widely communicate the decision to become a HPS;
4. Form a HPS committee comprising representatives from the school and the community;
5. Set goals and guidelines for the school;
6. Write an action plan;
7. Draw up a school health calendar;
8. Implement the action plan and monitor and publicize progress;
9. Evaluate action plan outcomes;
10. Enter Phase 2 of the project.

SUPPORTING THE COUNTRIES

WHO consistently continued to support the Pacific countries in their effort to implement HPS throughout the schools of the region. This support included the development of materials such as the regional guidelines, which were finalized in 1996 (WHO, 1996) and distributed to Pacific schools. The regional HPS network coordinator visited Kiribati, Nauru, FSM, the Marshall Islands, the Solomon Islands, Vanuatu, and Fiji to assist the establishment of national HPS committees and to provide training in formulating and integrating projects into school activities and/or to revitalize national or school efforts.

A survey of the extent to which the participating countries were building on or linking up with existing programs and activities revealed that much was already happening but that the efforts were largely being carried out in isolation and without consultation with other key players in school health. Accordingly, WHO increased its efforts to support countries in their efforts to secure links with existing programs and to limit duplication of (i.e., consolidate) activities.

One key initiative that the HPS national programs were able to capitalize on was that of the Australia–South Pacific (ASP) 2000 Sports Program, which at least eight Pacific nations adopted. However, the cessation of the coordinator position slowed down the momentum in regards to networking and activities.

REGIONAL NETWORKING

The regional HPS network was also represented at subsequent workshops, notably the SPC's Development of Indicators for Health Promotion workshop held in Noumea (New Caledonia) in December 1998, and the Healthy Islands Meeting workshop organized by WHO and held in Suva (Fiji) in February, 1999. The inclusion of HPS network representatives in forums that had traditionally been limited to health personnel and health programs was a positive sign of sector collaboration between health and education in the region.

By this time, information sharing had become an added dimension of the HPS network. For example, countries were now documenting their experiences for circulation to others through a newsletter and gaining greater awareness of and ideas for resources and activities, such as the comprehensive school program in the Republic of Palau, which included school health screening, dental care, development of a health curriculum, coordination of health promotion, in-service training for teachers and nurses, and sports training.

EXAMPLES OF HPS INITIATIVES FROM SELECTED COUNTRIES

Fiji

Fiji signaled its commitment to the HPS concept in the mid-1990s by setting up school health teams charged with planning and monitoring HPS activities in the country's 374 kindergartens, 700 primary schools, and 147 secondary schools. The activities included health-based advice, inspection and monitoring of school lunches, personal hygiene, dental health, height to weight ratios, environmental sanitation, school gardening, and district workshops. During the late 1990s, Fiji also extensively revised its senior primary school curriculum, a process that provided an excellent opportunity for including HPS issues and concepts in classroom programs.

Another initiative implemented around the same period was the Australia–Fiji Healthy Islands program, which subsumed the Kadavu Rural Health Project that ran from 1994–1997 (Roberts, 1997). Even though the project was embedded in the activities of the Ministry of Health, its primary health care approach meant its reach extended into rural administrative systems and communities, providing much needed support for HPS to build on. The health and safety awareness policies and campaigns that the government ran under the program helped keep schools free of health risks for those attending them.

In 2009, teachers from selected schools were invited to attend a national HPS workshop in order to help them implement the program in their schools. The Ministry of Education and Ministry of Health also signed a memorandum of understanding to strengthen the implementation of HPS in Fiji.

More recently, national school nutrition policy and canteen guidelines have been produced for use in participating HPS schools. Another pleasing development is that of schools that had volunteered to take part in research focused on obesity prevention in the community signing up for the HPS program.

Republic of the Marshall Islands

At the time the HPS program was being promoted throughout the Pacific region, the Republic of the Marshall Islands already had in place a policy regarding school education on HIV/AIDS and sexually transmitted infections, and it was field testing modules containing information on these matters in selected schools. As such, it was already attuned to issues of school health.

In July 1996, the nation's Ministry of Health and Environment introduced the HPS concept to 40 school principals, school supervisors, and elementary school teachers, in the presence of assistant secretaries of education. The initiative was immediately taken up by the Ministry of Education as a priority area of focus for schools. In August 1996, health education officers presented their HPS groundwork to the Pacific Educational Conference 1996, thereby generating interest in sharing information with other Pacific nations and territories. At the beginning of the 1996/1997 school year, staff from the Ministry of Education and Ministry of Health and Environment visited schools where they distributed fluoride tablets and Vitamin A capsules, conducted a de-worming program, measured students' heights and weights, and conducted programs designed to raise awareness of health issues. Schools also started clean-up activities in their grounds and their communities. These nationwide health initiatives provided good entry points for implementing HPS in each school. Somewhat later, seven schools on the atolls of Majuro and two on Ebeye began developing and implementing health plans of their own, with these encompassing issues particular to these communities.

Niue

At the time the HPS concept gained the attention of Pacific nations, Niue had a number of initiatives running that complemented HPS very well. The WHO-supported ASP 2000 Sportstart program called Junior Sports had been in place since 1995. Niue was also one of the participants in the Australian Government's Overseas Aid Program, the AusAID-funded Healthy Islands program. Members of the nation's eventual HPS committee, drawn from Niue's two schools, also participated in the national committee for that program.

Under the HPS umbrella, Niue carried out compulsory health checks of all students and instituted healthy food policies in the country's two schools. Action plans drawn up for the schools were implemented at both schools. Niue also completed the Global School-Based Student Health Survey, a surveillance tool developed by WHO in order to aid evaluation of HPS activities. Niue was the first country to conduct the survey.

Palau

In Palau, the Ministry of Health and the Ministry of Education formally agreed to establish a HPS program. One of the program's first activities was a survey of all high school students and 20% of elementary school students in order to provide baseline data for the program. Subsequent activities included training and certifying a "school-based" nurse to work with the national health promotion coordinator, establishing a "dispensary-based" nurse as a contact person for the outlying villages, and completing a computerized database containing health information on all students in Palau. The aim of the last of these three activities was to facilitate information exchange about immunization and other health matters between the Ministries of Health and Education. The first school audit and assessment of the HPS implementation and monitoring began in January 1997.

Samoa

Samoa already had a history of health education in schools, but this was reinvigorated by the prospect of developing this area of education into a HPS initiative. A national HPS committee was set up, with the national coordinator and chair selected from the senior ranks of the Department of Education, and with the chief health educator of the Department of Health assisting as technical adviser.

In September 1995, a week-long in-service training program for teachers was held under the banner, School Health in Transition to HPS. Key stakeholders in primary schools, school inspectors, and district nurses were trained and introduced to WHO's HPS guidelines. Further workshops were held for HPS stakeholders, culminating in a national HPS symposium in May 1997.

Over time, the national HPS committee has organized a number of activities, among them the following:

- National School Boys' Under-17 and Under-19 Smoke-free Rugby Tournament, May 1996;
- National School Girls' Smoke-free Netball Tournament, May 1997, in collaboration with the Samoa Rugby Football (School Boys') Union and the Samoa Netball Association; and
- The WHO-supported ASP 2000 Sportstart program called FiaFia Sport.

The committee was also instrumental in securing Samoa's participation in the AusAID-funded Healthy Islands program, one focus of which was HPS. A significant milestone for Samoa with respect to HPS was the government's decision to include funding for the initiative in the nation's 1998/1999 national budget.

Tonga

Tonga has a long-standing health education program as well as involvement in school gardens and healthy school-compound projects. Health studies are compulsory for Forms 1 and 2 students in all schools. After Form 2, health is incorporated in home economics studies. A broad cross-section of people from government and community agencies are involved in school health promotion.

The Ministry of Health and the Ministry of Education agreed to jointly carry out a health behavior study of schoolchildren. Around the same time, Tonga's parliamentary cabinet approved implementation of a "health and weight awareness program" as part of fitness instruction in Nuku'alofa primary schools. The program, which was initiated by Tonga's Central Planning Department and Ministry of Education, included fitness instruction, health promotion (through the medium of television), aerobics competitions, and development and distribution of education materials.

Follow-on activities within primary schools since that time have included those aligned with Tonga's National Weight-loss Competition and with information drawn from the country's National Nutrition Survey. Tonga also went on to develop a National Food and Nutrition Policy and a National Plan of Action for

Nutrition. (UNICEF assisted this initiative in 1997.) The country also participated in the Healthy Islands project, which included HPS activities.

Cook Islands

The Cook Islands reinvigorated its HPS-related work when it conducted a curriculum review in 2004, commensurate with the signing of a memorandum of understanding between the Ministry of Education and the Ministry of Health. The memorandum resulted in development the Cook Islands Health and Physical Well-being Curriculum, the content of which is based on two key questions:

- What does being healthy mean to you?
- What makes it hard to be healthy in the Cook Islands?

All schools were required to develop a plan setting out how they would implement the two essential learning areas of the curriculum. They have also, since that time, been required to produce a biannual health education long-term plan and an annual physical education long-term plan.

As part of its implementation of the curriculum document, the Ministry of Education and the Ministry of Health have continued to work closely together in many different ways. One example is a pilot project which aims to address obesity through encouraging physical activity and sport at school.

CONCLUSION

The shift in approach from health education to health promotion across the island nations of the Pacific has placed greater responsibility on schools, teachers, and administrators to create environments, relationships, and policies that support HPS. The success of health promotion can be measured in terms of the extent to which it becomes integrated into national governments' planning and funding, into ministry of education policies and priorities, and into school ethos, behavior, and activities. There is great hope throughout the Pacific Islands for the continued success of HPS. But this success relies on all participants, especially children, being empowered to make and act on decisions that promote their health and the health of those around them. Realizing this state of affairs should lead to generational changes that will ultimately help the Pacific nations achieve their vision of healthy islands populated by healthy people.

REFERENCES

Erben, R. (1998). *Regional strategies for the development of health-promoting schools.* Keynote address to the National Conference on Health-Promoting Schools in Brisbane, Australia, November 15–17, 1998.
Pacific Network of Health Promoting Schools. (1997). *Health promoting schools manual.* Suva, Fiji: Institute of Education, University of the South Pacific.
Roberts, G. (1997). The Kadavu health promotion model, Fiji. *Health Promotion International, 12*(4), 283–290.

World Health Organization (WHO). (1995a). *New horizons in health*. Manila, the Philippines: Regional Office for the Western Pacific, WHO.

World Health Organization (WHO). (1995b). *School health promotion: Report of the workshop on school health promotion*. Manila, the Philippines: Regional Office for the Western Pacific, WHO.

World Health Organization (WHO). (1995c). *Yanuca Island declaration*. Manila, the Philippines: Regional Office for the Western Pacific, WHO.

World Health Organization (WHO). (1996). *Regional guidelines for the development of health promoting schools*, Manila, the Philippines: Regional Office for the Western Pacific, WHO.

World Health Organization (WHO). (1998). *WHO's global school health initiative: Health promoting schools*. Geneva, Switzerland: Author.

Sereana Tagivakatini
Secretariat of the Pacific Board for Educational Assessment
Suva
Fiji
email: stagivakatini@spbea.org.fj

Temo K. Waqanivalu
World Health Organization
Suva
Fiji
email: WaqanivaluT@wpro.who.int

ABDULLAH AMBUSAIDI AND SULAIMAN AL-BALUSHI

3. HEALTH EDUCATION IN THE SULTANATE OF OMAN

Towards Sustainable Health for Students

INTRODUCTION

Geographically, the Sultanate of Oman is one of the Gulf Co-operation Countries. It is surrounded by three Arab countries—the United Arab Emirates, Yemen, and Saudi Arabia. The population is almost three million, of which around one million are expatriates, mainly from South Asia (India, Pakistan, and Bangladesh). The Omani government has a long-term vision to shift the country's economy from one that is highly dependent on oil and gas to one that is more diverse, with tourism as a key contributor.

As a response to Oman 2020, Oman's vision for the future that was adopted in 1998 (Ambusaidi & El-Zain, 2008), the Sultanate of Oman adopted a new education system consisting of 10 years of basic education and two years of post-basic education (Ministry of Education, 2003). These changes marked a major redevelopment of the education system. The major subjects taught within it are science, mathematics, Arabic language, and English language. In addition, students have become the cornerstone of the educational process, with the Ministry of Education giving priority to learner-centered approaches in teaching and assessment. Teachers are now required to use different methods of teaching, such as cooperative learning and inquiry-based learning. Students are assessed formatively and summatively (Ambusaidi & Al-Shuaili, 2009).

Since 1970, modernization has reached into all corners of life in the Sultanate of Oman. A well-treated water supply and a well-designed sewage system are being built to minimize waterborne diseases. However, in the last 10 years, there has been a rapid increase in what are termed "lifestyle diseases," such as heart disease, high blood pressure, and diabetes. Another concern in the Sultanate of Oman is widespread smoking amongst school students. A study investigating the attitudes of 2,297 Omani 13- to 15-year-old students toward taking tobacco (Ministry of Health, 2007) found that 1 out of 10 students (14.5% of the males and 5.7% of the females) had already smoked tobacco. Furthermore, 5.7% of students admitted to using tobacco products besides cigarettes. Comparison of these findings with those of a similar survey conducted four years earlier (Ministry of Health, 2003) made evident a decline in tobacco use amongst school students. However, the researchers agreed that tobacco use still needed to be addressed. The 2007 study revealed other results relating to the desire to give up smoking, the effect of peers on tobacco use, and the extent to which the respondents agreed that smoking should be prohibited in public places.

N. Taylor, F. Quinn, M. Littledyke and R.K. Coll (eds.), Health Education in Context, 17–26.

Another current issue of concern in Oman is the spread of drugs among school students. The Sultanate of Oman is an open country in terms of expatriates and tourists and has long land and sea borders, factors that make it relatively easy for drug dealers to promote drug use to school students. These problems have led the Omani government to place more emphasis on health education not only in schools but also in institutions of higher education. The Ministry of Education opts to embed or include the concepts and themes of health education in science and life skills curricula instead of as a separate subject area, probably because these concepts and themes are closely related to these two subjects.

The Omani science curriculum has been under review many times since the adoption of the new education system in 1998. Given that health education is largely part of the science curriculum, it also has been under review, a process that has seen new concepts and themes included in the curriculum. In addition, several health education projects have been implemented in schools with the aim of supporting this part of the science curriculum on the one hand and of improving students' attitudes toward a healthy life on the other. Some of these projects have come into being as a result of cooperation between Ministry of Education, Ministry of Health, and international organizations such as the United Nations Children's Fund (UNICEF) and the World Health Organization (WHO). These projects include Peer Education for the Human Immuno-Deficiency Virus (HIV), Prevention of Tobacco in Schools Project, Girls' Health Project, and the Health Promoting Schools Project. Another initiative, Preserving Cleanliness and Health in the School Environment, is run as a contest.

HEALTH EDUCATION IN GENERAL EDUCATION

The Ministry of Health, with strong cooperation from the Ministry of Education, positions the health of school students as its priority. The first school health program launched by the Ministry of Health was signaled in the ministry's fourth five-year plan, from 1991 to 1996 (Ministry of Health, 2006). At the beginning of the program, the ministry established (within its Directorate General of Health Affairs) a new department—the Department of School Health. The aim of this department is to develop and implement, in collaboration with other government, private, and international organizations, the polices and strategies needed to provide health care to school and university students.

In 2006, the Ministry of Health, Ministry of Education, and WHO proposed a national strategy for school health in Oman, effective from 2008 to 2015 and operating under the banner of Better Health for School Communities. The strategy's mission is for relevant organizations to work together in order to enhance the health of school communities. According to the Ministry of Health (2006), the aims of the strategy—to be achieved by the end of 2015—are:

- Giving all members of schools the opportunity to enhance health;
- Developing school health services so that they are more effective and of better quality;

- Making available people who have skills related to school health;
- Developing a supportive, safe, and healthy learning and working school environment; and
- Periodically observing and remedying dangerous behaviors among school students.

It is assumed that these aims will be fulfilled through several activities and initiatives implemented in schools. Directives in line with these aims call for the following:

- Greater emphasis paid to students' health education and health awareness in order to help students acquire better health-related skills;
- Provision of general health care for students, with that care including
  – general check-ups for students in Grades 1, 7, and 10,
  – eye checks for students in Grade 4,
  – mouth, teeth, eye, and ear checks for students in Grade 1,
  – treatment of simple diseases, and
  – a first aid service;
- Achieving and maintaining a healthy school environment;
- Encouraging students to do regular physical exercise and sports;
- Educating students about health nutrition and how to preserve food;
- Encouraging parent participation in school health programs; and
- Enhancing the health of school workers (teachers, administrators, and the like).

Health Education in Omani Science Textbooks

Among the concepts and themes of health education presented in the science curricula for Grades 1 to 12 are those presented in Table 1. The examples given in the table come from Omani science textbooks.

Al-Hajji's (2005) content analysis of science textbooks for Grades 5 to 8 identified the extent to which health education concepts and themes exist in these resources. The results of the study showed that about 37% of the content of the textbooks contained health education concepts and themes. Most of the content dealt with personal health care. However, the results also showed that these concepts and themes did not follow a pattern or show continuity.

The science textbook for Grade 9 contains one chapter about human reproduction. It contains topics related to the male and female reproductive systems, the menstrual cycle, fertilization, and other related issues. The textbook for Grade 10 incorporates other topics pertaining to human health. One concerns human body systems (skeletal, digestive, respiratory, circulatory, excretory), which are presented in terms of their components, their functions, the diseases that attack them, and how to protect them from such diseases.

In addition to containing general biology topics, the textbooks for Grades 11 and 12 contain many topics related to human health. Grade 12 students can also study a curriculum called science and environment. This curriculum is offered to those students who do not want to study the three traditional sciences (biology, chemistry, and physics). Science and environment contains two units that deal with human health. Disease defense and human health, the first unit, encompasses two chapters. The first covers diseases and the second, titled reproduction and genetics, consists of two sections, the first of which focuses on human reproduction and the second on genetics. Both chapters present various topics related to human health.

Table 1: Examples of concepts and themes of health education incorporated in Omani science textbooks

Major concepts and themes	Examples
Human Body Health	• Human body systems and organs and how to preserve them • Diseases that attack human body systems and organs, how to take care of these and how to prevent diseases
Healthy Food	• What is meant by "healthy food" • The importance of healthy food • How to preserve food from a health perspective
Healthy Air	• The importance of healthy air for human health • How to prevent air pollution • Diseases caused by air pollution
Plant Health	• The importance of vegetables in one's diet • The importance of fruit • General guidelines to observe before eating vegetables and fruit
Health of the Environment	• The environment and how to preserve it (a variety of topics)
Safety on the Road	• How to protect oneself from car accidents

Extracurricular Projects in Health Education

To support those components of the science curriculum and other curricula (e.g., Islamic education, Arabic and English, life skills, and physical education) that focus on health education, several projects are being implemented in schools. Brief descriptions of these follow.

Prevention of Tobacco in Schools Project This project was initiated after the results of the aforementioned 2003 Global Youth Tobacco Survey of Omani students (Ministry of Health, 2007). The aim of the project is to provide young people with knowledge regarding health-related aspects of tobacco use and to dissuade them from smoking. Booklets, leaflets, guides, CDs, video tapes, and other materials focused on these matters are distributed to students. In an effort to garner wider support for these aims, the ministry holds public meetings and workshops. Some social events and interactive activities are also included in the project, such as games, competitions, drawings, role-plays, and puppet plays.

The project started out as a trial during school year 2003/2004. Forty-eight schools (24 for males and 24 for females) were randomly chosen from four of Oman's 10 educational regions. The schools represented 20% of the schools in these four districts. One classroom was randomly chosen from each school. This stage of the project was sponsored by the Ministries of Health and Education and WHO. Its effectiveness was evaluated via pre- and post-achievement tests and attitudes surveys. The results of the tests and surveys showed a significant gain in students' knowledge about the health hazards of tobacco use. The project was then implemented in all Omani schools, under the joint supervision of the Ministry of Health and the Ministry of Education. The main goal for the first implementation stage (2006 to 2010) was to reduce smoking among school students by 30%.

Each school involved in the project has a teacher responsible for coordinating its activities (Department of School Health, 2009). These teachers receive intensive training on the methods and activities used in Prevention of Tobacco in Schools. On returning to their respective schools, the teachers bring together a team of people responsible for organizing project activities within the school. The team also liaises with parents and local foundations such as mosques, youth clubs, and companies, and encourages their involvement in the project. The implementation stage of the project was being evaluated at the time of writing.

Life Facts Book Project This global project was initiated by several international organizations such as UNICEF, the United Nations Educational, Scientific and Cultural Organization (UNESCO), and WHO at the beginning of the 1990s. It began in Oman in 1996 and operates under the auspices of the Ministry of Health in cooperation with UNICEF and the Ministry of Education. The main objective of this project is to promote students' awareness of the most prevalent and serious health-related behaviors in the local community, such as poor dietary and lifestyle habits, including smoking, drug use, and little if any regular exercise, and the manifestations of these behaviors, notably diabetes, obesity, high blood pressure, cancer, and overall lack of fitness (Department of School Health, 2008). The *Life Facts* book is the main vehicle for providing information about these issues. The book is comprehensive in its explanations, which are presented in clearly laid out text and illustrations, and so readily accessible by both students and adults. The book is updated regularly and is published in both Arabic and English.

The project also operates an article-writing competition for Grades 9 and 10 students. Articles must be based on the topics of the book, and each student who enters the competition is restricted to exploring one topic only. The main objective of the competition is to enhance students' knowledge of both local and personal health matters. About 100,000 articles have been submitted since the competition began in 2001. The number of articles submitted has increased every year, and an interactive website based on the book is under construction. The project is currently being evaluated by the Ministry of Health and UNICEF.

Girls' Health Project   The goal of this project is to enhance 11- and 12-year-old girls' (generally fifth and sixth graders) awareness of the physiological changes that their bodies undergo during puberty and how they can best handle these changes (Department of School Health, n. d.). Another aim is to promote female self-esteem, personal health, and good dietary habits. The Ministry of Health, in cooperation with the Ministry of Education and Procter and Gamble (a pharmaceutical company that manufactures, among other products, sanitary pads), operates the project.

The project, which is implemented and overseen in schools by school health doctors and nurses, school health education supervisors, and volunteer health educators, also makes available various other educational and social activities. The girls have access to booklets, leaflets, guides, CDs, and video-tapes and receive samples of Proctor and Gamble products such as sanitary pads.

Pre- and post-tests and surveys regarding the health issues featured in the project are administered to the girls before and after their participation in the project. Results consistently show a significant gain from pre- to post-test in the students' knowledge of the health topics, especially those relating to physiological changes during adolescence, personal health, personal hygiene, sexual health, menstruation, and psychological handling of the stresses and fears associated with adolescence. The project also facilitates good relationships between the school doctors and nurses and the girls, who typically become less hesitant in asking questions about their personal health problems and expressing their fears and anxieties. The project has also helped correct the girls' misconceptions about several health issues. Parents have praised the project's activities and materials and expressed their support.

Peer Education Project   The philosophy underpinning this project draws on a social principle —"Young people listen to their peers." The project, which began in 2002, initially focused on AIDS. Success in meeting the objectives associated with this issue convinced the Ministries of Health and Education in cooperation with UNICEF to include other issues, such as diet control, physical fitness, tobacco use, road safety, sex-related diseases, and violence. The project has been implemented in six males' schools and six females' schools in each educational region. Students are selectively chosen for a rigorous training program that provides them with information focused on particular health issues. The program prepares these students to educate their friends about those issues. It also shows them how to convey information to their peers via a convincing approach that suits the personality of each individual, and how to deal with their peers from a psychological standpoint. Students furthermore receive advice and guidelines on communication skills, negotiation, problem-solving, dealing with personal struggles, and coping with peer influence (Department of Educational Counseling, 2008).

Health Promoting Schools Project   The main goal for this project is to promote a healthy environment for education by connecting health and education through a variety of inside and outside school activities (Department of School Health, 2006). These activities involve teachers, students, parents, and the wider community. This international project, which is organized by WHO, has been implemented in several countries around the globe.

The project has been in place in the Sultanate of Oman since school year 2004/2005, and is coordinated by a national team chaired by the Ministry of Health. Its members are drawn from the Ministry of Health, the Ministry of Education, UNICEF, and WHO. The team's work has included designing a detailed working plan for implementation of the project, preparing instructional guidelines, designing workshops directed at educating health educators in all educational regions about the project's principles and strategies, setting up criteria for the project's success, and evaluating the participating schools.

The project began in 19 schools around the country. Each year since has seen a 19% increase in the number of schools choosing to participate in it. The current number of participating schools is 109. When implementing the project, each school forms a team, chaired by the school principal, to coordinate the project's activities both within and beyond the school's boundaries. Team membership typically includes the school health supervisor (usually a science teacher), school social supervisor, school nurse, several teachers, two student representatives, two parent representatives, and two local-community activists. The participating schools undergo an annual process and impact evaluation. They also have opportunity each year to attend a symposium, during which they can share their ideas and experiences.

Positive Personality Project This project is a collaboration involving the Ministry of Health, the Ministry of Education, UNICEF, and Shell Oil in Oman. It targets students 13 to 15 years of age in order to enhance the positive aspects of their personalities and to help them evaluate themselves with respect to their strengths. The overall aim is for students to gain a more positive view of themselves and the world around them. To facilitate achievement of this goal, students work through seven booklets of life skills activities, designed by university professionals and health educators. The books focus on different themes, such as thinking and decisionmaking, good study habits, peer relationships, self-development, healthy lifestyles, and the art of good communication (Al-Kharousi, Sulaiman, & Al-Mashaikhi, n. d.),

Contest for Preserving Cleanliness and Health in the School Environment This contest was launched during school year 1991/1992 after His Majesty Sultan Qaboos bin Said directed that it be implemented in all Omani schools (Al-Shaibaniya, Ambusaidi, Al-Rwahi, & Al-Bulushiya, 2009). The contest focuses on three main elements:

- *Hygiene or cleanliness:* corporal hygiene (physical, moral) and cleanliness of school buildings;
- *Health:* physical and psychological; and
- *Environment:* cleanliness of the environment, types of pollutants, results of pollution, methods to prevent pollution.

The Ministry of Education uses the contest as a means of equipping students with the basic principles of health care, increasing their awareness of environmental issues, and helping them acquire positive attitudes and values. More specifically, the contest aims to:

- Bring health- and hygiene-related knowledge and facts to the school environment in a practical way;
- Develop positive attitudes among students toward health and hygiene in the school environment;
- Develop relevant skills and self-reliance among students by having them actively participate in activities related to hygiene and health in the school environment;
- Make clear to students the importance of a clean environment and of caring for school facilities and maintenance;
- Encourage closer links between the students by encouraging their cooperation in maintaining the cleanliness and safety of the school environment;
- Encourage closer ties between students, teachers, and school administrative staff by having them work together to achieve a hygienic school environment;
- Strengthen cooperation between the school and community with respect to the contest activities and program; and
- Prepare students for future challenges relating to hygiene, protecting the environment from pollution, and preserving a high standard of public health.

SUMMARY AND CONCLUSIONS

The Sultanate of Oman seems to have in place a sound system of health education, evident in both science curriculum content and supporting projects, and operating across all sectors of the education system. The science curriculum covers many concepts and themes related to health education. The supporting projects are varied and target students of different ages and stages. Both male and female students benefit from these projects. None of these projects could be implemented in the field and achieve its aims without the support and collaboration of the government, private-sector, and international organizations operating in Oman.

However, there is a need to evaluate the science curriculum and supporting projects in order to identify their strengths and weaknesses. One problem evident with respect to the science curriculum is the fact that some teachers do not teach health education topics in a manner likely to bring about the required changes in students' health-related behaviors and attitudes. There is a real need for such teachers to shift from teacher-dominated/oriented instructional approaches toward learner-centered approaches and to use appropriate teaching methods such as role-play, problem-solving, and story-telling.

The supporting projects also face some difficulties in schools. Most notable are lack of teacher capacity and lack of student cooperation. In regard to the first difficulty, the amount of work that each project requires sometimes extends beyond science teachers' capacities. This is understandable, given that these teachers have to coordinate and supervise the activities of the projects in schools alongside their teaching and other administrative duties. With respect to the second difficulty, some students do not cooperate and/or cope with the requirements of some projects. For example, one part of the Prevention of Tobacco in Schools Project calls on students to declare and provide information about their experiences in relation to smoking. Not all students are prepared to disclose this information.

Despite these difficulties, there is much to learn and emulate from Oman's experiences to date in health education. We are confident that the health education Oman has in place provides a strong platform upon which to build and further promote health attitudes and behaviors that will secure a healthy future for all Omanis, present and future.

REFERENCES

Al-Hajji, S. (2005). *Analysis study of the content of the Sultanate of Oman basic education science textbooks according to the health education domains.* Unpublished Master's thesis in Science Education, College of Education/Sultanate Qaboos University.

Al-Kharousi, H., Sulaiman, S., & Al-Mashaikhi, A. (n. d.). *My positive personality.* Muscat, Sultanate of Oman: Ministry of Education/Sultanate of Oman.

Al-Shaibaniya, M., Ambusaidi, A., Al-Rwahi, N., & Al-Bulushiya, A. (2009). *Towards a sustainable world: Focus on education for sustainable development in Oman.* Muscat, Sultanate of Oman: Ministry of Education/Sultanate of Oman.

Ambusaidi, A., & Al-Shuaili, A. (2009). Science education development in the Sultanate of Oman. In S. BouJaoude & Z. Dagher (Eds.), *The world of science education: Arab States* (Vol. 3, pp. 205–219). Rotterdam, the Netherlands: Sense Publishers.

Ambusaidi, A., & El-Zain, M. (2008). The science curriculum in Omani schools: Past, present and future. In R. K. Coll & N. Taylor (Eds.), *Science education in context* (pp. 85–97). Rotterdam, the Netherlands: Sense Publishers.

Department of Educational Counseling. (2008). *Preparing trainers in peer education: A workshop.* Muscat, Sultanate of Oman: Ministry of Education.

Department of School Health. (n. .). *Girls' Health Project: "I am grown up."* Muscat, Sultanate of Oman: Ministry of Health.

Department of School Health. (2006). *Training guide for school teams in the Health Promoting Schools Project.* Muscat, Sultanate of Oman: Ministry of Health.

Department of School Health. (2008). *Life facts* (12th ed.). Muscat, Sultanate of Oman: Ministry of Health, Sultanate of Oman.

Department of School Health. (2009). *The prevention of tobacco in schools: A project training guide.* Muscat, Sultanate of Oman: Ministry of Health.

Ministry of Education. (2003). *Basic education in the Sultanate of Oman: The theoretical framework.* Muscat, Sultanate of Oman: Author.

Ministry of Health. (2003). *Global youth tobacco survey (GYTS).* Muscat, Sultanate of Oman: Ministry of Health.

Ministry of Health. (2006). *The national strategy of school health in the Sultanate of Oman.* Muscat, Sultanate of Oman: Ministry of Health.

Ministry of Health. (2007). *Global youth tobacco survey (GYTS).* Muscat, Sultanate of Oman: Ministry of Health.

Abdullah Ambusaidi and Sulaiman Al-Balushi
Sultan Qaboos University
Muscat
Oman
email: ambusaid@squ.edu.om

MAYADA KANJ

4. HEALTH EDUCATION THROUGH EXTRACURRICULAR ACTIVITIES IN LEBANON

Process and Challenges

INTRODUCTION

This chapter describes the extracurricular health club initiative in public schools in Lebanon, the challenges encountered, and the impact on the health of its youth members. In the context of this discussion, health is defined in its broader, more holistic sense in line with much contemporary research and the Ottawa Charter for Health Promotion (WHO, 1986) as encompassing aspects of students' physical, psychological, and social wellbeing.

COUNTRY BACKGROUND

Lebanon is located at the eastern end of the Mediterranean Sea. Its land area of 10,452 square kilometers makes it one of the world's smallest countries. It has a population of approximately four million, over 80% of whom live in urban areas (Daher et al., 2002; WHO, 2006). About 1.6 million people live in the capital Beirut and its surroundings (Daher et al., 2002; WHO, 2006). Lebanon is home to various cultural, ethnic, and religious groups.

In October 2005, the World Health Organization (WHO) surveyed Lebanese students in Grades 7, 8, and 9. With respect to dietary behavior, the survey, known as the Global School-Based Student Health Survey (GSHS) (WHO, 2007), revealed that almost 15% of the students risked becoming overweight. Their diets lacked various nutrients, notably calcium, and the majority of them had a very poor intake of fruit and vegetables (no more than one portion per day). This situation could be mostly explained by the regular intake of fast food and eating outdoors. Good hygienic practices were widespread, but dental health was poor because many students were failing to brush their teeth at least three times a day and just over one in four had not seen a dentist in the previous two years. About 20% of the students had never heard of HIV/AIDS. However, half of them supported discussing sexual and reproduction topics in class.

The survey also showed an alarming increase in alcohol consumption and more students in the younger age brackets taking up drinking; almost 20% of the surveyed students had experienced the negative consequences of getting drunk, while 3% reported having used drugs. About one third of the students

N. Taylor, F. Quinn, M. Littledyke and R.K. Coll (eds.), Health Education in Context, 27–36.

reported not being taught about the dangers of drinking alcohol or using drugs in any of their classes during the past year. The GSHS data on youth mental health indicated that 16% of the students had seriously thought of committing suicide and 11% had actually attempted suicide. Girls were more likely than boys to report suicide ideation. Risk factors for suicide ideation included poor mental health (felt lonely, worried, sad, or hopeless), substance use (got drunk, used drugs), victimization (bullying, sexual harassment), and lack of parental understanding (see also Mahfoud, Afifi, Haddad, & Dejong, in press, in this regard).

RESEARCH ON HEALTH EDUCATION

Schools have always been recognized as a focal setting for health education (Laurence, Peterken, & Burns, 2007; Mukoma & Flisher, 2004; Yang, 2010). Extensive literature exists suggesting that extracurricular activities in schools can be associated with improved academic achievement and enhanced social capital; these claims have not, however, been systematically tested, and there is little known about their effects on health-related behaviors and wellbeing.

According to Shulruf, Tumen, and Tolley (2007), there is little research offering theoretical justification for extracurricular programs in schools. Although research of this kind has not been conducted to the same extent as that relating to formal education theoretical frameworks, what has been done suggests that participation in extracurricular activities generally has positive effects on student outcomes across a range of domains (Barber, Eccles, & Stone, cited in Shulruf et al., 2007). Studies arguing primarily for the positive impact of extracurricular activities refer to positive associations, rather than causal relations, between partaking in extracurricular activities and educational attainment, student motivation, aspiration, and attitudes (Broh, 2002; Shulruf et al., 2007). Fredricks and Eccles (2008) suggest that participation in school clubs and out of school recreational activities is associated with higher self-esteem, higher grades, and less adoption of risk-taking behavior.

Conversely, lack of participation in extracurricular activities has been associated with adoption of risky behaviors such as smoking tobacco, marijuana use, and very low consumption of fruits and vegetables (Kaplan et al., 2003). Feldman and Matjasko's (2005) comprehensive literature review on extracurricular activities for high school students in the United States indicates that while these extracurricular activities are viewed as important for adolescents' development and academic achievements, the exact features of how participation in these activities contributes to students' outcomes remain unclear.

On the whole, sustainable programs promoting mental health are most valuable when implemented through the health promoting schools' framework and complemented with a supportive psychosocial climate within the school (Buijs, 2009; Cushman, 2008). However, it is worth differentiating between health promoting activities and health promoting schools. A school may implement different interventions and programs to address various health issues, but if these interventions are not implemented as a comprehensive approach involving the whole community, their outcome will be distinct from those evident in health promoting schools (Cushman, 2008). Lee, Wong, Keung, Yuen, Cheng, and Mok (2008) compared students' health profiles in health promoting schools and in non-health promoting schools; their findings revealed a more positive health profile among students in the health prompting schools, although no causal relationship was established.

HEALTH EDUCATION CONTEXT IN LEBANESE PUBLIC SCHOOLS

The educational system in Lebanon is composed of general education, vocational and technical education, and higher education. General education comprises pre-elementary kindergarten, elementary (Cycles 1 and 2), intermediate (Cycle 3), and secondary (Cycle 4). With each cycle consisting of three years, the total number of school years (excluding pre-elementary kindergarten) is 12. General education is public, private, or subsidized free education. According to the Ministry of Education and Higher Education (MEHE) (2010), the total number of enrolled students is 942,391, of whom 47% are in public schools and 52% in private schools.

The Lebanese public education system is centralized. Public schools are supervised by regional education bureaus that exist in each governorate and serve as the liaison with the MEHE. Despite the fact that the MEHE is expected "to carry out its mandate by looking after the public interest in both the public and private educational sectors, its role in private schools is mostly limited to administering national examinations and recording the names of students enrolled" (Mneimneh, 2010, p. 643). As such, private schools are more independent and autonomous than public schools. In essence, they are only "mentored" by the MEHE.

Traditional health education has concentrated mainly on providing knowledge to help students make healthy choices and avoid risky behaviors. Health education in Lebanese public schools began in 1985, when the government created a Health Education Unit within the MEHE. The unit was charged with improving the skills of primary public school teachers, within the context of the Alma Ata goal of "Health for all in year 2000."

In 1986, the first health education curriculum for primary classes was launched; health education was allocated one hour per week. Each public school nominated one teacher to become the "health educator" based on several criteria. These health educators then received intensive training designed to provide them with the necessary skills to teach health.

This process continued until 1998 when the health education curriculum was revised and an integrated approach was adopted. Health messages were integrated in all classes of general education from Grade 1 through to high school. In 2000, an evaluation of the integrated curriculum revealed gaps in the sequence of topics covered at different grades and in the relevance/appropriateness of the learning objectives (Center for Educational Research and Development, 2000).

In 2009, and based on the results of the GSHS, the MEHE developed a life skills curriculum for reproductive health and gender-related issues. School health supervisors received training as to which health-related extracurricular activities they could appropriately use in their schools. This process also initiated the supervisors into how to deal with awareness activities within the health domain.

THE ROLE AND DEVELOPMENT OF HEALTH CLUBS

An independent ministerial decree in 2000 led to the creation of "school health clubs" in every public school. Although clubs were open to students in all grades, implementation of this decree was possible only for elementary and intermediate classes (Grades 1 to 9). This was because until this time health educators had been working only with these grades and not in high schools. The aim of the clubs, which were to function under the supervision of each school's principal and in collaboration with parents, teachers, and students, was to teach students about health behaviors and to train them to become actively involved in identifying health and environmental issues.

Curricular and extracurricular activities were designed to help achieve these objectives. The former have been integrated within the curriculum since 1998 while the latter entail awareness campaigns for health issues such as dental health, healthy snacks, importance of breakfast, personal hygiene, school environment, and participation in national health campaigns (e.g., No Tobacco Day, HIV/AIDS, environment days) and in environmental health clubs in order to build up students' life skills outside the classroom.

Establishment of the health clubs required school administrators to fulfill certain conditions, such as garnering the commitment of themselves, teachers, and students to club precepts, employing a competent and well-trained school health educator, offering an appropriate physical setting where club members could meet, and ensuring that at least 20 to 25 students initially join the club.

The absence of a long-term plan for the clubs meant that their survival and development depended on ad hoc decisionmaking and availability of funds. Thus, in 2002, and with support from WHO, trainers from the YMCA implemented a workshop to train club facilitators. The three-day intensive training provided knowledge about environmental issues as well as practical sessions on establishing and running a club, interactive teaching, facilitation skills, collaborating with the community, and developing a strategy and plan for club activities.

Almost a year later, in December 2002, another workshop took place. This, too, received support from WHO, which contracted a YMCA training team to conduct the workshop. During the three days of sessions, club facilitators reported on and shared their experiences throughout the year. They noted, in particular, difficulties and challenges encountered and lessons learned. The University of Balamand also participated in the capacity-building initiative by running training sessions for club facilitators (MEHE & Directorate of Guidance and Counseling, 2002; MEHE, School of Public Health at Balamand University, & Greek Orthodox International Charity Association, 2005).

Almost every year since 2002, new schools have been contacted and clubs established. In the absence of a law forcing schools to host a health club, the presence of such a club in a school depends solely on the principal's motivation and willingness to collaborate with the MEHE. School principals also play a key role in maintaining clubs once set up in the schools. They are in charge of choosing the club facilitators and securing or allocating resources. Once recruited, the club facilitators attend a training workshop to prepare them for the new endeavor. Clubs can shut down if the facilitator resigns, if the challenge is overwhelming, or if the principal decides on this action. Seven health education coordinators (one for each governorate) together with their respective team of supervisors are responsible for supervising and following up on the club facilitators, and for providing support and training as needed. They can also recommend that a club closes if found inactive.

There are currently around 100 school health clubs in 100 primary public schools. The number changes every year when new clubs open and others close down. The number of students who join a club averages around 25, but there is wide variability among schools. Club membership is open to students from Grades 1 to 9. Members are usually chosen randomly by the facilitators but at times demand to join can be so high that club facilitators have to select members based on criteria that they set, such as students having particular skills (e.g., theater, art). At times, special committees are formed to support the club and accommodate the excess demand for membership. In other cases, members change every semester to allow a larger number to join.

HEALTH CLUB ACTIVITIES

Because the nature and scope of activities varies among the different clubs, they can potentially address a wide range of issues. Several clubs are developing annual work plans for their activities, which occur mostly on national days such as World AIDS Day and No Tobacco Day. The health issues that a club selects are usually based on an existing or emerging need that the club facilitator identifies in collaboration with other school personnel or with the Health Education Unit of the MEHE. Overall, few physical health issues beyond nutrition, dental health, and environment are being addressed.

In schools where a health educator exists, club facilitators admit that they do not focus on health issues per se because it is up to the health educator to address these matters within class. Instead, the facilitators tend to focus on activities such as field trips, competitions (art, poetry), carnivals, and the like. Club activities such as health fairs, competitions, healthy snack sales, and health lectures, although planned for and facilitated by club members, are open to all students to attend and are usually very well received.

Although, in urban areas, most activities happen inside the school, the situation in villages is different. Often schools or community members from other villages are invited to attend events such as health fairs or art exhibitions that make visible students' talents. These events help create a competitive spirit among other schools that want to replicate the event. Successful events also give recognition to the teachers (club facilitators) who organize and supervise them, a situation that heightens the confidence of these teachers. Club activities that involve the whole village provide opportunities for collaboration among different partners, such as the school, municipality, local non-government organizations (NGOs), and the community at large. In some villages, the whole community is mobilized, in part because the reputation of the village is at stake. Community-wide events also open up each village to other people and cultures because they attract visitors.

THE CHALLENGES

The challenges so far experienced by the health club initiative relate to limited financial and physical resources, a low level of commitment from facilitators and school principals, and an absence of community support. However, these same factors, when present, function as success factors.

Funding

Limited funding is repeatedly reported as a challenge because public schools have no allocated budgets for health clubs. Securing money to carry out activities depends on each school's principal and the initiative and resourcefulness of the club facilitator. Collaboration with civil society is important in countries with limited resources. Acknowledging this, NGOs sometimes give the MEHE seed money for club activities. This aid is distributed to all schools. In other instances, club facilitators manage to procure, through their own contacts, small amounts of funding for specific activities. Availability of funds usually results in visible and attractive activities that appeal to community members and accordingly motivate parents who show their support for the club by, for example, donating money and participating in fund-raising activities.

Supportive School System

Club facilitators are mostly teachers who have teaching and/or administrative responsibilities and so have little time left for facilitating club activities. Also, most facilitators are recruited very close to their retirement age, which makes it very hard to invest in and train them before they leave. The choice of club facilitators and eventual success is very much the province of the school principal and the extent to which he or she is willing to recommend and support the right person for the job. This difficulty could be resolved if health clubs became mandatory rather than optional, as is the case at present.

Support and Recognition for Club Facilitators

Clubs are typically successful only when their respective facilitators are willing to put in the extra effort needed. However, facilitators are not compensated for the expenses they incur when planning and implementing club activities, and their efforts are rarely acknowledged or appreciated. Community support, including that from parents, is more prevalent in rural than urban areas. In cities, many parents do not want their children to participate in after-school activities because of transportation costs and concerns relating to distance, traffic, and security. These issues are not so problematic in villages in rural areas, where distances are not great and social networks are strong. As such, club outreach activities are more abundant in rural areas than in big cities.

IMPACT OF HEALTH CLUBS

The fact that no formal structured evaluation of the impact of health clubs on student health has yet been implemented is a limitation of the program. Club facilitators continuously report on their activities but the information collected is descriptive only (number of sessions, issues addressed, number of participants, etc.) and is used only for report writing. Although individual supervisors use process indicators, this information is not collected or collated beyond the personal observation of the club facilitators and supervisors. However, these descriptive reports, anecdotal evidence from teachers and participants, and information procured during three focus group meetings with health education coordinators, facilitators, and members suggest a range of positive health impacts for participants.

For students, clubs appear to provide space for talents to emerge and be cultivated. Club facilitators frequently use non-traditional methods in their health activities so that they can adopt and encourage creative activities, and thereby provide opportunities for non-traditional activities such as art, theatre, drama, sports, and so forth. As one teacher commented, "The students are happy; they work and enjoy themselves ... They have no opportunities outside. The club is their space to express what they want." When considered against holistic health principles, this comment gives credence to the positive impact of the clubs on the overall health and wellbeing of their participants.

Further evidence of the positive impact of health clubs on students' emotional wellbeing is evident among several children who have been able to overcome disciplinary problems and improve academically. As one facilitator commented, "I used to hear complaints about him every day—now he has changed." Joining a club appears to give some students a sense of belonging, which changes their attitudes toward school. "I like school now!" said one student. "Ms. ... likes me, and she made me like the school and also the work we did." Another way that club membership seems to enhance participants' emotional wellbeing is the formation of social networks. Teachers observe that members become more sociable and their self-confidence increases. A comment from one student confirmed this observation: "I feel good in the club. I have more friends, and we are very close to each other. We do things together." Club membership additionally seems to enhance students' confidence and self-esteem by giving them appropriate opportunities to participate, perform, and even excel.

On the basis of this kind of evidence, it appears that a range of emotional and general wellbeing aspects of health are enhanced for students attending the clubs. However, there is no documented evidence that health clubs are fulfilling their original aims with respect to the overall physical health, health knowledge, and health behavior of participants. Nor is there documented evidence indicating that the clubs are helping lower the incidence of mental health problems among young people. The paucity of data on the health impact of the clubs in association with ongoing health-related problems among Lebanon's young people makes prominent the importance of closely monitoring club activities and preparing specified indicators for use in this work. This need certainly offers an avenue for further empirical research.

CONCLUSION

It is well documented that schools can be an ideal medium for bringing particular initiatives, such as those relating to health, to students, families, and communities at large. In recent years, and in line with comprehensive school health approaches, Lebanon has placed more and more emphasis on using the school to secure better health for all its citizens. School health clubs have the potential to help achieve this goal. The non-formal context that characterizes school clubs is ideal for attracting students and promoting interaction among them. When conducted in association with outreach activities, clubs can facilitate networking with and linking to the community, eventually enhancing the wellbeing of both. These influences, however, need to be confirmed through formal research. This research, in turn, needs to be part of a comprehensive health promoting school approach and not a standalone initiative.

REFERENCES

Broh, B. (2002). Linking extracurricular programming to academic achievement: Who benefits and why? *Sociology of Education, 75*, 69–91.

Buijs, G. (2009). Better schools through better health: Networking for health promoting schools in Europe. *European Journal of Education, 44*(4), 507–520.

Center for Educational Research and Development (CERD), WHO, & UNESCO (2000). *Results of a review of school books of the health education and environment curricula.* Beirut, Lebanon: Author.

Central Administration of Statistics (CAS). (2010). *Lebanon in figures 2008.* Beirut: Author. Retrieved from http://www.cas.gov.lb/index.php?option=com_ content&view=article&id=57&Itemid=65.

Cushman, P. (2008). Health promoting schools: A New Zealand perspective. *Pastoral Care in Education, 26*(4), 231–241.

Daher, M., Tabari, H., Stjernswärd, J., Ammar, W., Abounasr Nabhan, T., Bou Khalil, M., & Mansour, Z. (2002). Lebanon: Pain relief and palliative care. *Journal of Pain and Symptom Management, 24*(2), 200–204.

Feldman, A., & Matjasko, J. (2005). The role of school-based extracurricular activities in adolescent development: A comprehensive review and future directions. *Review of Educational Research, 75*(2), 159–210.

Fredricks, J., & Eccles, J. (2008). Participation in extracurricular activities in the middle school years: Are there developmental benefits for African American and European American youth? *Journal of Youth Adolescence, 37*, 1029–1043.

Kaplan, C. P., Zabkiewicz, D., McPhee, S., Nguyen, T., Gregorich, S., Disogra, C., & Jenkins, C. (2003). Health-compromising behaviors among Vietnamese adolescents: The role of education and extracurricular activities. *Journal of Adolescent Health, 32,* 374–383

Laurence, S, Peterken, R., & Burns, C. (2007). Fresh Kids: The efficacy of a health promoting schools approach to increasing consumption of fruit and water in Australia. *Health Promotion International, 22*(3), 218–226.

Lee, A., Wong, M., Keung, V., Yuen, H., Cheng, F., & Mok, J. (2008). Can the concept of health promoting schools help to improve students' health knowledge and practices to combat the challenge of communicable diseases: Case study in Hong Kong. *BioMed Central Public Health, 8*(42). Available online at http://www.biomedcentral.com/1471-2458/8/42.

Mahfoud, Z., Afifi, R., Haddad, P., & Dejong, J. (in press). Prevalence and determinants of suicide ideation among Lebanese adolescents: Results of the GSHS, Lebanon 2005. *Journal of Adolescence.*

Ministry of Education and Higher Education, Center for Educational Research and Development, *Statistical Bulletin 2009-2010.*

Ministry of Education and Higher Education, & Directorate of Guidance and Counseling. (2002). *Report of evaluation meeting for health, environment and population clubs.* Beirut, Lebanon: Author.

Ministry of Education and Higher Education, School of Public Health at Balamand University, & Greek Orthodox International Charity Association. (2005). *Activation of school clubs in public schools.* Beirut, Lebanon: Author.

Ministry of Finance. (2011). *Lebanon country profile 2011* (based on prospectus published 12 May 2011). Beirut, Lebanon: Author.

Mneimneh, N. A. (2010). *Lebanon.* In P. Peterson, E. Baker, & B. McGaw (Eds.), *International encyclopedia of education* (3rd ed., pp. 636–655). Amsterdam, the Netherlands: Elsevier.

Mukoma, W., & Flisher, A. (2004). Evaluations of health promoting schools: A review of nine studies. *Health Promotion International, 19*(3), 357–368

Shulruf, B., Tumen, S., & Tolley, H. (2007). Extracurricular activities in school: Do they matter? *Children and Youth Services Review, 30,* 418–426

World Health Organization (WHO). (1986). *Ottawa Charter for Health Promotion: First International Conference on Health Promotion.* Retrieved from www.who.int/hpr/NPH/docs/ottawa_charter_hp.pdf.

World Health Organization (WHO). (2006). *Country cooperation strategy for WHO and Lebanon 2005–2009.* Retrieved from http://www.who.int/countryfocus/cooperation_strategy/ccs_lbn_en.pdf.

World Health Organization (WHO). (2007). *Lebanon 2005 Global School-Based Student Health Survey.* Retrieved from http://www.who.int/chp/gshs/2007_Lebanon_GSHS_Country_Report.pdf.

Yang, J. S. (2010). School health education. In P. Peterson, E. Baker, & B. McGaw (Eds.), *International encyclopedia of education* (3rd ed., pp. 547–553). Amsterdam, the Netherlands: Elsevier.

ACKNOWLEDGEMENT

I would like to thank Ms Nina Lahham of the School Health Program and the regional coordinators, club facilitators and children for agreeing to share their experiences with me.

Mayada Kanj
American University of Beirut
Beirut
Lebanon
email: mkanj@aub.edu.lb

GRAÇA S. CARVALHO

5. HEALTH EDUCATION IN PORTUGUESE SCHOOLS

The Contribution of the Health and Education Sectors

INTRODUCTION

Children and young people spend a large part of their lives in school. In this environment they eat, drink, smoke, fall in love, speak about AIDS and about drugs, face stress, and experience a wide range of emotions. It is during this formative stage of their lives that our students most need to experience education in their schools that is directed toward preventing physical and mental health problems. In this chapter, I describe and discuss the Portuguese system of school health education and health promotion, which is strongly inspired by the European Network of Health Promoting Schools (ENHPS) and Schools for Health in Europe (SHE). I begin by outlining and comparing the two main perspectives informing the general health education framework. The first perspective focuses on the biomedical model of health and the second on the social (holistic) model of health. I also pay special attention to the roles that the Portuguese health and education sectors play in implementing school health education and health promotion.

HEALTH VIEWS AND SCHOOL HEALTH EDUCATION PERSPECTIVES—GENERAL BACKGROUND

From the Biomedical Model of Health to the Holistic View of Health

The traditional view of health as the *absence of disease* derives from a medical concept of disease as a pathological condition (a deviation from measurable variables that represent *normal* parameters in the *healthy* body) that can be diagnosed and categorized (Katz & Peberdy, 1998). Evident within this model of health education is the assumption that the body works like a machine (Doyal & Doyal, cited in Birk & Silvertown, 1984). Thus:

- All parts of the body are connected but can be isolated and treated separately;
- Being healthy is to have all parts of the body in good working condition;
- Being ill is to have parts of the body working deficiently;
- Illness is caused by internal processes (age-related degeneration or deficient self-regulation) or external processes (invasion by pathogenic microorganisms);
- Medical treatment aims to restore the normal body functions, or health.

N. Taylor, F. Quinn, M. Littledyke and R.K. Coll (eds.), Health Education in Context, 37–46.

CARVALHO

In short, the biomedical model focuses explicitly on diseases and on their causes, treatment, and prevention. Health professionals, as the people equipped with the knowledge and skills to identify disease and its causes as well as to treat it, play a dominant role, often using persuasive and paternalistic methods during their work (Ewles & Simnett, 1999). Under this model, it is health professionals who are responsible for ensuring that patients comply with medical prescriptions and for encouraging the use of procedures that (presumably) prevent and reduce disease.

Those who ascribe to the biomedical model see health education as a preventive procedure wherein people make behavioral changes that allow them to live healthier lives. The aim of school health education under the biomedical model, then, is to teach children and young people how to keep their bodies in good physical condition and how to avoid disease.

Health education within this framework appeared in Portuguese schools—and also in French and Spanish schools—at the end of the 19th century. Content was ordered into "lessons of morals" and "lessons of things" (Csergo, 2002) and focused on three main themes: hygiene, tuberculosis, and alcoholism. The health messages were informative and presented as injunctive, authoritative prescriptions, that is, rules to be obeyed (Sandrin-Berthon, 2000). The implicit idea was that once people received information about and understood what constituted unhealthy behavior, they would embrace healthy behaviors.

Interested in what keeps people healthy, Antonovsky (1987) developed a model opposite in nature to the dominant biomedical one. His model is based on what is known as the "salutogenic" (health-seeking) approach. In addition to focusing on the question of why some people remain healthy and others do not, this approach emphasizes "that stressors and disruption [are] ... unavoidable aspects of life rather than the demons they are portrayed to be in the pathogenic account" (Katz & Peberdy, 1998, p. 31). The dynamic relationship between people and their environment is an essential element of this model, and emphasis is given to the personal resources that people need to cope with the challenges they face. In order to deal effectively with stressors, people need to create "a sense of coherence" for themselves by integrating three components: comprehensibility, manageability, and meaningfulness. According to Antonovsky (1987, p. 19), coherency is achieved when

1. The stimuli deriving from one's internal and external environments in the course of living are structured, predictable, and explicable;
2. The resources are available to meet the demands posed by the stimuli; and
3. These demands are challenges worthy of investment and engagement.

The salutogenic paradigm provides an interesting bridge between the biomedical model and the social model of health. The social model of health, in line with the salutogenic paradigm, assumes a holistic perspective and emphasizes the interaction between persons and the environment. It adopts the logic of multi-causal theories of health, and it assumes that health is influenced not only by biological factors but also by political, economic, social, psychological, cultural, and environmental factors (Carvalho, 2006; Ewles & Simnett, 1999; Katz & Peberdy, 1998; Naidoo & Wills, 1994).

The social model of health does not dispense with medicine; rather, it positions the medical model as just one part of the answer. Those adhering to the social model recognize that improving people's health requires early identification of the causes of ill-health in persons and communities, such as housing and nutrition and societal and personal hygiene factors (Katz & Peberdy, 1998).

The aim of health education within the social model of health is to develop positive attitudes toward and behaviors associated with good health and wellbeing. While this approach may lead to people taking on a healthier lifestyle in order to improve some facet of their health, the focus is not on disease prevention, as it is in the biomedical model of health education. Health education predicated on a social health model endeavors to provide people with knowledge and understandings that enable them not only to make well-informed decisions but also to explore their values and attitudes (Carvalho et al., 2008).

School-based health education likewise emphasizes skills development and behavior change rather than acquisition of facts. It thus takes a much broader view than traditional biomedical-based health education, which focuses only on formal classroom activities. Holistic school health education also addresses the development of healthy lifestyles and healthy environments, including the social and physical environments in schools. Thus, the aim of social (holistic) school health education is to help children and young people develop healthy living competencies within an environment that is conducive to their physical, mental, and social wellbeing (Carvalho, 2002; Carvalho & Carvalho, 2006; Ewles & Simnett, 1999).

School Health Promotion: From ENHPS to SHE

The health promoting schools notion is based on the World Health Organization's (WHO) view that health education and health promotion must take account of the particular nature of the communities and societies that the educational initiative is targeting. Although there are many models of health promoting schools, they are all based on the five strategies of the Ottawa Charter (WHO, 1986), albeit adapted to the school setting (WHO, cited in Colquhoun, 1997):

- *Ensuring practice is based on health promoting policy*—by drawing together biological, ecological, social, and environmental dimensions to ensure the development of coherent health-based education curricula;
- *Creating supportive environments*—by utilizing the setting of the school to encourage reciprocal support among teachers, students, and parents;
- *Strengthening community action*—by drawing on existing human and material resources in the community in which the school is set and involving that community in practical aspects of health education, decisionmaking, and planning;

- *Developing personal skills*—by providing students not only with information on and understanding about health but also opportunities to enhance life skills in the setting of the school community; and
- *Reorienting health services*—by involving school health services in project activities aimed at promoting health and by utilizing the skills of school health professionals on a basis broader than the traditional.

These precepts of the health promoting schools concept have inspired health education in Portuguese schools. Portugal is a member of the European Network of Health Promoting Schools (ENHPS), which was launched in 1991 as a joint and collaborative effort between the WHO Regional Office for Europe, the Commission of European Communities, and the Council of Europe.

According to the WHO Regional Office for Europe (cited in Parsons, Steers, & Thomas, 1996, p. 311), "The health promoting school aims at achieving healthy lifestyles for the total school population by developing supportive environments conducive to the promotion of health. It offers opportunities for, and requires commitments to, the provision of a safe and health-enhancing environment."

The overall aim of the ENHPS not surprisingly aligns with this aim. Its goal is to "influence and have impact on policy and decision making in the development, implementation and sustainability of health promoting schools in European countries. This aim is achieved through capacity building, resource development, research and evaluation, advocacy and dissemination" (ENHPS, 1997, p. 1).

Despite the diversity in culture and educational settings throughout Europe, there is general agreement across these settings on the aims of health promoting schools. According to Barnekow et al. (2006, p. 13), there are 10 such aims:

1. To establish a broad view of health;
2. To give students tools to enable them to make healthy choices;
3. To provide a healthier environment by engaging students, teachers, and parents, using interactive learning methods, building better communication channels, and seeking partners and allies in the community;
4. To have all members of the school community (students, their parents, teachers, and all other people working in the environment) clearly understand the "real value of health" (physical, psychosocial, and environmental)—both present and future—and how to promote it for the wellbeing of all;
5. To be an effective (perhaps the most effective) long-term workshop for practicing and learning humanity and democracy;
6. To increase students' agency with respect to health, that is, empowering them to take action, individually and collectively, for a healthier life and for healthier living conditions locally as well as globally;
7. To make healthier choices easier choices for all members of the school community;
8. To promote the health and wellbeing of students and school staff;

9. To enable people to deal with themselves and the external environment in a positive way and to facilitate healthy behavior through development and implementation of policies; and

10. To increase the quality of life.

In 2008, the International Union for Health Promotion and Education (IUHPE) clarified the concepts of health education and health promotion as they relate to schools. Health education is "a communication activity … [which] involves learning and teaching pertaining to knowledge, beliefs, attitudes, values, skills and competencies" (IUHPE, 2008, p. 3). Health promotion is "any activity undertaken to protect or improve the health of all school users" (IUHPE, 2008, p. 3). Although both concepts emphasize the participative approach to learning, the latter is a broader concept that goes beyond classroom activities and curriculum implementation.

The Schools for Health in Europe (SHE) network is the continuation of ENHPS. It began in January 2007. The network is currently present in 46 European countries, including Portugal (DGIDC, 2010a). Its aim is to support organizations and professionals in Europe who work in the field of school health promotion, by sharing with them good practice, expertise, and skills (SHE, 2008). All health promoting schools involved in the SHE network are expected to value and develop the following:

- *Equity*—equal access for all to the full range of educational opportunities;
- *Participation*—a sense of ownership brought about by students' participation;
- *Empowerment*—students developing their own ideas about healthy lifestyles and making active and healthy choices;
- *A healthy environment*—includes the physical environment, and the quality of the relationships among and between students and staff and with parents and the community;
- *Effective policies*—developed locally and reflecting local interests, problems, and priorities (SHE, 2008).

There is growing evidence that the health promoting schools approach has a positive impact on teaching and learning within the school. Advantages include higher academic achievement, a lesser likelihood of students leaving school early, and higher job satisfaction for staff (Barnekow et al., 2006; Leger, Kolbe, Lee, McCall, & Young, 2007; Mérini, Jourdan, Victor, Berger, & De Peretti, 2000; SHE, 2008).

HEALTH EDUCATION IN PORTUGUESE SCHOOLS

Different countries address educational policies in different ways for reasons relating to political orientation and to the goals, priorities, and organization of their respective education systems (Pommier & Jourdan, 2007). In some countries, regional or local authorities are responsible for developing education (including health) policies. In other countries, Portugal being one, policy (again including health) is formulated at the national level. In Portugal, the Ministry of Education translates national government policy into curricula and their associated guidelines and standards (DGIDC, 2010b). However, the health sector also works in partnership with the ministry to develop and implement health education.

Education Sector and Health Sector Tensions

In Portugal, the education sector's holistic view of the health education curriculum fits well with the health promotion approach set down by the health sector. However, tensions can arise because the limited time usually available for addressing the various areas of the formal national curriculum means that health issues can be pushed to one side. Despite this difficulty, it is encouraging to find that the broader view of health evident within the informal school curriculum supports the health promotion approach advocated by the health sector (Barnekow et al., 2006).

The particular words and terms that education specialists and health specialists use can be a source of difficulty and tension when the two sectors work in partnership (Kemm, 2006). For example, for the education sector, the term "curriculum" usually means the totality of learning experiences the school offers to children and young people (i.e., the formal and informal curriculum referred to previously). In contrast, the term curriculum for the health sector typically refers to syllabus guidelines or to classroom teaching and learning activities; the wider influence of the school is encompassed within "the whole-school effect" or the notion of health promoting schools.

Also, the education sector naturally gives priority to education, whereas the health sector gives priority to health. Each therefore has different starting points, generating different priorities and possibly different perspectives about which model of health promotion schools should adopt.

The spirit of partnership between the two sectors requires their respective professionals to be aware of these difficulties and to work with an open and positive attitude toward achieving their slightly different aims. These tensions between the sectors may be lessening, however, given evidence that health promotion initiatives are having a positive impact on students' learning outcomes (Barnekow et al., 2006; Leger et al., 2007; Mérini et al., 2000; SHE, 2008).

Health Sector Participation in School Health Education and Promotion

In Portugal, local health services meet their responsibility for providing children and young people with health care by providing their services directly to students or schools. The section on school health within the Portuguese National Health Plan 2004–2010 (Ministry of Health, 2010) requires health services and schools to work together to provide students with health-promotion and disease-prevention strategies throughout the academic year, and beyond. These activities include monitoring children's health (including vaccination uptake) according to standards set down in the National Health Plan; making sure that children's health needs are met quickly and efficiently (this includes ready access to medical facilities); promoting oral health; and encouraging healthy lifestyles.

Local health centers also collaborate closely with schools to deliver particular facets of the health education curriculum and to promote amelioration of several issues. Content focuses on healthy food (under the slogan, healthy eating means a healthy lifestyle); prevention of bullying; sex and emotions; HIV/AIDS; and prevention of substance abuse and dependency (alcohol, tobacco, and other drugs). The health centers furthermore work in partnership with local communities (i.e., municipalities) to improve health and safety conditions within schools (e.g., buildings) and their surroundings (Ministry of Health, 2010).

Table 1 outlines the school goals that the Ministry of Health set down for 2010 (Ministry of Health, 2010, p. 1). Over-arching goals were for all health centers in Portugal to have school health teams, all schools to experience hygiene and safety evaluations, and all health-promotion interventions to be supported by well-defined implementation guidelines.

Health education in Portugal is an important component of school activity, but it must take into account the setting in which it is conducted. The school is, first of all, a place of cognitive and social learning, and so not really a place of healing. Schools should therefore not focus on health risks and diseases. Ideally, they should be ever mindful that good health enhances learning outcomes (IUHPE, 2008) and offers experiences and teaches skills that enable children and young people to be agentic in improving their own health and wellbeing and that of others in their community. Tones and Tilford (1994, p. 11) capture this thinking:

> Health education is any intentional activity which is designed to achieve health or illness related learning, i.e. some relatively permanent change in an individual's capability or disposition. Effective health education may, thus, produce changes in knowledge and understanding or ways of thinking; it may influence or clarify values; it may bring about some shift in belief or attitude; it may even effect changes in behavior or lifestyle.

Education Sector Participation in School Health Education and Promotion

Changing to healthier behaviors is a relatively complex process that depends, among other factors, on each individual's personal attitudes toward general health, health risks, and health topics (nutrition, sexuality, etc.). Attitudes are, in this context, judgments that are more or less favorable with respect to health issues. These judgments depend on individuals' knowledge (health subject matters), beliefs, and social representations, as well as the generated emotional reactions and intended reactions (Larue, Fortin, & Michard, 2000). The Portuguese Ministry of Education (DGIDC, 2010b, p. 1) thus states that in "the school context, health education consists of providing children and young people with knowledge, attitudes and values that can help them select options and make decisions appropriate to their health and to their physical, social and mental wellbeing."

The Portuguese Ministry of Education, which is responsible for monitoring and assessing school health activities, pays particular heed to five priority topics, all of which align with health sector priorities (see above). These are healthy food and physical activity, prevention of alcohol and drug abuse, sex education, sexually transmitted infections, and mental health and prevention of school bullying (DGIDC, 2010c).

Table 1. School health goals for 2010

Indicator	Situation in 2009 (percentages meeting goals)	Goals for 2010 (target percentages)
• Health centers with school health teams	96	100
• Health status of six-year-old students monitored	71	90
• Health status of 13-year-old students monitored	31	75
• Preschool students up to date with vaccinations	82	95
• Six-year-old students up to date with vaccinations	90	99
• Thirteen-year-old students up to date with vaccinations	78	95
• Students with particular health needs have those needs addressed by the end of the school year	53	75
• Hygiene and safety in all schools evaluated	65	100
• Schools meet "good" standards of hygiene and safety	64	90
• School buildings and surroundings show "good" standards of hygiene and safety	18	60
• Health-promotion interventions supported by well-defined implementation guidelines	20	100
• Six-year-old students free of caries (tooth decay)	33	65
• CLFD index (number of adult teeth with caries, lost, or filled) conducted of all 12-year-old children	2.95	1.90
• Twelve-year-old children needing dental treatment, treated by end of school year	18	60

In Portugal, as in other countries, school health education tends to be based on a topic approach, which means each of the topics just mentioned is taught separately. Various stakeholders have criticized this approach. It can be "problematic or ineffective as such approaches are sometimes based on assumptions relating to human behaviour, which are difficult to justify and not supported by evidence" (IUHPE, 2008, p. 4). Because teaching the topics separately (and properly) represents a very large portion of teaching time—time that teachers usually do not have—teachers tend to respond by transmitting information only (Pizon, 2008). Therefore, instead of teachers taking on an exhaustive approach, topic by topic, a more effective approach is for them to develop children's and young people's life skills and competencies, so enabling them to consider different health topics within the reality of the social and environmental contexts of their lives (IUHPE, 2008).

CONCLUSION

When health education centers neither on disease nor on risk behaviors but on empowering people, mere transmission of knowledge in classrooms about different health-related risk behaviors is not enough. Sustainable and effective prevention of health risks supports people in ways that enable them to take responsibility for their own health and for the health of others in their families and communities (Pizon, 2008).

The health promoting schools concept places considerable emphasis on empowering students and building their capacity to make healthy choices (Leger et al., 2007). Children and young people can thus have an important role in healthy school initiatives, such as the food provided in the school canteen, a clean safe physical environment, and policies concerning social matters, such as bullying. When children and young people collectively work toward securing good health—physical, environmental, and social—they cannot help but work toward a healthier society, both within and beyond the school gates.

REFERENCES

Antonovsky, A. (1987). *Unravelling the mystery of health: How people manage others and stay well.* New York: Wiley.

Barnekow, V., Buijs, G., Clift, S., Jensen, B. B., Paulus, P., Rivett, D., & Young, I. (2006). *Health-promoting schools: A resource for developing indicators.* Copenhagen, Denmark: Council of Europe, World Health Organization, European Commission.

Birk, L., & Silvertown, J. W. (1984). *More than the parts: Biology and politics.* London, UK: Pluto Press.

Carvalho, A., & Carvalho, G. S. (2006). *Educação para a Saúde: Conceitos, práticas e necessidades de formação* [Health education: Concepts, practices and training needs]. Loures, Portugal: Lusociência.

Carvalho, G. S. (2002). Literacia para a Saúde: Um contributo para a redução das desigualdades em saúde [Health literacy: A contribution to reducing inequalities in health]. In M. E. Leandro, M. M. L. Araújo, & M. S. Costa (Eds.), *Saúde: As teias da discriminação social–Actas do Colóquio Internacional: Saúde e Discriminação Social* [Health: The webs of social discrimination. Proceedings of the International Conference on Health and Discrimination] (pp. 119–135). Braga, Portugal: University of Minho.

Carvalho, G. S. (2006). Criação de ambientes favoráveis para a promoção de estilos de vida saudáveis [Creating environments that promote healthy lifestyles]. In B. Pereira & G. S. Carvalho (Eds.), *Actividade Física, Saúde e Lazer: A Infância e Estilos de Vida Saudáveis* [Physical activity, health and leisure: Children and healthy lifestyles] (pp. 19–37). Lisbon, Portugal: Lidel.

Carvalho, G. S., Dantas, C., Rauma, A.-L., Luzi, D., Ruggier, R., Geier, C., Caussidier, C., Berger, D., & Clément, P. (2008). Comparing health education approaches in the textbooks of sixteen countries. *Science Education International, 19*(2) 133–146.

Colquhoun, D. (1997). The health promoting school in Australia: A review. *International Journal of Health Education, 35,* 117–125.

Csergo, J. (2002). Propreté et enfance au XIX siècle [Hygiene and childhood in the 19th century]. In D. Nourisson (Ed.), *Éducation à la Santé: XIXᵉ–XXᵉ siècle* [Health education from the 19th to the 20th centuries] (pp. 43–56). Rennes, France: Editions ENSP.

Directorate General for Innovation and Curriculum Development (DGIDC). (2010a). *SHE*. Retrieved from http://www.dgidc.min-edu.pt/SAUDE/Paginas/she.aspx.

Directorate General for Innovation and Curriculum Development (DGIDC). (2010b). *Educação para a Saúde* [Health education]. Retrieved from http://www.dgidc.min-edu.pt/saude/Paginas/default.aspx.

Directorate General for Innovation and Curriculum Development (DGIDC). (2010c). *Educação para a Saúde: Áreas Prioritárias* [Health education: Priority areas]. Retrieved from http://www.dgidc.min-edu.pt/SAUDE/Paginas/areas_Prioritarias.aspx.

European Network of Health Promoting Schools (ENHPS). (1997). [Website]. Retrieved from http://ec.europa.eu/health/ph_overview/previous_programme/promotion/networks_enhps_promotion_en.htm.

Ewles, L., & Simnett, I. (1999). *Promoting health: A practical guide.* London, UK: Baillière Tindall.

International Union for Health Promotion and Education (IUHPE). (2008). *Achieving health promoting schools: Guidelines for promoting health in schools.* Saint-Denis, France: Author.

Katz, J., & Peberdy, A. (1998). *Promoting health: Knowledge and practice.* London, UK: MacMillan.

Kemm, L. (2006). The limitations of evidenced public health. *Journal of Evaluation in Clinical Practice, 12*, 319.

Larue, R., Fortin J., & Michard J.-L. (2000). *Ecole et santé: Le pari de l'éducation, collection enjeux du système éducatif* [School and health: The challenge of education, critical issues in the education system.]. Paris, France: Hachette Education.

Leger, L. St., Kolbe, L., Lee, A., McCall, D. S., & Young, I. M. (2007). School health promotion: Achievements, challenges and priorities. In D. V. McQueen & C. M. Jones (Eds.), *Global perspectives on health promotion effectiveness* (pp. 107–124). New York: Springer.

Mérini C., Jourdan, D., Victor, P., Berger, D., & De Peretti, C. (2000). *Guide ressource pour une éducation à la santé à l'école primaire* [Guidelines for health education in primary schools]. Rennes, France: Editions ENSP.

Ministry of Health. (2010). *Plano Nacional de Saúde 2004–2010* [National Health Plan 2004–2010]. Retrieved from http://www.dgsaude.min-aude.pt/pns/vol1_531.html.

Naidoo, J., & Wills, J. (1994). *Health promotion: Foundations for practice.* London, UK: Baillière Tindall.

Parsons, C., Stears, D., & Thomas, C. (1996). The health promoting school in Europe: Conceptualising and evaluating the change. *Health Education Journal, 55*, 311–321.

Pizon, F. (2008). *Education et santé au lycée: Quelle contribution à la prévention du tabagisme pour les professionnels?* [Education and health in high schools: What influence does it have on preventing smoking amongst professionals?]. Unpublished doctoral dissertation, Blaise Pascal University, Clermont-Ferrand, France.

Pommier, J., & Jourdan, D. (2007). *La santé à l'école dans les pays Européens* [School health education in European countries]. Paris, France: Sudel.

Sandrin-Berthon, B. (2000). Approche historique de l'éducation pour la santé à l'école [Historical approaches to health education in schools]. *La Santé de l'Homme, 346.*

Schools for Health in Europe (SHE). (2008). Who is SHE? *SHE Newsletter*, September.

Tones, K., & Tilford, S. (1994). *Health Education: Effectiveness, efficiency and equity.* London, UK: Chapman & Hall.

World Health Organization (WHO). (1986). *Ottawa Charter for Health Promotion: First International Conference on Health Promotion, Ottawa, Canada.* Retrieved from http://www.who.int/hpr/NPH/docs/ottawa_charter_hp.pdf.

Graça S. Carvalho
University of Minho
Braga
Portugal
email: graca@ie.uminho.pt

MAGDOLNA CHRAPPÁN

6. THE POSSIBILITY OF HEALTH EDUCATION IN AN EDUCATION-BASED SOCIETY

The Case of Hungary

BACKGROUND

Hungary is located in Central Europe. Its area is 93,030 square kilometers and it has a population of 10,014,000 people (Hungarian Central Statistics Office, 2010). The country is ethnically homogenous. Thirteen nationalities other than Hungarians live in Hungary, but they make up less than 10% of the population. Hungary was the first of the former socialist countries to make the transition to a "capitalist system," which led to economic and social polarization. Although the country's environmental conditions are conducive to a healthy lifestyle, social changes in the last 20 years have resulted in a very high incidence of lifestyle-related (diabetes, heart conditions, cancer) and psychological diseases (stress, depression, and alcohol and drug addiction), a pattern similar to that in other Western European countries.

The data in Table 1 suggest that health education for both adults and children in Hungary needs to be much more effective than it is, although the situation seems to be somewhat better for children 15 years old and younger than for adults. This pattern is especially apparent when we compare these data with the results of national trends relating to eating habits and responsible sexual behavior (e.g., use of condoms in order to prevent sexually transmitted diseases, notably HIV/AIDS). These trends among Hungary's young people are positive in nature (Németh, 2007), and probably reflect health campaigns focused on specific issues (e.g., safe sex) as well as curriculum changes over the last two decades.

The only positive trends among the adult population have been decreases in the annual suicide rate and in smoking but they have been offset by a doubling in the rate of obesity since 1989 (Mladovsky, Allin, Masseria, Hernandez-Quevedo, McDaid, & Mossialos, 2010). These developments strongly indicate the advisability of offering much more intensive health education and health promotion programs for adults that align with best practice internationally (Clift & Jensen, 2005; Obilade, 2005; World Health Organization, 2001). Hungary, just like other countries in the European Union, considers adult education and lifelong learning as strategic to securing economic and social wellbeing. However, most education for adults comprises either formal training within the labor market or informal ad hoc courses run by the civil sector and focused on general interest topics. Nevertheless, this provision could be the best entry point for education directed at improving adults' health-related behavior (Obilade, 2005).

N. Taylor, F. Quinn, M. Littledyke and R.K. Coll (eds.), Health Education in Context, 47–56.

Table 1. Hungary's health indicator rankings relative to those of other OECD countries

Among adults	Hungary's ranking	Number of examined countries
Life expectancy at birth*	29	30
Mortality from heart disease*	28	29
Mortality from stroke*	29	29
Mortality from cancer*	28	28
Tobacco consumption among adults*	27	28
Alcohol consumption among adults*	27	30
Overweight and obesity among adults*	23	27
Suicide*	27	28
Treatable mortality**	17	20
Preventable mortality**	20	20
Among children (at ages 12, 13, and 15)		
Dental health*	27	28
Smoking consumption*	20	24
Alcohol consumption*	20	24
Overweight and obesity*	18	25
Nutrition (daily fruit eating)*	16	25
Physical activity*	10	25

Sources: *Organisation for Economic Co-operation and Development (2009), ** Mladovsky et al. (2010).

Concerns about the declining state of health amongst Hungarian adults and the fact that Hungary's population is an aging one (there is a higher proportion of people in older than younger age brackets) brings into focus an important question: how can the health education component of public education be increased and made more effective? Tones' (2005) maxim that "Health Promotion = Healthy Public Policy x Health Education" provides an answer. The implication here is that health education both within schools and beyond must be supported by strong state-sector policies and practices. While state-based legislation and strategies do champion comprehensive health promotion, these measures are undermined by controls and sanctions, powerless non-government organizations (NGOs), under-financing, and lobbying from commercial bodies and concerns (Tones, 2005). Piecemeal rather than coordinated initiatives are the outcome.

HEALTH EDUCATION IN THE HUNGARIAN PUBLIC EDUCATION SYSTEM

Basic health education is taught at school and is part of the regular curriculum. The current school system is compulsory for children between ages 6 and 18. Children attend kindergarten from three to six years of age, and then enter primary school (Classes 1 to 8). Post-primary, children can choose to enter different types of school: secondary general, secondary vocational, and vocational. The following sections discuss how the different levels of the formal education system in Hungary position health education.

Kindergarten

Health education is an important part of kindergarten programs, which are developed at the central government level. The prominence given to health education in kindergartens is not surprising because the aim of most activities in these institutions is to develop children's physical and emotional wellbeing. More specifically, kindergarten programs focus on helping children develop good eating and personal hygiene habits, providing children with an environment in which they feel socially and emotionally safe, and allowing children plenty of scope for physical activity so that they can enhance their motor-coordination and kinesthetic skills and abilities. Help with developing other everyday skills, such as dressing oneself, along with more broad-based sensibilities, such as learning how to look after the natural environment, is also a typical part of kindergarten programs (ÓNOAP, 2010).

Hungarian kindergartens employ a combination of pedagogies, notably Montessori, Freinet, and Waldorf, all of which are underpinned by the concept of "learning by doing." Staff consequently encourage the children to become self-reliant (e.g., take responsibility for their personal hygiene), and they take them on visits to places such as shops, markets, dentists, food-producing farms, and factories. Regular use is made of projects focused on improving the children's understanding of a healthy lifestyle (eating habits, physical activities, hygiene) and environmental sustainability. The children's parents frequently participate in these activities, and the kindergartens have strong relationship with agencies in the public sector and with NGOs. The latter include foundations, associations, and charitable organizations, all of which organize programs (mainly healthy eating, sports, and protection of the environment) for preschool children and their parents.

Health and educational officials see these various initiatives at the kindergarten level as changing not only the children's health-related attitudes and habits but also their parents'. They also consider that health-promoting activity in kindergartens has a more positive influence on parents than any kind of information campaign.

The School System in General

The Hungarian school system's traditions are rooted in traditional knowledge-focused pedagogy, which means that school is a place where teachers transmit the curriculum exactly as it is set down, and students learn it. The school curriculum therefore typically comprises "neatly packaged" content relating to different arts- and science-based subjects.

This approach hinders the development of better health education for several reasons. First, the strict adherence to the subjects contained in the curriculum means that extracurricular activities receive little, if any, attention. Second, schools are suspicious of working with people not qualified as teachers, even if those people have expertise in various knowledge domains. The law aids this situation because it strictly limits teaching to qualified teachers. Third, the teaching and learning process at school positions students as passive recipients. Student-centered activities are rare, especially in the middle and secondary schools. The opportunities that children in the early years of schooling have to actively engage in their learning almost disappears at the higher levels, where all but a very few teachers employ a transmission model of pedagogy.

The "body and mental health" section of the national curriculum focuses on forming positive attitudes, behaviors, and habits among children, training them to make the right lifestyle decisions, showing them how to prevent dangerous situations at home and other places, advising them on how to avoid harmful addictions, giving them guidance on safe and appropriate sexual behaviors, and helping them appreciate the value of a supportive, well-functioning family life. Appropriate behavior for teachers is also stressed (Ministry of Education and Culture, 2007). The national curriculum frequently emphasizes that teachers need to model healthy lifestyles for their students, and it reminds teachers that their everyday behavior must support what they teach.

In 2004, the Ministry of Education published resources that advised schools on developing health education programs that would align with the strategic purposes of the national curriculum. Schools were encouraged to set up health-development teams consisting of the principal, a health educator, the school drugs counselor, the school doctor or nurse, a physical education teacher, the after-school activity coordinator, and the educator responsible for child and youth protection (Ministry of Education, 2004). These professionals would be responsible for organizing health education and liaising with families and health and social organizations.

In order to comply with the requirements of the national curriculum, school health-education programs have to meet five conditions:

1. The program must be comprehensive, it must be developed by teachers and the other professionals mentioned above, and it must work in association with a NGO.
2. Its content must be based on credible and accessible content that is informed by best practice and research findings.
3. It must allow for the active participation of students.
4. It must have built-in longevity (because of the time needed to facilitate attitudinal changes), have school-wide support, and be taught in a way that is non-threatening and comfortable for all concerned.
5. All program stakeholders (children, school staff, family, media, local policymakers, companies, health and social welfare agencies) must buy in to the program and feel that they own it.

Those involved in planning the program need to ensure that they establish a program that is coherent and that its goals and content accord with those specified by central education authorities. Coherency is important to ensure that the contributions of the various agents associated with health education—educators, outside professionals, school textbook writers, health agencies and foundations, and other civilian organizations—are melded together into a program that serves the needs of the school, its students, and the local community.

Primary Schools

Table 2 summarizes health education content and pedagogy in primary schools. The data in it relate to the curriculum issued by the Ministry of Education and used by most Hungarian schools (Ministry of Education, 2003). The few remaining schools use a variety of other accredited curricula.

Table 2. Healthcare content within primary school subjects

Subject	Grade	Content	Activities
Environmental studies	1–2	• Rhythm of the body (heartbeat, breathing, sleeping, waking) • Role of sensory organs with respect to experiencing the environment • Seasons, weather, clothing, personal hygiene • Observation of the living body, building up of daily routine • Dental and bodily hygiene • People with physical and/or mental disabilities	• Observations, games • Situation and role-playing games • Measuring of body parts • Practicing techniques • Discussions, role plays
Household studies	1–2	• Using household appliances Allocating time, resources, and money	• Exercises • Discussions • Role plays
	3–4	• Effects of environmental change on our lives • Healthy lifestyle—the daily routine • Symptoms of illness (pain, fever, vomiting, diarrhea, bleeding) • Infectious diseases, importance of vaccinations • Tidy/untidy homes and surroundings • Sources of infection, prevention • Waste management • Habits that endanger one's health (alcohol, drugs, smoking, excessive eating), learning how to avoid them • Effects of advertising on our lives	• Observations, measurements • Exchanging experiences with classmates • Role plays directed at forming appropriate habits • Finding causal relationships • Simple investigations, examinations, experiments • Analysis of advertisements
Physical education (PE)	1–4 and 5–8	• Development of physical abilities • Importance of exercises and relaxation • Personal hygiene	• Games, sports • Discussions

Table 2. Healthcare content within primary school subjects (contd.)

Household studies	6, 8*	• Importance of constructed spaces, energy-saving house construction • Role of plants and the garden in our surroundings • Healthy eating habits • Ingredients in the food • Modern kitchen techniques, importance of tidiness • Household organization, waste management	• Project work • Excursions, field days, observations • Practicing cooking, workshop activities • Experiments
Health education (HE)	5–8 (>12) #	• Keeping safe • Healthy nutrition • Exercises and personal hygiene • Psychoactive substances, alcohol, smoking • Sexuality, stereotypes • Family life and relationships, conflicts • Effects of the environment and evolving technology	• Group work • Project work • Collecting information, interviews • Role plays
Personal and social education (PSE)	7	• Way of life and healthcare • Decisions regarding personal health • Struggles for independence and healthcare • Personal responsibility for the future • Healthy lifestyles and teen life • Me and others (our place in the world) • Observing the rules, deviancy • Responsibility for the community	• Project work • Role plays • Research, discussions
	8	• Importance of bacteria to our healthcare • Human anatomy and physiology, including healthcare information relating to different organs in the body	• Presentations, discussions • Experiments, observations • Group work
Chemistry	7	• Importance of microelements within the living body • Air and water pollution • Fats, carbohydrates, proteins • Plastics, selective waste management	• Presentations • Experiments, observations
Ethics	7	• Instincts, temper, emotion, thinking • Necessities and interests • Preconceptions and tolerance • Values and norms, morals • Appropriate way of life • Social relationships, sexual identity, love • Personal and community values	• Creative work • Project work • Role plays • Research, discussions

Note: *18 lessons per school year; #10 lessons per school year.

Secondary Schools

At secondary grammar, secondary vocational, and vocational schools, health education is subsumed within biology and, to some extent, chemistry and ethics. Biology is offered for one year only in secondary vocational and vocational schools. Because the main emphasis at the secondary level is on academic knowledge, health education is side-lined. Yet health education at this level is especially important, given the health areas of particular relevance to teenagers, notably sex, drugs and alcohol, HIV, and bullying. According to Batár (2003), the sex education that is available to young people is not effective in Hungary. There is thus an urgent need to allocate more time to health education in secondary schools and to increase the number and type of after-school health education activities.

EXTRACURRICULAR ACTIVITIES AND THE ROLE OF OTHER ORGANIZATIONS

Another cornerstone of health education could be school-based extracurricular activities, the most obvious of which is traditional student sport. School sports provide students with cost-free opportunities to enhance their physical fitness. Recent research, however, shows that schools differ greatly in the sports facilities they offer. Seventy-five to 80% of schools meet only the minimum sports infrastructural and equipment requirements (Education Authority, 2010).

Most primary and secondary schools do engage in extracurricular activities, campaigns, and programs related to health issues. One example is a program that is based on an American model and targets drugs, alcohol, smoking, and HIV/AIDS. Run by the Hungarian Police, the program is offered in every school. Children in preschools and primary schools all learn about recycling. Programs about condoms and use of condom machines feature in secondary schools, as does a program that champions the "healthy life."

Programs such as these are usually collaborations between schools and various NGOs. According to Hungarian Justice Courts' records for 2010, 475 registered private organizations in Hungary list health education among their activities (Courts of Justice, 2010). The majority of these organizations are foundations connected to schools; the rest (about 150) focus on various aspects of healthcare and social wellbeing. The activities that these organizations undertake include campaigns directed at, for example, drug-use prevention, safe and sensible alcohol consumption, not smoking or quitting smoking, and ways of avoiding and limiting cancer, heart, and vascular diseases. There are also organizations that provide mental and psychological support. Limited funding, however, compromises the work that these NGOs do. All are financially dependent on private personal pledges, tax deductions, company and corporate donations and grants, and small contributions from government. The fact that the NGOs are operated by volunteers also limits their efficacy.

Organizations in the commercial sector, such as food, biochemical, and other such companies, carry out various health education campaigns. Although there are no data showing the extent to which these agencies target adult (both parents and teachers) and school-age populations, it is clear that they do direct high-volume health education and behavioral campaigns at young people. These campaigns employ modern marketing tools such as company products placed in schools, sponsoring of after-school activities, and conducting programs and competitions likely to appeal to children and young people.

Government-funded health-education-oriented institutions are also of decisive importance within the health education arena because they have the facilities and resources to conceptualize and develop programs, conduct research, and provide professional support. Their efficiency in this regard is, however, variable, as they tend to be stymied by bureaucracy and centralized control, factors that have also prevented the creation of a comprehensive, easily implemented health public policy.

The same can be said of organizations considered to be direct partners of schools. These include not only government ministries but also local health authorities, the police, and social welfare agencies. There is considerable overlap of tasks across these agencies, which makes for inefficient (in terms of time, finances, and personnel) management of drug prevention campaigns, drug addiction rehabilitation initiatives, and HIV/AIDS prevention. This consideration is highlighted when it is realized that five government ministries, each with its own management team, financing, and programs, currently engage in health education. Fewer organizations, less bureaucracy, and more targeted resourcing are needed if health education is to be more successful.

Lack of finance is probably the main reason why health education is not as effective as it could and should be in Hungary. Health education tends to have been an especially expensive area of educational provision in the country, not only because of the unnecessary expense associated with too many agencies trying to do the same thing but also because of the steady decline in government funding over the last years. Poorly executed and implemented health-related initiatives have also added to the expense. Promotion of healthy lifestyles and health behavior does not, however, need to be a financial problem. The value systems that children develop during their socialization in preschool and school have a considerable long-term influence, so it is here that health education is likely to be most effective, and cost-effective. This early grounding not only supports the influences that families, educators, and peers can have on facilitating good health, but also feeds into those influences.

The Role of Teacher-Training Institutions

The only teacher training programs in Hungary where students receive tuition in health education and promotion of healthy lifestyles and behaviors are those for preschool and primary Grades 1 to 4 teachers. Pre-service middle and high school teachers therefore receive no such training, except for drug use prevention, which is included in pedagogy courses.

Since the introduction of the national curriculum, a major portion of in-service teachers' professional development has focused on health education and drug prevention training, and there are now, in every primary and secondary school, at least three or four teachers who have the requisite knowledge and skills. But these teachers remain too few in number because they still have to teach their own subjects, and cope with a heavy workload (15 to 18 lessons weekly). The fact that other teachers rarely see health education as their responsibility adds to the burden.

CONCLUSION

The health data statistics presented in Table 1 of this chapter make it very clear that Hungary's citizens need to change their health-related behavior, and that they need support to do so. Comprehensive education directed at fostering good health habits and skills needs to begin in pre- and primary schools and to continue on, as an important subject, through all levels of the school system. The closed nature of the school system in Hungary means that social agencies can do little at present to support school-based health education, except in preschools and the junior grades of primary school. The weakest point of the school system is the secondary school. There, little time is allocated to health education and formation of healthy lifestyle approaches, even though health education is particularly important at this stage of schooling because it helps students see, and avoid, the consequences of the unhealthy lifestyles evident amongst the adult population.

Schools have to become more receptive to health education and open to support from agencies outside the school. Health professionals need to be strongly involved, and measures need to be put in place so that they can legally work with and within schools. Schools also need to form collaborative relationships with parents, and to draw on parents' and other community support to develop and implement comprehensive health education action programs. Making health education a strong component of teacher education (both pre- and in-service and across all levels of the education system) is likely to be one of the most resource-efficient and quickest catalysts for change. Health education is too important to be left to just a few teachers or for aspects of it to be simply incorporated within other subjects, such as biology. A school environment supportive of health education can only be achieved if all teachers within it work together to create and sustain that environment.

REFERENCES

Batár, I. (2003). Sex education in Hungary. *Entre Nous: The European Magazine for Sexual and Reproductive Health*, *56*, 19–22.

Clift, S., & Jensen, B. B. (Eds.). (2005). *The health promoting school: International advances in theory, evaluation and practice.* Copenhagen, Denmark: Danish University of Education Press.

Courts of Justice. (2010). *Homepage.* Retrieved from http://www.birosagok.hu/engine. aspx?page=tarsszervsearch.

Education Authority. (2010). *Jelentés a tanórán kívül szervezett iskolai sportkörök, sportfoglalkozások országos szakmai* ellenőrzéséről [Report on supervision of extracurricular sports activities in primary and secondary schools]. Budapest, Hungary: Retrieved from http://www.oh. gov.hu/kozoktatas/kozoktatasi-hatosagi/elvegzett-hatosagi.

Hungarian Central Statistics Office. (2010). *Népességadatok* [Hungarian population data]. Retrieved from http://portal.ksh.hu/pls/ksh/docs/hun/ xstadat/xstadat_hosszu/h_wdsd001a.html.

Ministry of Education. (2003). *Kerettanterv az általános iskolák számára* [Curriculum framework for primary schools]. Budapest, Hungary: Author. Retrieved from http://www.nefmi.gov. hu/kozoktatas/tantervek/kerettanterv-2000.

Ministry of Education. (2004). *Segédlet az iskolai egészségnevelési, egészségfejlesztési program kidolgozásához* [Resources for creating health education programs in schools]. Budapest, Hungary: Author.

Ministry of Education and Culture. (2007). *Nemzeti alaptanterv* [National curriculum]. Budapest, Hungary: Author. Retrieved from http://www.okm.gov.hu/letolt/kozokt/nat_070926.pdf.

Mladovsky, P., Allin, S., Masseria, C., Hernandez-Quevedo, C., McDaid, D., & Mossialos, E. (2010). *Health in the European Union: Trends and analysis. Observatory Studies Series, No. 19.* Brussels, Belgium: European Observatory on Health Systems and Policies, World Health Organization.

Németh, Á. (Ed.). (2007). *Serdülőkorú fiatalok egészsége és életmódja* [Health behavior of Hungarian teenagers]. Budapest, Hungary: National Institute of Child Health.

Obilade, O. O. (2005). Health education. In L. M. English (Ed.), *International encyclopedia of adult education* (pp. 274–277). Basingstoke, UK: Palgrave-Macmillan.

ÓNOAP. (2010). *Az Óvodai nevelés országos alapprogramja* [National curriculum for education in kindergartens]. Retrieved from http://net.jogtar.hu/jr/gen/hjegy_doc.cgi?docid=99600137.KOR.

Organisation for Economic Co-operation and Development (OECD). (2009). *Health at a glance.* Paris, France: Author. Retrieved from http://www.oecd-ilibrary.org/content/book/health_glance-2009-en.

Tones, K. (2005). Health promotion in school: The radical imperative. In S. Clift & B. B. Jensen (Eds.), *The health promoting school: International advances in theory, evaluation and practice* (pp. 23–41). Copenhagen, Denmark: Danish University of Education Press.

World Health Organization (WHO). (2001). *Skills for health: Skill-based health education including life skills: An important component of a child friendly/health-promoting school* (WHO's Information Series on School Health, Document 9). Retrieved from http://www.who.int/school_youth_health/media/en/sch_skills4health_03.pdf.

Magdolna Chrappán
University of Debrecen
Debrecen
Hungary
email: chrappanm@gmail.com

7. AN OVERVIEW OF FORMAL AND NON-FORMAL HEALTH EDUCATION IN TURKEY

INTRODUCTION

When the Ottoman Empire collapsed after the First World War, a new republic named Turkey was established in 1923. Since then, Turkey has paid considerable attention to keeping up with the standards of developed countries—in education, science, health, economics, and commerce. Effort directed at achieving these standards in education was initially signaled by the Act of the Law of Unification of Instruction 1924. The Act centralized the Turkish educational system by placing its governance under the control of the Ministry of National Education. This centralized oversight encompassed all schools, including religious schools. The only exceptions were schools for ethnic minorities living in Turkey, namely, Armenians, Greeks, and Jews (Ayas, Çepni, & Akdeniz, 1993).

The establishment of health education was another step along the standards pathway. Initially provided for under the Act of Public Health 1930, health education was successively modified in line with developments within the government sector. These included the establishment in 1936 of the Social Welfare Works Department within the Department of Education Affairs and Executive Approval, which, in 1960, became the General Directorate of Professional Supervision and Training. The following year, the Grand National Assembly of Turkey made health education a compulsory part of school curricula.

In 1978, Turkey signed the Declaration of Alma-Ata.[1] The declaration expressed the need for urgent action by all signatory governments, all health and development workers, and the world community to protect and promote the health of all the people of the world. In signing the declaration, Turkey agreed to meet the precepts of primary health care, that is, adequate food supplies and proper nutrition, adequate supply of safe water, immunization against major infectious diseases, basic sanitation, and health education (Öztek & Eren, 2006). In 1982, restructuring of the Ministry of Health led to the General Directorate of Professional Supervision and Training being renamed the General Directorate of Education. One of its goals was to promote and implement a more robust system of health education.

Pursuit of this goal gained momentum in the 1990s with the launch of the Reconstruction of Health Education Project. Its establishment grew out of Turkey's desire to meet European Union standards for a healthy workforce, and it aligned with Turkish health goals identified during an earlier round of health sector reforms. As part of the project, a three-year health-education institute supervised by the Ministry of Health was replaced in 1994 with the current Faculty of Health

N. Taylor, F. Quinn, M. Littledyke and R.K. Coll (eds.), Health Education in Context, 57–66.
© *2012 Sense Publishers. All rights reserved.*

Education. The faculty offers undergraduate programs and operates under the auspices of Turkey's Higher Education Council.

In 2000, the Ministry of Health published public health education regulations in an effort to make people more aware of the importance of health education. The ministry also wanted to inform its own employers about their obligations with respect to public health education.

Despite the relevance that these various developments have for health education, and despite health education being a subject in its own right in certain contexts,[2] this area of educational provision remains largely embedded in the curricula of preschools and primary and secondary schools. This is true even of Turkey's recently released new science curriculum, the content and design of which aligns with Turkey's practice, as a developing country, to draw on innovative developments worldwide, including those pertaining to health. Here, we might expect to see health education gain prominence, given the six aims that underpin the curriculum.

1. Help students become scientifically literate;
2. Develop student-centered learning;
3. Raise the educational-attainment level (and thereby the quality) of Turkish society;
4. Keep up with advances in technology and contemporary science;
5. Help students link theoretical knowledge to daily-life experiences; and
6. Bring new developments in pedagogy and assessment of learning to the classroom.

However, as the following findings of our analysis show, health education remains an embedded rather than a prominent part of the curriculum.

ANALYSIS OF CURRICULA RELATED TO HEALTH EDUCATION

To examine the extent to which preschool, primary, and secondary school curricula incorporate health education, we decided to use each of the five principles informing the work of the World Health Organization as themes denoting health education. These themes are as follows:

• Theme 1: Ensure that people understand the significance for them and society of good health (both physical and mental);
• Theme 2: Encourage individuals and society to solve their own health problems;
• Theme 3: Enable individuals and society to make effective use of health foundations and companies;
• Theme 4: Encourage individuals and communities to adopt healthy habits and lifestyles; and
• Theme 5: Persuade individuals and society to look after their own health.

We used these themes as a means of identifying content within the various subjects of Turkey's preschool and school curricula that could be labeled health education. Table 1 provides a summary of our findings with regard to preschool and primary school courses, while Table 2 does the same for secondary school courses. Each table cites course name, the grades at which each course is taught, and the health themes evident in that course.

Table 1. Health education themes evident in preschool and primary school courses

School	Name of course	Grade	Theme number
Kindergarten		Preschool	1, 4, 5
Primary	Knowledge of life*	Grades 1–2	1, 4, 5
		Grade 3	4, 5
	Turkish language*	Grade 4	1, 5
	Science and technology*	Grade 4	2, 4, 5
		Grades 5 & 7	1, 4, 5
		Grade 6	1, 5
		Grade 8	1
	Social science*	Grades 4–5	3
	Sports activities**	Grades 1–8	2, 4
	English*	Grade 4	4
		Grade 5	1, 2, 5
		Grade 6	5
		Grade 7	1
	Culture of religion and ethics*	Grade 4	1, 5
		Grade 6	5
		Grade 7	1, 2, 5
	Physical education*	Grades 1–3	5
		Grades 4–8	4, 5
	Computer**	Grade 2	5
	Agriculture**	Grades 6, 7, 8	4
	Traffic and first aid*	Grades 4–5	2, 5

Note: *These courses are compulsory. **These courses are elective.

Table 2. Health education themes evident in secondary school courses

Course	Grade	Theme number
Biology*	Grade 9	5
	Grade 12	4,5
Psychology**	Grade 10	1, 5
Contemporary Turkish and world history**	Grade 12	2
Human anatomy**	Grade 9	1
Sport and nutrition**	Grade 11	1, 5
Fundamental sports training**	Grade 9	1, 5
Physics*	Grade 9	4
	Grade 12	5
Health knowledge*	Grade 9	1, 2, 3, 5

Note: *These courses are not only common courses but also compulsory. **These courses are generally compulsory for Grade 9 but those in Grades 10–12 are compulsory for students who must attend their main subject-matter interests.

As is evident in Tables 1 and 2, only one course, health knowledge, relates directly to health education. It contains all themes except Theme 4. Of the other courses with an implicit focus on health education, the only course that incorporates Theme 3 is social science (effective use of health agencies).

ANALYSIS OF HEALTH-RELATED SPECIAL EVENTS

We also used the five themes to conduct an analysis of health-related special days and weeks in the Turkish calendar, the findings of which appear in Table 3. These activities are a part of informal health education, and the intention behind them is to enhance social awareness of health issues. Information is disseminated primarily through the media, and schools and adult education programs often create activities and challenges in response to these events. Taken together, these events create a health education environment. Another intention behind these special promotions is to coordinate the activities of governmental and non-governmental organizations (NGOs), and particularly those of the Ministries of National Education and Health, which play a significant role in planning and implementing these events.

When we look at Table 3, we can see that all of the events that we analyzed concentrate mainly on Theme 1, except for World Food Day. Table 3 also shows that the themes apparent in these days and weeks overlap somewhat with the themes evident in primary and secondary school curricula courses, evidence that the informal education associated with these events reinforces what is taught in formal education.

Table 3. Health education themes evident in health-related special days and weeks in the Turkish calendar

Name of special days/weeks	Date	Theme(s)
Public Health Week	September 3–9	1, 3, 5
Tuberculosis Education Week	January 3–9	1, 5
Green Crescent Week	March 1–7	1, 5
Cancer Week	April 1–7	1, 4, 5
World Health Day	April 7	1, 5
Health Week	April 7–13	1, 3, 4
World No Tobacco Day	May 31	1, 5
World Food Day	October 16	4
World AIDS Day	December 1	1, 5

KEY ORGANIZATIONS INVOLVED IN HEALTH EDUCATION

In this section, we take a closer look at some of the key organizations that have endeavored to lead the development of health education in Turkey. The first group of organizations considered here includes governmental and the second non-governmental.

Government Organizations and their Scope

The two main government agencies responsible for health education today are the Ministry of National Education and the Ministry of Health Affairs. Although both ministries share certain responsibilities, the Ministry of National Education has primary responsibility for health education in schools and the Ministry of Health concentrates primarily on public health education.

One of the responsibilities of the General Directorate of Health Affairs, established in 1958 under the Ministry of National Education, was health education. Later, the directorate was renamed the Office of Health Affairs. It has been serving the Ministry of National Education since 1982. The role of the office is to help bring up healthy generations of children by providing health education for teachers and students in all schools. The office oversees health vocational schools, which provide courses for students wanting to work in the health sector. All students in the vocational schools receive some training in health education. The office designs and conducts health education programs in schools related to reproductive health, substance abuse, food security, and mother and child health. The office also collaborates with many other national and international organizations and institutions when developing and implementing these programs. These other agencies include the following:

- Turkish Radio and Television (an official media foundation)
- International Child Center
- Universities
- AIDS Prevention Association
- Mother–Child Education Foundation
- Human Resource Development Foundation
- Cancer Research Institute, KASEV-Kadıköy
- Health Education Foundation
- Red Crescent Society (Ministry of National Education, 2011).

In 2000, the Ministry of Health released a regulation on public health education. The terms of this regulation require the ministry not only to heighten public understanding of health issues but also to improve people's health-related attitudes and behaviors. The ministry also provides people with ideas on how they can protect their health. The emphasis, under the regulation, is on ensuring that the public can readily access health services and that they know their rights in relation to health. The regulation also provides guidance for staff responsible for managing health education work carried out by the ministry's central and provincial offices.

In July 2009, the Grand National Assembly of Turkey approved a "smoke-free" law. Smoking is now forbidden inside public transport, particularly aircraft, buses, and trains, as well as other enclosed vehicles, restaurants, bars, cafes, traditional teahouses, and air-conditioned public places.

Non-Governmental Organizations and their Scope

NGOs promote public understanding and awareness of health issues. They do little in the way of formal health education. For example, the main focus of the Red Crescent Club is to promote the importance and benefits of blood donation and to help people recognize and protect themselves against certain dangerous diseases. The Green Crescent Club addresses the adverse effects of alcohol and cigarettes on public and personal health, and offers means of overcoming dependency on or abuse of these products. To raise public consciousness of these issues, the club conducts some formal information dissemination activities. These include conferences, press releases, road trips, courses, and seminars, as well as publication of journals, writing of articles for publication in other print media, car bumper stickers, and so forth. The club also organizes and implements regular education activities and distributes its own teaching and learning materials to schools.

The Mother–Child Education Foundation carries out activities relating to family health. One of its main initiatives is its Mother–Child Education Program. The foundation's main aim is to promote and enable the optimal physical, cognitive, and social development of young children. A particular sub-aim is to facilitate the conditions that allow children to feel emotionally secure and to develop good self-esteem. The foundation also works to keep mothers informed about family planning, reproductive health, and the vital role they play in their children's development.

The foundation furthermore, through public-oriented health education, provides education and training for mothers and doctors in neonatology, a subspecialty of pediatrics that comprises the medical care of newborn infants, especially those who are ill or premature. The foundation also sets up and has oversight of mother–infant training centers—the agencies that carry out the foundation's objectives.

The Turkish Association for Cancer Research and Control works collaboratively with the Cancer Control Department of the Ministry of Health. A particular area of responsibility for the association is raising public awareness of cancer and its causes. Working under the slogan "War on Cancer," the association carries out its information campaign through the public health services and other institutions and organizations.

The Smoking and Health National Committee, founded in 1995, was set up to fulfill the aim implicit in the inspiring "United for a Tobacco-Free World" slogan of the World Health Organization. The committee, which represents over 40 official and civil institutions, maintains that all sectors of society should work together to broadcast the dangers of tobacco and to encourage people to give up cigarettes and other tobacco products. According to the Global Adults Tobacco Survey (2008), nearly 16 million adults in Turkey (a number that represents 31.2% of the country's total adult population) are smokers. Just under 48% of Turkish men and a little more than 15% of Turkish women currently smoke tobacco. Use of tobacco products is associated with approximately 100,000 deaths per year in Turkey (Ministry of Health, 2008). These statistics continue to give urgency to the committee's efforts to disseminate information about the dangers of smoking.

Typical dissemination outlets are conferences, seminars, radio and television programs, and specific events, such World No Tobacco Day, which is held on the 31st of May each year.

SOME REFLECTIONS ON THE CURRENT STATE OF HEALTH EDUCATION

Alkan, Ertem, Hatemoğlu, Hülür, and Mollahaliloğlu (2005) point out that despite initiatives directed at improving the health-related behavior of people in Turkey, the standard of behavior evident remains unsatisfactory. Their claim is evident in various studies conducted during the first decade of this century. For example, Ögel and Liman's (2003) study of 24,000 primary and secondary school students from throughout Turkey found that about 50% of all these students were habituated smokers and drinkers of alcohol. They also found that 19% of primary school students and 54% of secondary school students were addicted to drugs. Ekici (2000) found that only about 15% of the children under investigation said they brushed their teeth regularly while around 75% disregarded basic hygiene rules.

These types of data along with the facts that Turkey has nearly 16 million students ranging from 6 to 18 years of age and 700,000 teachers give prominence to the need for comprehensive health education in schools (Baysal, 2010). Because Turkey, as a developing country, tracks innovative developments, it is somewhat behind in terms of implementing more robust and effective health education measures; the same can be said of the country's environmental and science education provision (see, for example, Çalık, 2009; Çalık & Ayas, 2008; Kaysılı, 2006).

We might assume that Turkey would have developed a more effective system of health education by now, given that health education was established under the fundamental law on health, which was enacted some 17 years before the Declaration of Alma-Ata. It seems reasonable to say that Turkey has done relatively well in terms of informal health education, but that considerably more work is needed with respect to developing and implementing formal education.

To date, the only formal provision has been the subject called health knowledge, but its effectiveness is diffused because of its integration across school curricula; it is not a separate subject. This integrated approach is not surprising given that the focus of the newly released school curricula is on intra-discipline and inter-subject topics, as well as scientific literacy. However, before making a final determination on how well this approach is working, we should wait to see the learning outcomes of the new curricula: international experience suggests that a new curriculum can take as long as 10 to 15 years before improvements in learning occur (Çalık & Ayas, 2008).

Although the school curricula are built on constructivist learning theory, conceptual understanding, multiple intelligence theory, active learning, reflective thinking, and cooperative learning (Çalık & Ayas, 2008), there is a shortage of teachers, including health education teachers, familiar with the pedagogies associated with these frameworks (Turhan, 2004). Furthermore, because the subject health knowledge is not assessed by high-stakes national examinations, notably the Selection and Placement of Students in Secondary Schools (SBS) and the Selection and Placement of Students in Higher Education Institution (YGS and LYS), it is likely to remain marginalized in school curricula.

LOOKING AHEAD

The Ministry of Health's health education strategy is highly centralized, which means it operates a top–down model of information dissemination. However, the ministry has recently been planning to give a more active health-education role to NGOs such as the Green Crescent Club. That it is doing so signals its intention to share its health education responsibility with such organizations. The Ministry of Health, in our view, also needs to work more collaboratively with the Ministry of National Education and the universities to provide dedicated health education in schools. We consider that the Ministry of Health must pay more attention to the health-related themes of WHO when developing health-related activities and programs.

Although the Office of Health Affairs within the Ministry of National Education claims that it works collaboratively with various national and international organizations and institutions, we think the office still takes an overly centralized role with respect to health education. For example, the universities that the office engages with are in metropolitan cities, such as İstanbul, Ankara, and Adana. There is a need for this engagement to occur right across the country.

For us, the Ministry of National Education is essentially a first step toward creating an interactive collaborative environment amongst government agencies, NGOs, and other relevant institutes. But this type of cooperation needs to move beyond a focus on theory and policy concerns to a focus on practical initiatives. For example, Çalık (2009) calls for a new course—community education—to be offered within the Faculty of Education's teacher-training programs. This course would give people specialist training in the means of enhancing public and student understanding of health issues at the community level. Elements of the course could also provide teachers, students, and parents with practical resources and ideas related to sustaining good health.

There is a need not only to position health education more firmly within communities but also to make sure that this type of education is made prominent early in children's schooling. Because young children are particularly likely to share their learning with parents and their communities, this approach could be a very effective way of spreading health education from bottom–up.

This grassroots approach would also, we think, work for public health education. Both the Ministry of National Education and the Ministry of Health need to act more as coordinators of the health-education initiatives of other organizations and institutes. The ministries might also consider promoting the idea of having students spend time working voluntarily in local health-education organizations, which would allow for two-way exchanges of information and, in essence, bring school-based health education and public health education together.

A possible name for this initiative might be along the lines of "integrating school health-education curricula into local communities." Students would benefit from gaining a first-hand understanding of what is meant by good public health and how their own attitudes and behaviors contribute to or detract from it. The organizations would benefit by gaining a clearer idea of the types of issues facing students and their communities, which would allow these agencies to develop more targeted health-education programs.

Working with students, especially the younger ones, in this way needs to be conducted carefully. For example, teaching students about the hazardous effects of tobacco or alcohol and the addictive nature of drugs without taking into account student age and stage may simply arouse students' desire to try these products. Thus, all agencies involved in health education should ensure that their activities are complementary and align with respect to what is taught and when within both schools and communities. One implication of this consideration is the need for the work of health vocational high schools and the Faculty of Health Education to be tied in more firmly with—and to help inform—the health-related policies and practices of the Ministry of National Education, the Ministry of Health, and the Council of Higher Education.

NOTES

[1] For a copy of the declaration, go to http://www.who.int/hpr/NPH/docs/declaration_almaata.pdf.
[2] Health education is evident as a compulsory course for Grade 9 students. This course, called health knowledge, comprises two class hours per week and has been in place since 1996 (Kaysılı, 2006). Health education is also seen in high schools offering vocationally oriented health courses.

REFERENCES

Alkan, E., Ertem, A. A., Hatemoğlu, E., Hülür, Ü., & Mollahaliloğlu, S. (2005). *Okullarda sağlık eğitimi* [Health education in schools]. Ankara, Turkey: School of Public Health Directorate.

Ayas, A., Çepni, S., & Akdeniz, A. R. (1993). Development of the Turkish secondary science curriculum. *Science Education, 77*(4), 433–440.

Baysal, S. U. (2010). *Okul sağlığı* [School health]. Istanbul: Turkey: University of Istanbul. Retrieved from oubs.iu.edu.tr/doc/167.doc.

Çalık, M. (2009). An integrated model for environmental education in Turkey. In N. Taylor, R. K. Coll, M. Littledyke, & C. Eames (Eds.), *An international perspective on the development and implementation of environmental education and its impact on student knowledge, attitudes and behaviour* (pp. 109–122). Rotterdam, the Netherlands: Sense Publishers.

Çalık, M., & Ayas, A. (2008). A critical review of the development of the Turkish science curriculum. In R. K. Coll & N. Taylor (Eds.), *Science education in context: An international examination of the influence of context on science curricula development and implementation* (pp. 161–174). Rotterdam, the Netherlands: Sense Publishers.

Ekici, B. (2000). *Çocukların uyku-dinlenme gereksinimleri ve alışkanlıkları* [Sleep–rest requirements of children and their habits]. Paper presented at the National Nursing Congress, Antalya, Turkey.

Global Adults Tobacco Survey. (2008). *Fact sheet Turkey 2008*. Retrieved from http://wwwcdc.gov/tobacco/global/gats/countries/eur/fact_sheets/turkey/2009/pdfs/turkey_2009.pdf.

Kaysılı, B. (2006). *Tanzimat'tan Cumhuriyet'e Türkiye'de sağlık eğitimi üzerine bir araştırma (1839–1938)* [Health education in Turkey from Tanzimat to Republic (1839–1938)]. Unpublished Master's thesis, Institute of Social Sciences, Selçuk University, Konya, Turkey.

Ministry of Health. (2008). *National tobacco control program and action plan for Turkey 2008–2012.* (2008). Ankara, Turkey: Author.

Ministry of National Education. (2011). *Business sectors cooperating with the Office of Health Affairs* (2011). Ankara, Turkey: Author. Retrieved from http://sdb.meb.gov.tr/ calistigimizsektorler html.

Ögel, K., & Liman, O. (2003). *Gençlerde madde kullanım yaygınlığı ve özelliklerinin değerlendirilmesi 2001 araştırması sonuçları.* [Assessment of the prevalence of substance use in young people: 2001 survey results]. İstanbul, Turkey: Yeniden Health and Education Society.

Öztek, Z., & Eren, N. (2006). Sağlık yönetimi [Health management]. In Ç. Güler & L. Akın (Eds.), *Halk sağlığı temel bilgiler [Public health: Basic information]* (pp. 993–1017). Ankara, Turkey: Hacettepe University.

Turhan, K. (2004). Sağlık eğitim fakülteleri'nin durumu [Status of health-education faculties]. *Bilim, Eğitim ve Düşünce Dergisi, 4*(2). Retrieved from http://www.universite-toplum.org/text.php3?id=189.

Muammer Çalik
Fatih Faculty of Education
Karadeniz Technical University
Trabzon
Turkey
email: muammer38@hotmail.com or muammer38@ktu.edu.tr

Gamze Çan
Faculty of Medicine
Karadeniz Technical University
Trabzon
Turkey
email: gcanktu@yahoo.com

MARINA GVOZDEVA AND VALENTINA KIRILINA

8. EDUCATION FOR HEALTHY LIFESTYLES IN THE EUROPEAN NORTH OF RUSSIA

Developments and Dilemmas

INTRODUCTION

Significant changes in the social, political, and economic life of Russian society demand high-quality education for individual and social development. Ecological and social cataclysms, social instability, and deterioration of family foundations and moral principles are particularly detrimental because they result in growth of violence, crime, drug and alcohol addiction, and development of various chronic and acute diseases, especially among children and youth. It is challenging at the best of times for young people to achieve their physical and mental potential, to complete school, to secure a decent job, and to become successful, economically productive and socially responsible adults who can contribute to the wellbeing of their local community, region, and country. The fact that the health of the population in various regions of Russia has deteriorated under the influence of the above factors makes the challenge even greater for many young people.

The Republic of Karelia is located in the area of the European north of Russia and is considered to be a difficult area in which to live (Dorshakova, 1993). This is because the significant fluctuation in weather conditions that characterize Karelia lowers people's immune systems, making them more susceptible to illness, including cardiovascular disorders. The Republic of Karelia has the dubious distinction of having the highest incidence of influenza and the fifth highest rate of diphtheria in the Russian Federation. A more detailed analysis of sickness patterns in the republic shows a high incidence of nearly all types of diseases among adults and children. Average life expectancy in Karelia is 66.7 years (59.7 years for men and 74.2 years for women), which is lower than the Russian average of 68.3 years (Federal Statistics Agency, 2010).

These facts have generated considerable concern among both the medical profession and the general public. Promotion of healthy lifestyles has become ever more important, especially with the relatively recent recognition in Karelia that heredity and parental awareness of healthy behaviors and practices also has a considerable impact on the health of children and young people. To give an example: during the period between 2004 and 2008, one third of newborns were found to have been adversely affected by maternal ill-health while they were in the womb. In general, maternal illness was associated with heredity factors or the

N. Taylor, F. Quinn, M. Littledyke and R.K. Coll (eds.), Health Education in Context, 67–76.

negative impact of exogenous factors, such as smoking. Maternal ill-health also had an impact on breastfed newborns.

Many children in Karelia remain vulnerable during their first year of life, particularly with respect to so-called adaptation diseases. These include, amongst others, neonatal weight loss, allergic dermatitis, intestinal diseases, kidney problems, and neurological difficulties. These conditions generally do not require specific treatment, and the children usually recover fairly quickly. However, lack of necessary preventive measures, disregard of the basic precepts of good child care, and sometimes simple ignorance can lead to these diseases thriving and developing into chronic forms. According to data from the Ministry of Health Care and Social Development of the Republic of Karelia, five percent of newborns per annum have a congenital anomaly, including rachitis (rickets), six percent suffer from neurological diseases, and eight percent from digestive disorders.

As with children throughout Russia, Karelian children continue to face increasingly serious challenges to good health as they grow up. Over the last five or so years, the incidence of illness among children 0 to 17 years of age in the Republic of Karelia has grown by just under 13%. The two main types of illness among children in this age bracket are those of the respiratory system and the gastrointestinal tract. Between 2004 and 2006, diseases of the skin and hypodermic tissue were the third most prevalent type of illness among children, but this ranking was taken over by diseases of the nervous system between 2007 and 2008. The overall incidence of illness among children and young people during this period increased by 12.2% due to growth in nearly all classes of disease. The growth rates for two such classes—neurological diseases and cancers—were particularly alarming, 49% and 46.7%, respectively. Blood and blood-clotting disorders also grew during this time, by 43.7%. The rate of increase for musculoskeletal disorders was 29.8%, and for the endocrine system was 26.6%.

In addition, too many adolescents in Karelia, and in Russia more generally, continue to make choices that have a negative impact on their physical and mental wellbeing. It is essential that students learn how to manage the health problems they already face and avoid additional health problems in the future. Russia therefore needs to address issues relating to health education, particularly the importance of promoting healthy lifestyles and the need to implement up-to-date medical knowledge and technologies. In an effort to provide understanding as to why Russia is experiencing health difficulties, we outline in the next section some of the ideas about health and health education evident in Russia over time.

HEALTH EDUCATION IN RUSSIA: AN HISTORICAL VIEW

As early as 1850, Dr. Symashko, the editor of the journal *Family and School*, emphasized the need to promote healthy lifestyles. His medical textbook (Symashko, 1850) included information about good nutrition, cleanliness (e.g., the need to have regular baths), and disease prevention. In 1883, Alexander Gerd proposed an integrated course for primary school children that would cover the basics of a healthy lifestyle (Gerd, 1928). However, it was not until 1923 that the so-called hygiene syllabus in Russian schools stressed that the main goal of this type of education was to promote behaviors and attitudes favoring holistic health.

Issues surrounding sex education, personal hygiene, and harmful habits were covered by B. E. Raikov in his text *Sexual Education at School* (1927 edition). In it, Raikov not only pointed out the importance of sex education and prevention of at-risk behaviors but also discussed gender relationships.

The famous Russian teacher and writer Konstantin Ushinsky, credited as the founder of scientific pedagogy in Russia, wrote extensively about the beneficial influence of a healthy lifestyle on personal development. In his three-volume work, *The Human as a Subject of Education*, which he began writing in 1876, Ushinksy advocated for schools to teach the foundations of a healthy lifestyle. This, he said, would enhance people's physical, mental, and moral welfare (Ushinsky, 1950). Pavel Kapterev (1982), a prominent representative of empirical psychology in Russia, also argued for regular exercise as an important means of maintaining good health.

Peter Lesgaft, born in 1837, was the founder of the modern system of physical education, which was informed by both his medical (particularly his anatomical) and pedagogical knowledge. He promoted the following components of a healthy lifestyle: a reasonable standard of hygiene, normative child development, well-regulated daily routines, including the school schedule, regular physical check-ups, and vaccination (Lesgaft, 1951). Lesgaft wrote that both physical education and everyday education in the classroom should be such that they aided rather than hindered children's physical and mental development, and thus improved their overall health.

The work of these men during the 19th century and early part of the 20th century brought together ideas and practices from medicine, ecology, psychology, and physical training, which remained influential throughout much of the 20th century. This melding created the foundation of current health education and promotion in Russia.

Throughout much of the 20th century, health education and disease prevention in Russia was the province of medical institutions, medical doctors, and school nurses. All pre-service teachers, no matter what subjects or grades they were to teach, were mandated to complete a two-year medical course and a two-semester internship in hospitals. Once teaching, these individuals were expected to incorporate their medical knowledge into classroom content, again no matter what subject or grade they were responsible for.

During the Soviet period, all teachers were certified as medical nurses liable for military call-up. Medical doctors and specialists in the area of classical medicine balked at what they saw as an incursion into their domain. They also resisted being themselves responsible for school-based health education, in part because of their lack of pedagogical skills, inability to link health-related issues to school subjects, and dislike of ongoing contact with students. To aggravate the situation, around 60% of schools in Russia did not have proper medical facilities and nurses, and most schools offered little in the way of school-based health-related activities.

D. V. Kolesov's call for "health through education" brought a new pedagogical direction to health education in the latter part of the 20th century (see, for example, Kolesov, 2000). This direction is informed by a relatively new discipline called valeology, or the scientific study of health. One of its main implications for health education is the notion that children need to be acculturated into good health (see Khripkova & Kolesov, 1984). Kolosov's thinking suggests a more encompassing, holistic approach to health promotion and improvement than the current approach where these matters are still addressed in different school subjects.

Toward the end of the 20th century, various analyses of available data indicated that lifestyle accounted for the health problems of just over half of all people presenting with illnesses (see, for example, Lisitsyn, 1992; Lisitsyn & Sakhno, 1989). It is highly likely, given the statistics cited earlier in this chapter, that the proportion is much higher now.

RECENT THINKING AND DEVELOPMENTS

Although promotion of good health is a fundamental principle of Russian educational policy and is provided for in the Law on Education (Ministry of Education of the Russian Federation, 1992), it seems that children's awareness of and understanding of health development and healthy living remains rudimentary in many parts of Russia (Khrutchev, 2006). Certainly, school children in the Republic of Karelia do not appear to understand the connection between their health and their way of life, and so do not know even the rudiments of good health, such as the need to engage in regular physical exercise. They are thus unable to evaluate their own state of health and are commonly physically inactive and display unhealthy eating habits. Even secondary school graduates in Karelia appear to lack comprehensive knowledge about long-term health protection, do not understand the principles of health promotion and prevention and treatment of illness and injury, and cannot evaluate the impact of environmental factors on their health (Aisman & Abaskalova, 1996).

During the last decade there has been growing interest in the role of physical education in the development of healthy lifestyles in Russia. However, the present system of physical education in most Russian schools is unlikely to be effective unless it enables students to see the personal value of good health. In line with the understandings developed from valeology noted above, physical education needs to acculturate students into good health by providing them with activities and opportunities that they find relevant within the context of their own lives and those of their peers and communities.

More specifically, the goals of school-based physical education should be for students to acquire movement skills, understand what constitutes health-enhancing physical activity (and then engage in it), set themselves physical fitness targets, and self-monitor their progress toward achieving them. Activity should also focus, on the one hand, on showcasing, through team sports, the importance of collaborative effort and, on the other hand, on helping students value and take pride in themselves. Over time, these approaches should lead to students appreciating the need to develop and maintain healthy lifestyles.

Contemporary science considers human physical and mental welfare from both biological and social perspectives. As "biosocial" creatures, we constantly interact with the physical and social dimensions of our environment. Family, as immediate environment, is instrumental in teaching children healthy skills. Just as they guide and monitor their children's academic health, parents need to take responsibility for their children's physical health and social and emotional wellbeing. This means making sure that their children, from the time they are born, are raised in a clean and physically and emotionally secure environment. It also means helping children develop healthy habits from a very young age.

Schools serve as an ideal setting from which to positively affect children's health. This is because they reach young people at a critical age of development, during which lifestyles are tested, developed, and adapted through social interactions with peers, teachers, parents, and others. Collaboration between family, school, and other stakeholders is therefore essential to securing good health for children. Without such effort, health deteriorates because of lack of alignment between what happens at school and what happens at home (Bazarny, 2005). Health education is thus most effective if it takes place in a supportive environment, with students, teachers, and parents ideally working together to maintain their own health as well as the health of their families and communities.

In Russia, we need a new framework to guide health promotion, and this framework must be one that takes account of regional and cultural variation. We consider that this framework is foregrounded by a program launched in the Republic of Karelia in 2005. The aim of this initiative, called *Healthy Lifestyles* (Government of the Republic of Karelia, 2005), was to lift the overall health of the local population by encouraging people to adopt healthy lifestyles. Program activities included the following:

- Providing administrators in all state and municipal schools of the Republic of Karelia with the information and support they needed to establish healthy school nutrition programs and school meals;
- Providing students and inmates in all state and municipal kindergartens, secondary schools, vocational schools, hospitals, orphanages, and boarding schools with the recommended daily intake of iodized salt;
- Making the ingestion of foods high in Vitamin C mandatory in all state and municipal kindergartens, secondary schools, vocational schools, hospitals, orphanages, and boarding schools;
- Developing medical and social standards against which to regularly monitor the physical and mental health of children, young people, and their families, with particular emphasis placed on priority health outcomes and the behaviors (both positive and negative) that influence those outcomes;
- Identifying and endeavoring to prevent or reduce habits harmful to good health;
- Actively recognizing WHO-promoted events, such as World No Tobacco Day, World AIDS Day, World Health Day, and engaging in other relevant educational and cultural activities;

- Participating in initiatives organized by the republican government, including "Healthy Families" (promotion of healthy families and healthy lifestyles) and "Healthy School Environments";
- Taking part in contests supported by the republican government such as "The Best School Sports Ground of the Year" and "The School with the Healthiest Lifestyles"; and
- Developing resources designed to support health education teachers run "Healthy Lifestyle" workshops and schools for children at summer camps.

HEALTH EDUCATION IN RUSSIAN SCHOOLS

Late in the 1990s, the Ministry of General and Vocational Education of the Russian Federation announced its intention to implement a new curriculum in Russian secondary schools in 1999 (Ministry of General and Vocational Education of the Russian Federation, 1997, 1999). This curriculum, which is still in force, sets out the compulsory fields of study in schools: humanities, with a special emphasis on Russian language, literature, social sciences, and physical culture; natural sciences, with priority given to mathematics; and technology. The curriculum also provides for subjects and topics to be selected and taught according to local and regional discretion. While ministry guidelines recommend that schools include the subject basic safety/security skills and cover other health-related issues in relevant mandatory subjects, schools tend to favor instead inclusion of discretionary content of particular relevance to their locality, such as the languages of the ethnic minorities in the region. As a result, health education is generally incorporated within the educational area termed physical culture. Statements in official documents that physical culture and basic safety/survival skills are complementary areas also contribute to health education being incorporated within physical culture (Petrov, 2005).

Our analysis of the content of physical culture as well as three other subject areas containing elements of health education, that is, basic safety/survival skills, nature studies, and biology, shows "across the board" coverage not only of habits and practices that favor good health but also of issues relating to healthy lifestyles. The content of the subject called physical culture gives students opportunities to assess, improve, and maintain their level of physical fitness, to gain and demonstrate knowledge of fitness concepts, principles, and strategies, and to acquire responsible personal and social behaviors.

At the beginning of September 1991, the school subject basic safety/survival skills was introduced to the secondary school curriculum in accordance with the Decree of the Council of Ministers of the Russian Federation No. 253. Its syllabus contains a section devoted to the rudiments of a healthy lifestyle, issues pertaining to health care, and first aid and appropriate behavior in emergency situations (see Ministry of General and Vocational Education of the Russian Federation, 1997, 1999; Smirnov, Vishnevskaya, & Voloshinov, 1997). Nature and biology provide understanding of the scientific underpinnings of good health as well as knowledge about the human body and how it works. This content is particularly important because research demonstrates a direct relationship between individuals' attitudes toward their own health and their level of knowledge about human physiology and physical wellbeing (Mash, 2000).

Because all of the above information is presented in a piecemeal way (in separate subjects) to students rather than as an integrated course, children are prevented from developing a comprehensive model of a healthy lifestyle. This situation also limits teachers' ability to provide children with clear understanding of basic concepts related to health promotion and disease prevention, even though, under curriculum requirements, students are expected, during their schooling, to learn to do the following:

- Demonstrate ability to access valid health information and health-promoting products and services;
- Engage in health-enhancing behaviors and know how to reduce health risks;
- Analyze the influence of culture, media, technology, and other factors on health; and
- Use goal-setting and decisionmaking skills in order to enhance one's own health and to advocate for personal, family, and community health.

THE NEED FOR INTEGRATED HEALTH EDUCATION

Given the concerns just mentioned, what is obviously needed in schools is integrated health education provision, a claim that is supported by various researchers, including Lubysheva (1997), Maksimova (1988), and Mamgetov and Popova (2000). According to Lerner (1987), awareness of the intertwined nature of the health-related issues relies on synthesizing knowledge from various disciplines. Dyatlova (1997) likewise argues that the complex nature of health-related issues can be revealed only through interdisciplinary integration and the application of a regional approach. The latter, explains Dyatlova, means that global problems can be contextualized to local issues and cultural concerns. The piecemeal approach to health education that comes from placing it within different subjects undermines these sorts of approach. In short, integration of content areas is the prerequisite for health literacy.

Awareness of the need to localize content makes evident another important aspect of comprehensive health education, and that is ensuring that both children and parents hold the same views of what constitutes good health. This consideration again points to the need for schools, families, and communities to work in partnership to promote and maintain healthy living.

Because, in Karelia, there is presently no means of establishing health education as a separate subject that integrates content from all relevant existing courses, the only way to teach students a model of health-enforcing behavior is to *firmly* integrate the content, instruction, extracurricular activities, and community involvement into all aspects of the curriculum. But just how easily and effectively integrating the content of such subjects as physical culture, basic safety/survival skills, and biology might be accomplished has yet to be determined. Reference to time-proven methods and modern pedagogical techniques should help find a way forward in this regard.

In the meantime, all teachers can help students maintain healthy lifestyles by employing the following strategies:

- Encouraging students to self-evaluate and assess their own, their peers', and their family members' physical, mental, and emotional health;
- Enabling students to see that health choices are affected by a variety of influences, and that the ability to recognize, analyze, and evaluate internal and external influences is essential to protecting and enhancing health;
- Engaging students in health behaviors that are the foundations of healthy lifestyles and healthy communities.

Development of these competencies has other advantages. Managing health behaviors requires critical thinking and problem-solving. Practicing healthy behavior builds competence and confidence to use learned skills in real-life situations. Ability to use knowledge and skills to manage health helps students avoid risk-taking behaviors. The ability to use decisionmaking skills to guide healthy behavior fosters a sense of control and promotes acceptance of personal responsibility for one's health.

CONCLUSION

Analysis of educational standards pertaining to the subject areas of physical culture, basic safety/survival skills, and biology shows that the essential health-related knowledge and skills that students in the Republic of Karelia are expected to acquire during their schooling relate to hygiene, maintaining a healthy lifestyle, preventing diseases, making healthy choices, and avoiding high-risk behaviors. Our analysis of these subjects with respect to these outcomes suggests that separating out elements of health education into these three subject areas has marginalized health-related issues within school curriculums. One of the prerequisites of an educational program that is effective in developing and maintaining a healthy lifestyle is to take an interdisciplinary approach wherein content relevant to health education is taken from all relevant disciplines and integrated into one comprehensive program of study. This development must also take account of the need to provide all teachers with comprehensive health education training. Although there is as yet no ready curriculum-based means of adopting this approach in Karelia, these measures, if eventually adopted, should go some way to ameliorating some of the major health issues still confronting the Republic of Karelia.

REFERENCES

Aisman, R. I., & Abaskalova N. P. (1996). Medical, social and psychological aspects of health development. In E. N. Viner (Ed.), *Valeology education: Problems, research and solutions* (pp. 3–12). Lipetsk, Russian Federation: LSPU.

Bazarny, V. F. (2005). *Health and a child's development: Express control at school and home.* Moscow, Russian Federation: ARKTI.

Dorshakova, N. V. (1993). *Quality of the environment and human health in Karelia.* Petrozavodsk, Russian Federation: PSU.

Dyatlova, V. I. (1997). Valeology at school. *Valeology, 2*, 58–66.

Federal Statistics Agency. (2010). *The Republic of Karelia.* Retrieved from http://krl.gks.ru/default.aspx.

Gerd, A. Y. (1928). *Construction and life of the human body*. Leningrad, USSR: State Publishing House.

Government of the Republic of Karelia. (2005). *Target program "Healthy Lifestyles"*. Petrozavodsk, Russian Federation: Government of the Republic of Karelia.

Kapterev, P. F. (1982). In A. M. Arseniev (Ed.), *Selected pedagogical works*. Moscow, USSR: Pedagogika.

Khripkova, A. G., & Kolesov, D. V. (1984). *Hygiene and health: Textbook for schoolchildren*. Moscow, USSR: Prosveshcheniye.

Khrutchev S. V. (2006). *Physical culture of children with diseases of the respiratory system*. Moscow, Russian Federation: Academia.

Kolesov, D. V. (2000). Health through education. *Biology at School, 2*, 20–22.

Lerner, I. Y. (1987). Ecological issues in the topic "human body and health". *Biology at School, 3*, 41–43.

Lesgaft, P. F. (1951). *Guidelines on the physical education of schoolchildren*. Moscow, USSR: Physkultura y sport.

Lisitsyn, Y. P. (1992). *Social hygiene and organization of health care: Issues lectures*. Moscow, USSR: Medicine.

Lisitsyn, Y. P., & Sakhno, A. V. (1989). *Human health as a social value*. Moscow, USSR: Mysl.

Lubysheva, L. I. (1997). Contemporary value potential of physical training and sport for individuals and society. *Theory and Practice of Physical Training, 6*, 26–37.

Maksimova, V. N. (1988). *Interdisciplinary connections in the educational process*. Moscow, USSR: Prosveshcheniye.

Mamgetov, K. Y., & Popova, S. A. (2000). Health of the population of the Republic of Adygeya. In S. P. Lysenkov (Ed.), *Medical, social and health problems of the population of the Northern Caucasus*. Maikop, Russian Federation: CSMA.

Mash, R. D. (2000). *The human body and health: Biology experiments and activities for Grade 9 of secondary schools*. Moscow, Russian Federation: Mnemozina.

Ministry of Education of the Russian Federation. (1992). *Law on Education*. Moscow, Russian Federation: Author.

Ministry of Education of the Russian Federation. (1999). *Order # 56: Compulsory content of secondary general education*. Moscow, Russian Federation: Author.

Ministry of General and Vocational Education of the Russian Federation. (1997). Letter # 974/14-12: *Compulsory content of the secondary school curriculum*. Moscow, Russian Federation: Author.

Ministry of General and Vocational Education of the Russian Federation. (1999). *Information letter: Content of the subject "basic survival skills" in secondary schools in Russia*. Moscow, Russian Federation: Author.

Petrov, S. V. (2005). *Basic survival skills: State educational standards. Bibliography, visual aids*. Moscow, Russian Federation: ENAS.

Raikov, B. E. (1927). *Sexual education at school*. Leningrad, USSR: Leningradskaya Pravda.

Smirnov, A. P., Vishnevskaya E. L., & Voloshinov A. M. (1997). *Syllabus of the subject "basic survival skills" for Grades 1 to 11*. Moscow, Russian Federation: Prosveshcheniye.

Symashko, Y. I. (1850). *Russian fauna or description of the animals that live in the territory of the Russian Empire*. Saint-Petersburg, Russia: K. Vingeber.

Ushinsky, K. D. (1950). *The human as a subject of education: Pedagogical anthropology*. Moscow, USSR: Publishing house of the Academy of Pedagogy.

Marina Gvozdeva and Valentina Kirilina
Karelian State Pedagogical Academy
Petrozavodsk
Karelia
Russia
email: gms@onego.ru

JOOST PLATJE AND KRYSTYNA SŁODCZYK

9. THE ROLE OF EDUCATION IN PREVENTING DISEASES

A Case Study from Poland

BACKGROUND

Political change in Poland since the 1990s has involved not only transformation of the economy but also social policy, including that pertaining to the structure, financing, and functioning of the health care system. Health education and promotion is gaining in importance and increasingly is being seen as a strategy that is effective in limiting the incidence of certain diseases. Health education is effective because it helps make people aware that it is better to prevent disease than to cure it. As Sen (1999) reminds us, health is a vital component of human capability.

In general, Polish citizens' state of health has been improving over the past two decades (Central Statistical Office, 2010; Opole Provincial Office, 2009). Between 1996 and 2009, life expectancy increased by 4.0 years for women and 4.6 years for men. By 2009, women could expect to live to 79.4 years of age, and men could expect to live to 70.8 years. The infant mortality rate has also dropped in recent years. In 2009, 6.4 babies died for every 1,000 born. Another trend evident between 1999 and 2009 are changes to the proportions of older and younger people in the population. By 2009, there were proportionately more older than younger people, with the decrease in the younger age brackets particularly evident among people 20 years of age and under.

In general, although the state of public health in Poland has improved, and may be better than in many European countries, it is still not as good as in more developed western-European countries, where average life expectancy for women is higher by four to five years and for men by as much as eight years. The main reasons for death in Poland are the "civilization ailments," which include diseases of the cardiovascular system, cancer, injuries, and poisoning. These accounted for about 77% of all deaths in 2008.

A closer look at the statistics for these various causes of death show that the main one is cardiovascular disease, although its prevalence has been declining in recent years. In 2004, it accounted for 41.1% of all deaths among men and 52.6% among women. However, the rate of death due to this type of disease is three times higher for men below the age of 45 than it is for women 45 years of age and under. The next main cause of death is malignant cancer (26.4% of male deaths and 22.8% of female deaths), the incidence of which showed an ever upwards trend from 1989 on. In 2008, 214 people per 100,000 inhabitants died from cancer.

N. Taylor, F. Quinn, M. Littledyke and R.K. Coll (eds.), Health Education in Context, 77–88.

Colon cancer, prostate cancer, and, in particular among women, lung cancer are the most prevalent types of cancer leading to death, and the incidence of each is increasing. The third important cause of death, showing a decreasing trend, is misadventure (injuries and accidents). It accounted for 9.7% of all male deaths in 2008 and 3.7% of female deaths (Central Statistical Office, 2010; Opole Provincial Office, 2009).

The case study presented later in this chapter focuses on the Opole province in the southern part of Poland, where the number of people hospitalized for malignant cancer climbed from 81.5 per 10,000 inhabitants in 2004 to 95.3 in 2006 and 100.7 in 2008 (Niemiec, 2007). Among women, the most common malignant types of cancer for which hospitalization was needed in this same period were of the reproductive organs (26%), breast (24%), digestive organs (17%), respiratory organs and thorax (7%), and lymphatic tissue, bone marrow, and related tissues (7%).

HEALTH CONCERNS PARTICULAR TO WOMEN

Health issues particular to women are of special concern in Poland because of the implications of these for reproduction and for children's physical and mental wellbeing. In Poland, women often neglect important female-specific health matters (Niemiec, 2007). There seems to be a culture among women that works against them actively monitoring their health and addressing any issues that arise.

As already noted, women's health, as well as their attitudes toward and behaviors relating to health matters, have a considerable influence not only on their immediate family but also on the development of the whole society. The health situation of Polish women of reproductive age (taken to be 15 to 49 years of age) in 2006, reported in a study cited in Niemiec (2007), gives some insight into this situation.

Trend data from this study for the period 1989 to 2006 showed a steady decline in the number of children being born to women right across the age group, and a particularly evident drop in the maximum number of children born to women ages 20 to 29. This continuous decline in the number of children born is causing concern in Poland because it means the population is not replacing itself.

While one might assume the drop in birth numbers is a product of women electing not to have children, contraception and infertility data suggest otherwise. Although there is a lack of research on contraception use in Poland, research reported in Niemiec (2007) shows that, between 2003 and 2005, of the proportion of women using contraception, only 19% were taking the most reliable form of contraception, the pill, a percentage that is half that in other European Union countries. Also, as in many developed countries, infertility has become increasingly prevalent in Poland. As yet, no epidemiological research has been carried out in order to estimate the actual need for the methods used to help redress this problem, such as in vitro fertilization.

Another concern, which may have some bearing on the reduction in birth numbers and the increased incidence of infertility, is the high level of cervical cancer and mortality in Poland due to the human papilloma virus (an etiological factor of cervical cancer). Although cytological examinations are generally accessible, the incidence of this disease in Poland is one of the highest in Europe (Niemiec, 2007), in part because there is no national screening program. And although the vaccination against the papilloma virus became available on the Polish—and European—market in November 2009, it is unlikely that this vaccination will be given out as a readily available preventative measure, mainly due to its cost.

According to the research discussed in Niemiec (2007), approximately 50% of 18-year-old girls (the age at which most finish secondary school) are having sex. Of this group, more than 10% of the girls reported having had three or more sexual partners, and 1 in 10 said she or her partner had not used contraception. Those who were using contraception were generally relying on the less reliable forms. However, the number of teenage girls giving birth has declined systematically, from 44,000 in 1990 to about 20,000 in 2004 (Central Statistical Office, 2010; Opole Provincial Office, 2009).

HEALTH EDUCATION

While the health concerns cited above can potentially be addressed by improving public health services, pro-health activities remain a crucial component of long-term amelioration of such concerns. Sidorowicz, Maroszek, and Kiedyk (2002) estimated that of the factors influencing people's health, personal behavior accounts for about 53% of the total influence, lifestyle (including physical and social aspects and the work environment) contributes about 21%, and genetic predisposition about 16%. The public health system accounts for only 10%. Thus, educational programs which aim to change behavior and lifestyle may have the highest potential for improving people's health.

In 1998, Poland ratified the World Health Declaration (Karski & Kozierkiewicz, 2001), which positioned good health as a fundamental human right. Poland also ascribes to the European Commission's policy on health education (Juszczak, 2006), which is underpinned by the assumption that preventing diseases is better than trying to cure people who contract them. (The commission's policy is evident in European Union programs in the field of public health.)

Those activities that are in place with respect to public health education and promotion in Poland are set out under the country's national health plan (Ministry of Health, 2007), development of which was informed by the World Health Organization's (WHO) banner of "Health for All in the 21st Century." The plan emphasizes that well-organized health education is that which is based on clear identification and good understanding of the factors that influence health for better or for worse. Health education is also more likely to be successful if it is complemented with legislation directed at ensuring the health care system meets its obligations, not only in terms of tending to people when they are ill but also in terms of educating society about how to avoid contracting diseases in the first place.

Health education as an element of the Polish Government's health policy is expressed in several documents. One such is the National Plan of Activities for the Benefit of Children 2004–2012 (Ministry of Education, 2004). Another sets out an agreement between the Ministry of National Education and Sports and the Ministry of Health to support health education through such initiatives as health promoting schools, evident in many countries around the world (Małkowska-Szkutnik & Mazur, 2009). One strategic goal of this program is monitoring Polish citizens' state of health. Monitoring provides information that allows health policymakers and practitioners, along with health education stakeholders, to identify the sources of health problems and thereby develop targeted and (hopefully) effective health education.

Despite achievements both nationally and internationally in the fight against a wide range of diseases, and despite the money and institutional resources that Poland has expended on this fight, there is little evidence of these efforts having had a positive impact. Perhaps this is because Poland's health care and health education are inefficient, or perhaps the country simply cannot afford to meet expectations.

Analysis of the existing system of health education suggests this argument has some merit. Educational programs are carried out at different levels of government administration (from local self-government through to central government level) and by different agencies, including the Polish health service, the education system, and non-governmental organizations. Health education, moreover, is directed by Poland's Department of Health and Epidemiology in cooperation with, for example, the Polish Red Cross, the Polish Sanitary Association, the Association for Family Development, and the Association for Common Knowledge, as well as publishers of health resources and various other cultural and/or educational organizations (Lewicki, 2006).

According to Juszczak (2006), modern health education, if it is to be effective, needs to be based on "positive health" policies that call for the implementation of innovative educational approaches and techniques. Health education thus needs to take into consideration social involvement and activities and the societal and environmental aspects influencing people's health-related decisions. It needs to employ a multi-sectoral and multi-disciplinary approach, and to develop new ways of conducting the health-related activities typically conducted at different levels of society (government, legal, professional, social).

We consider that efforts to develop more effective health education in Poland also need to be based on answers to this question: why do current methods of health education often fail, particularly in relation to specific female issues, despite the considerable sums of money spent on them and the use of engaging forms of health promotion? Analysis of the data arising out of the Opole case study (see below) and related literature (e.g., Leowski, 2008; Woynarowska, 2008) leads us to agree with other commentators in the literature that particular non-medical factors, such as lack of general education, lack of employment opportunities, and poor housing conditions, determine the success of health education. These are all socioeconomic factors, and they are ones that, for various reasons (e.g., lack of government will or ability), health education programs generally fail (or do not have sufficient "teeth") to address.

In line with work by and comments from Stoto, Abel, and Dievler (1996) and Woynarowska (2008), we agree that health education programs must pay equal heed to these three elements—knowledge, attitudes, and skills. Knowledge needs to encompass the determinants of good health and information about diseases (their prevention and treatment). Attitudes need to be ones that enable individuals to look after their own health and that of family and community members. Attitudes also need to be ones that promote concerns affecting wider society, such as care for the natural environment. And both knowledge and attitudes need to be transformed into skills.

Furthermore, differences among people in a society, such as level of education, economic situation, and ethnicity, make it necessary to explicitly identify target groups and tailor education programs to their understandings and sensibilities. Another issue requiring consideration is that disease incidence can be mediated by various factors—behavioral, social, economic, and political. For example, the risk of mortality and illness is much higher among lower-income groups than among higher-income groups, while chronic diseases are two or three times more prevalent. Special health education programs are necessary to address these matters (Juszczak, 2006). Those developing health education and health intervention programs need to design these programs so that they operate effectively at the level of the individual, of the community, and of society, and use a variety of strategies in such a way that synergy effects appear.

Three models of health education can typically be applied: those that are disease-oriented, those that are risk-factor-oriented, and those that are health-oriented (in the more traditional sense). Modern approaches toward health education focus not only on changing individual behavior, which can be considered a risk factor (Woynarowska & Sokołowska, 2001), but also on bringing in measures likely to stimulate social and environmental changes, with the aim of improving public health. These approaches require mindset changes within health care institutions as well as organizational change, a point strongly made by groups advocating for improved health among women and for environmental protection. In short, "education for change" relies on the creation of a more humane, democratic, healthy, and equitable society.

HEALTH EDUCATION IN SCHOOLS

Health education is an important component of the educational programs of Poland's nursery and primary schools (Stawiński, Jaworowicz-Szczepaniak, & Marcinkowski, 2006). As has been the case with environmental education, it has been implemented in primary schools as a part of the "didactic path," meaning that its elements are included in other subjects (Wiśniewska-Śliwińska, 2010). A new, valuable initiative is the module "health education," which has been included in the elementary program for physical education (Woynarowska & Sokołowska, 2001). As a result, physical education has become the most important vehicle for implementing health education. In 2008, a group of experts from the medical sciences and public health sector proposed that the Ministry of National Education include a subject called "health" or "health education" in the elementary program. However, this proposal was not acted on (Stawiński, Jaworowicz-Szczepaniak, & Marcinkowski, 2006).

There is no dedicated subject called "sexual education" (or similar) within the school curriculum, although some information is imparted in the elective subject "education for family life" (*wychowanie do życia w rodzinie*), as well as in biology. In the main, though, sex education barely registers in schools, even though girls living in urban areas and attending technical, trade, and other vocationally-oriented schools face particularly high risks of contracting infections and experiencing other deleterious effects associated with early sexual initiation (Niemiec, 2007, p. 86).

If Poland is to reduce these problems, its political and policy agencies must agree on implementing sexual education in secondary schools and on what the content of that education should be. They also need to provide accessible "teenager-friendly" medical advice in accordance with the principles of the European Strategy for Child and Adolescent Health and Development (World Health Organization, 2005).

The current state of affairs with respect to sex education in Poland, especially the fact that there is no uniform and stable policy, may not surprise outside commentators. However, there are many within the country who remain highly concerned about and are actively agitating for the implementation of a good general sex education program in order to advance the reproductive health of Poland's people (Juszczak, 2006).

HEALTH EDUCATION PROGRAMS IN OPOLE: A CASE STUDY

Development and stimulation of pro-health behavior is a complicated issue, requiring cooperation among the different stakeholders. While education in this field may measurably improve public health, it tends to be stymied by attitudes and stereotypes. The traditional models of health care implemented in Poland focus on the illness itself and its treatment. We consider that such models implicitly assume that people's health-related behaviors and disease-prevention measures are not as important as the process of treatment. Our analysis of different health-education and health-promotion programs in the province of Opole, some of which target women, show that there are programs within Poland that are trying to deal with the issues discussed in this chapter. The particular aims of these programs are to increase awareness of factors detrimental to good health, to popularize personal hygiene and healthy eating habits, and to advance knowledge about methods of preventing illness, including vaccination. These programs are thus behavior directed because they encourage people to take ownership of their health and to engage in habits and activities characteristic of a healthy lifestyle.

In Opole, the Opole Health Center (*Opolskie Centrum Zdrowia*) is responsible for overseeing and monitoring implementation of health programs within the province as well as undertaking tasks assigned under the auspices of the National

Health Program. Jurisdiction of health programs within the province is thus vested with provincial authorities.

The main organization responsible for health education in Opole is an organization popularly known as the Sanitary Station (*Stacja Sanitarna*).[1] The role of this organization is captured in its full title, the Section for Health Promotion and Education of the Sanitary Station. Established in 2005, the section carries out its role by disseminating information, training health education personnel, supplying educational resources, and monitoring and assessing the effects of its activities. Its target groups are children and their parents, teachers, medical employees, and other employees and citizens in general. Activities focused on healthy lifestyles and food, prevention of smoking, promotion of physical activity, prevention of different types of illness, and so forth are mainly aimed at children, and at adults bringing up or educating children.

Although the section does not directly target women, except in relation to breast and cervical cancer and health considerations during pregnancy, women are usually the main participants in its activities. This is not surprising, given that women are in the majority among secondary school teachers and medical personnel in hospitals, and that they continue to have primary responsibility within their families for bringing up children.

The section carries out its activities in cooperation with a wide range of organizations, such as provincial and local authorities, youth groups, institutions of higher education, the mass media, and the various agencies involved in specific health issues. Because the section's primary target group is children, most of the programs operating under its jurisdiction have been or are aimed at youngsters. Examples (pertaining to both children and adults) include the following:

- *Happy Smile, Happy Future:* this program addressed primary school children in the second grade. It involved 109 teachers and 1,906 students province-wide, as well as all 83 primary schools in the city of Opole. Forty-four nurses and seven dentists were also involved in the program.
- *Breathe Easy, Prevent Asthma*: this program focused on children in the first three years of primary school and the children's parents. Eighteen primary schools, 1,309 students, 1,012 parents, and 210 teachers took part in the program.
- *Keep in Shape:* this program targeted students in the first three years of secondary school. As with the previous two programs mentioned, participation rates were very high.
- *Don't Smoke in My Presence, Please:* this program is directed at students during their first three years of primary school. The aims of the program are to make children aware of the harmful effects of smoking and to help them develop skills that enable them to deal with situations where adults smoke in their presence.
- *Clean Air Around Us:* this program has the same aims as Don't Smoke in My Presence, but is aimed at nursery school children.
- *The ABCs of Healthy Nourishment:* as the name of this program indicates, the focus is on food products and food consumption. The program's primary target

group is women because they are still the family members most responsible for deciding what the family should eat and for then buying and cooking the food. The aims of the program reflect the aims of the National Health Plan.

- *HIV/AIDS Prevention:* This program targets young people.
- *Get Accustomed to the Gynecologist* (a literal translation of *Oswoić Ginekologa*): The main aim of this very important program in terms of women's reproductive health is to limit apprehension about visiting gynecologists. Young women are introduced to the idea and the importance of seeing a gynecologist. Trepidation is addressed by having support people take women on a first visit to a gynecologist's office, where they have opportunity to get accustomed to the atmosphere and process of coming to such a place. This program is of particular importance in rural areas, where going to a gynecologist can still be regarded as a slur on a woman's character.
- *Menopause with a Smile:* this program promotes measures designed to prevent ill health among women 40 years of age and over.
- *Examine Your Breasts and Have Your Cervix Checked*: the aims of these programs are evident in their titles.

This list suggests a fairly comprehensive targeting of women's health-related concerns. However, we found a greater prevalence in Opole province of programs directed at children and young people, possibly because these groups are easier to reach. In essence, efforts to address female issues seem to be accorded lesser importance.

Our investigations in Opole showed that effective health education and promotion programs are possible. Our experience there also confirmed for us that one of the main problems facing the development of effective health education programs throughout Poland is people's attitudes. Many people, particularly in rural areas, only go to a doctor when a problem becomes visible, by which time, as can occur with cancer, it may be too late for treatment. Many women do not take part in preventive examinations, not only because they think such visits are unnecessary, but also because they fear that visiting a doctor will make apparent a previously undetected illness. This way of thinking—that if we do not see the problem, the problem does not exist—has to change.

Another fundamental and urgent issue that health education needs to address, and that was also made evident during our time in Opole, is that people need to be taught how to understand medical information. It has been estimated that more than half of all adults do not understand such information. Rather than learning how to look after their health, people are more likely to visit a doctor or call for an ambulance, by which time they often require hospitalization, which adds to the cost of the health care system. It seems that people's lifestyles, which reflect the relationship between health values and activities, still contain too few elements conducive to good health. Although most people say health is the most important value (Nowakowska, Mędrzycka-Dąbrowska, Leoniuk, & Lemska, 2005), this sentiment is not reflected in the lifestyles and activities of the majority of the Polish population.

CONCLUSION

The state of public health in Poland, compared to the state of public health in more highly developed countries, is poor overall. Although health in general is improving, health indices show an increasing prevalence of some diseases, notably those of the cardiovascular and respiratory systems, as well as malignant cancers, diabetes, and mental illness. This situation seems to be the product of a series of unfavorable conditions that have developed over the last few decades and left the Polish health care system in poor shape. The present system is underfunded and overly bureaucratic, and people seeking and needing treatment typically experience long waiting times. The less than satisfactory circumstances under which many people work and the higher incidence of unhealthy lifestyles are compounding the problem.

Unhealthy lifestyles are particularly concerning given that people have better access to some aspects of healthy living than they did two decades ago under the former socialist economy. An example is the far greater availability, since the early 1990s, of vegetables and other healthy foods. While this availability may have changed the nutrition patterns of some people, it appears not to have changed their overall attitudes to healthy eating. Because change is most easy to facilitate among young children, it may take decades before Poland witnesses a level of health amongst its people equivalent to the level amongst people in the more highly developed countries of the European Union.

While health education in Poland is prioritized at a relatively high level of government, lack of finance and educational resources have made the implementation of many preventive measures impossible. Officials seem to readily acknowledge that well-implemented and well-resourced health care and disease prevention programs, especially within rural areas, promote the types of attitudes and behaviors favorable to good health, and so have tried to embed in them efficient health education. They also acknowledge the importance of targeted health education programs within schools and other venues. But again, various factors (e.g., too few teachers qualified to teach in this area and many teachers failing to model pro-health behaviors and habits) present barriers to the implementation and maintenance of such programs. Lack of localized educational policy, lack of clarity (especially among teacher education institutions) about teacher competencies with respect to health education, and wasted expenditure arising out of duplication of health-promotion activities also serve as barriers.

We consider that if Poland is to lower these barriers, it needs to establish strong links between health education and health promotion. Such a move would create a basis for shifting the focus from policy and administration toward local people undertaking activities commensurate with their needs and conducted in cooperation with other individuals and groups in the locality. In other words, there is a need for grassroots development so that people can take ownership of their own and their community's health, and find local solutions to local concerns. Realizing this state of affairs is undoubtedly a challenge, but a variety of health education and promotion programs, such as those (past and present) in the province of Opel, shows that it is not impossible.

NOTE

[1] We are indebted to Anna Gawęda-Żylińska from the Sanitary Station for the information on the station's activities.

REFERENCES

Central Statistical Office. (2010). *Life expectancy tables of Poland 2009*. Warsaw, Poland: Author.
Juszczak, K. (2006). Wokół problematyki edukacji zdrowotnej [On health education issues]. In M. Gwoździcka-Piotrowska & A. Zduniak (Eds.), *Edukacja w społeczeństwie:„ryzyka”: bezpieczeństwo jako jakość* [Education in the at-risk society: Safety as a quality issue] (pp. 114–121). Poznań, Poland: Wydawnictwo Wyższej Szkoły Bezpieczeństwa.
Karski, J., & Kozierkiewicz, A. (2001). *Zdrowie 21: Zdrowie dla wszystkich w XXI wieku [Health 21: Health for everyone in the 21st century]*. Warsaw/Krakow, Poland: CSIOZ, Uniwersyteckie Wydawnictwo Vesalius.
Leowski, J. (2008). *Polityka zdrowotna a zdrowie publiczne* [Health policy and public health]. Warsaw, Poland: CeDeWu.
Lewicki, Cz. (2006). *Edukacja zdrowotna: systemowa analiza zagadnień* [Health education: A systemic analysis of issues]. Rzeszów, Poland: Wydawnictwo Uniwersytetu Rzeszowskiego.
Małkowska-Szkutnik, A., & Mazur J. (2009). *Zdrowie i edukacja młodzieży polskiej w świetle badań międzynarodowych w Polityka młodzieżowa* [Health and education of Polish youth in the light of international research on youth policy]. In G. Zielińska (Ed.), *Studia BAS* (Vol. 2). Warsaw, Poland: Biuro Analiz Sejmowych Kancelarii Sejmu.
Ministry of Education. (2004). *Narodowy plan działań na rzecz dzieci 2004-2012 „Polska dla dzieci”* [National plan of activities for the benefit of children 2004–2012: "Poland for children"]. Warsaw, Poland: Author. Retrieved from http://men.gov.pl/index. php?option=com_content&view=article&id=914&Itemid= (in Polish).
Ministry of Health. (2007). *Narodowy Program Zdrowia na lata 2007–2015 [National Health Plan 2007–2015]*. Warsaw, Poland: Author. Retrieved from http://www.mz.gov.pl/wwwfiles/ma_struktura/docs/zal_urm_ npz_90_15052007p.pdf (in Polish).
Niemiec, T. (Ed.). (2007). *Raport „Zdrowie kobiet w wieku prokreacyjnym 15–49 lat. Polska 2006* [Female health in the reproductive age bracket 15–49: Poland 2006]. Warsaw, Poland: United Nations Development Programme. Retrieved from http://www.mz.gov.pl/wwwfiles/ma_struktura/docs/15032007_raport.pdf (in Polish).
Nowakowska, H., Mędrzycka-Dąbrowska, W., Leoniuk, K., & Lemska, M. (2005). The influence of education on wholesome behavior changes of the sick with Diabetes Type 2. *Annales Universitatis Mariae Curie-Skłodowska Lublin, Polonia, 60*(16), 358, 101–104.
Opole Provincial Office. (2009). *Nowotwory złośliwe: wybrane dane z chorobowości hospitalizowanej w województwie opolskim w latach 2004-2008* [Malignant cancer: Selected data on hospitalization in the Opole province 2004–2008]. Opole, Poland: Opolski Urząd Wojewódzki.
Sen, A. (1999). *Development as freedom*. New York: Alfred A. Knopf.
Sidorowicz, W., Maroszek, J., & Kiedyk, D. (2002). *Analiza społeczna w polityce zdrowotnej* [Social analysis in health policy]. Krakow, Poland: Uniwersyteckie Wydawnictwo Medyczne Vesalius.
Stawiński, M., Jaworowicz-Szczepaniak, M., & Marcinkowski J. T. (2006). Efekty wdrażania programu edukacji zdrowotnej w jednym z poznanskich przedszkoli [Effects of the introduction of health education in a kindergarten in Poznan]. *Zdrowie publiczne, 2*, 319–321.
Stoto, M., Abel, C., &, Dievler, D. (1996). *Healthy communities: New partnerships for the future of public health*. Washington DC: National Academies.
World Health Organization (WHO). (2005). *European strategy for child and adolescent health and development*. Copenhagen, Denmark: Author. Retrieved from http://www.euro.who.int/_data/assets/pdf_file/0020/79400/E87710.pdf.

Wiśniewska-Śliwińska, H. (2010). Głos w dyskusji nt. najnowszych trendów w edukacjizdrowotnej [Giving voice to the latest trends in health education]. *Problemy Higieny i Epidemiologii, 91*(2), 335–337.

Woynarowska, B. (2008). *Edukacja zdrowotna* [Health education]. Warsaw, Poland: PWN.

Woynarowska, B., & Sokołowska, M. (2001). *Scieżka edukacyjna: edukacja prozdrowotna i promocja zdrowia w szkole* [Learning paths: Health education and health promotion in schools]. Warsaw, Poland: KOWEZ.

Joost Platje
Opole University
Opole
Poland
email: joost@magma-net.pl

Krystyna Słodczyk
Opole University of Technology
Opole
Poland

GILBERT R. PHIRI

10. LIFTING THE LID ON HIV/AIDS AND TUBERCULOSIS IN MALAWI

INTRODUCTION

Malawi, a member of the Southern African Development Community block, is bordered by Tanzania (north), Zambia (west), and Mozambique (south). Malawi's population increased from 6 million in 1966, when the first post-independence Population and Housing national census was conducted, to just over 13 million in 2008 (National Statistical Office, 2008). The Malawi nation has remained a predominantly rural society. The proportion of the population living in rural areas ranged between 60% and 80% in the last five decennial censuses—1966, 1977, 1988, 1998, and 2008. Also, the rural communities have remained predominantly poor, with poverty levels in the range of between 60% and 65% being registered (Blackie, Conroy, Malewezi, Sachs, & Whiteside, 2006; Friends of Malawi, 2004; Malawi Economic Justice Network, 2003). There are equally high levels of illiteracy of up to 5,000,000 people. Africa has been reported as having the largest number of out-of-school young people in the world (Zodiak Broadcasting Station, March, 2010), and Malawi is typical in that respect.

In line with these socioeconomic trends, Malawi's development plans and national budgets have consistently been prepared and presented as pro-rural and pro-poor. By design, therefore, economic development policies in Malawi have focused on keeping rural–urban migration rates down. The establishment of rural growth centers has consistently been high on the economic development agenda of Malawi, and all social amenities and services are rurally oriented. However, cities and towns have not been left to fend for themselves.

Malawi has an extremely highly localized health service, with hospitals and health clinics confined to cities and towns. Because most health centers in rural service areas have average radii of 10.2 kilometers, the centers refer complicated cases to district hospitals, whose radii average 30 kilometers. When accessing health service delivery, patients have to wait for as long as four hours (especially in cities and towns) before being attended to. In another extreme case, patients often have to buy drugs from private pharmacies (Malawi Economic Justice Network, 2003).

What comes out of the history of Malawi's health care system and its weak socioeconomic status is the disjointed manner in which education about HIV/AIDS and tuberculosis continues to be implemented.

N. Taylor, F. Quinn, M. Littledyke and R.K. Coll (eds.), Health Education in Context, 89–98.
© *2012 Sense Publishers. All rights reserved.*

THE STATUS OF HEALTH EDUCATION IN MALAWI

Since 1964, Malawi has been signatory to many international resolutions, treaties, and conventions. In 1987, for example, Malawi became a signatory to the Alma Alta Health for All in the Year 2000 resolution (Last & Chavunduka, 1988). Just like any other serious signatory, and despite the country's weak economic position and its rural-based society, Malawi immediately engaged in designing programs for implementation under the Health for All resolution. The disease prevention and early warning systems that Malawi went on to develop are those that acknowledge the socioeconomic ills facing its communities. This response includes health education.

The country's health services center primarily on four categories of service providers:

• Public hospitals and health centers under the Ministry of Health and Population (MOHP);
• Faith-based hospitals and health centers under the Christian Health Association of Malawi (CHAM) hospitals;
• Dispensaries run by retired medical assistants; and
• Shrines run by traditional healers (THs) and traditional birth attendants (TBAs).

Hospitals and health centers under MOHP and CHAM serve as main hubs in the health sector. These are supported by smaller satellite hubs. Together, the two sets of hubs, 140 in total, serve as centers for coordinating all health and health-related activities in the country (Chavula, 2009).

Malawi relies heavily on in-country trained health personnel, ranging from doctors, graduate nurses, and state-registered nurses, clinical and medical officers, through to auxiliary nurses and surveillance assistants. MOHP and CHAM are jointly responsible for training medical personnel. One target of these institutions is an annual output of 500 nurses (Kaunda, 2009).

The dramatic shift in the country's health policy currently encompasses the professionalization of African medicine by incorporating THs and TBAs in its hospitals and those run by CHAM (Zere, Moeti, Kirigia, Mwase, & Kataika, 2007). Because they are community-based, herbalists have proved to be excellent and effective vehicles by which to reach the rural and urban poor. For its part, MOHP has prioritized training THs in areas such as the administration of basic drugs and making referrals. The MOHP is also empowering TBAs by providing them with basic child delivery kits to enable them to handle low-risk cases. The TBAs also receive training in how to make referrals.

The significance of the merger of traditional and Western practices is considerable because Malawi is not an urban society and because every Malawian has strong ties with rural communities. These ties mean that Malawians across social and economic classes hold traditions and customs, including the rich fund of knowledge and competencies of rural communities, in high esteem. Bringing the THs and TBAs together with medical personnel under the same roof reduces patients' waiting time.

Two key observations can be cited here to support this claim. First, when reporting on what they call Malawi's socialized health care system, Friends of Malawi, a grouping of persons who are interested in monitoring the country's achievements/hurdles pertaining to national socioeconomic development, have applauded Malawians as proud people with strong cultural roots (Friends of Malawi, 2004). The group makes clear that Malawians often turn to herbal remedies provided by an "African doctor." The second observation is the significant power of THs and TBAs. Through their practice, these practitioners provide individuals and communities with opportunity to interrogate, accommodate, adapt to, reject, or appropriate new ideas. The ability to go through a mental journey, which involves integrating traditional and Western medical practices, is a social feature of great value for health education providers in Malawi.

The value of this integration can be expressed in a slightly different way. Development experts have long concurred that "The source of power is not money in the hands of a few individuals, but information in the hands of many." As expected, therefore, the multiplier effect of the opportunity to interrogate, accommodate, adapt to, reject, or appropriate new ideas goes beyond enhancing health education in Malawi. Therefore, the gains made in health education through a wide information base impact on all spheres of national development.

Malawi is endowed with a rich network of mostly home-grown non-governmental watchdog organizations. These organizations busy themselves with activities that allow them to "blow the whistle" each time service delivery is not satisfactory. Because health, education, agriculture, and infrastructure are the top priorities of these organizations, they have formed a coalition whose aim is to provide a systematic response to issues pertaining to Malawi's economic development priorities, which include the above listed areas.

The key watchdog organizations in Malawi are the Malawi Economic Justice Network, the Civil Society Coalition for Quality Basic Education, the Civil Society Agriculture Network, and the Malawi Health Equity Network. All have a relevant role to play in providing health education in the country. What is even more satisfying is that these organizations reflect a sector-wide approach to topical issues (Malawi Economic Justice Network, 2003).

From the time (2007) that prevention, control, and management of HIV/AIDS and human nutrition were listed as components of the six priority areas of economic development within the Malawi Growth and Development Goals, a full ministerial position has been in place. The personnel involved in the Malawi Growth and Development Strategy are drawn from a wide range of line ministries and accredited private training institutions.

In Malawi, the main thrust of health care is disease prevention, management, and risk reduction through a number of closely related programs. One such is the Extended Program on Immunization (Sekeleza, 2010). This ongoing program, which was inherited from Britain, has kept pace with Malawi's growing population and advances in technology. A second program is health surveillance, which was developed in 2002. Health surveillance involves many activities, including detection of signs and monitoring of epidemics, collecting information on the nutrition status of children, and giving appropriate guidance on feeding, general hygiene, and home-based care in its broadest sense. To date, health care services, reacting to the ever increasing numbers of orphaned and vulnerable children, have been expanded to include the provision of decent housing for children, as well as persons with disabilities and the elderly (Twea, 2010).

Health care delivery also includes the dissemination, through a wide range of experts, of educative information on emerging health issues. Health education is coordinated by the Health Education Unit of the MOHP and a very large number of governmental (i.e., sub-sectors in government ministries that have competence in health matters) and non-governmental organizations. Agriculture and food security, the central aim of which is to reduce malnutrition by ensuring that every household has available to it adequate, balanced nutrition at all times, is an essential element of health care in Malawi. An additional component is the provision of water and appropriate sanitation. The aim of their inclusion is to reduce the incidence of waterborne diseases.

THE TRACK RECORD OF HIV/AIDS AND TUBERCULOSIS IN MALAWI

When news about the first case of an HIV positive person was announced in Malawi in 1985, the government refuted it. Since then, experience has shown that, in the majority of cases, the public sector has adopted a wait and see, reactive approach to natural and human-induced disasters (Bunda College of Agriculture, monitored by Zodiac Broadcasting Station, March, 2010). To date, the denial syndrome has been so widespread that many communities in Malawi take appropriate action only when they realize that ignoring problems is no longer the solution (Banda, 2004).

The most recent manifestation of Malawi's denial syndrome is the overt refutation that homosexuality and bisexuality are practiced in the country. This rebuttal comes against a background in which homosexuals and bisexuals are among the most vulnerable persons with respect to the spread of HIV/AIDS and opportunistic diseases such as tuberculosis. A conducive environment is needed to enable Malawians to seriously engage in advocacy, dialogue, and debate before any attempt to repeal laws governing homosexuality and bisexuality is made (*Mwakasungula*, monitored by Zodiak Broadcasting Station, May, 2010).

Between 1985 and 1994, the denial syndrome fueled the fast spread of HIV/AIDS and associated opportunistic diseases. During the governmental administration of that time, the general public was completely ignorant about how HIV/AIDS is contracted and spread. The few people who were aware of HIV/AIDS treated it as an ordinary sexually transmitted infection or reproductive tract infection. The main catalyst for awareness of the problem arose out of ignorance about the use of disposable syringes. This situation was worsened by numerous regular political measures that encouraged promiscuity because large numbers of people were continually dislodged from their homes and members of those households and families separated. The long and frequent temporary separations of women from their husbands raised their vulnerability to sexual abuse. On their part, men felt deserted, so they frequently turned to other women for sexual gratification.

During the second administration (1994 to 2004), the Bill of Rights (Chapter IV) was enshrined in the country's constitution. The Bill of Rights provided freedoms that some sectors of the Malawi population were unable to interpret appropriately. The hardest hit sector comprised youths and men in the 14 to 49 age bracket. These men were those who most engaged in risky behaviors, including unsafe sex. The health hazards associated with this behavior were colossal, and included contracting communicable diseases such as AIDS.

The following examples illustrate the magnitude of the net effect of the denial syndrome and the liberation highlighted above. By 1999, over 53,000 AIDS cases had been officially reported in the country (National AIDS Commission of Malawi, 2000). This number has since been treated as a gross underestimation of the true situation because many more cases, especially in rural areas, were not reported to hospitals and clinics due to cultural beliefs and the denial syndrome. The Malawi National Aids Control Program has since estimated the actual number of AIDS cases from the start of the epidemic to 1998 to be over 265,000 (National AIDS Commission of Malawi, 2000).

The third administration (2004–2014) has institutionalized Malawi's initiation (into adulthood) ceremonies. The government has rescheduled its school and university calendar to accommodate the season for initiation ceremonies. Despite the fact that the initiation ceremonies act as forums for providing sex education to children below the age of adolescence, circumcision exposes the affected children to HIV/AIDS through the use of untreated razor blades and other non-disposable sharp objects.

STRATEGIES FOR SENSITIZING/EDUCATING MALAWIANS ABOUT HIV/AIDS AND TUBERCULOSIS

Ideally, health is not the absence of disease. Instead, health is physical, mental, social, and economic wellbeing. This state is a continuous one because being healthy on one day does not necessarily mean being healthy on the next. Being infected by HIV or tuberculosis has many implications for infected people and their society, up to and beyond their death, should the infection lead to a terminal disease. This situation has had particularly strong implications for the wellbeing of boys and girls and led to the Government of Malawi lining up multiple programs to educate its citizens about various aspects of health, including HIV/AIDS and tuberculosis.

Government Programs

Working against the threat of HIV/AIDS, the Government of Malawi was quick to establish the Guidance, Counseling, and Youth Development Center for Africa in the country's capital city, Lilongwe, in 1994. The center was established under the auspices of UNESCO. The center's main purpose is to reduce the vulnerability of boys and girls to HIV/AIDS and opportunistic diseases, including tuberculosis, by empowering them through the provision of a comprehensive support service. Major fields of emphasis in this support service are guidance, counseling, gender issues, adolescent reproductive health, entrepreneurship, research, and behavioral change.

The support service provided by the Ministry of Education, Science, and Technology (MOEST) aligns with the approach taken by Dr. Techlemichael (a former Malawian WHO representative). This approach champions the involvement and empowerment of young people in what has hitherto been termed the World AIDS campaign by encouraging them to listen, learn, and live (Chitosi, 1999). It also heeds former United Nations secretary general Koffi Annan's call to governments of United Nations member states to fight HIV/AIDS as a health issue, a political issue, an economic issue, and a social issue ("Koffi Annan Calls on Governments," 1999).

The support service that the center provides is echoed by a series of interrelated curricular, co-curricular, and extracurricular activities that collectively contribute to a life skills training program. One of the aims of this program is to equip schoolboys and girls with personal tools that enable them to adapt and perform effectively in an ever-changing environment. The second aim of the program is to train boys and girls to identify personal visions and formulate strategies for realizing those visions.

One central relevant extracurricular activity named WHY WAIT? is aimed at enabling school-age youths to appreciate the importance of abstinence and the need to avoid indulging in premarital sex. The skills acquired through the WHY WAIT? program are expected to be applied later in life with the aim of reducing the incidence of extramarital sex and potential exposure to HIV. The WHY WAIT? messages are, however, restricted to abstinence only.

The MOHP runs its own health education programs, which are coordinated by its health education unit. Two of these programs are joint radio and television programs. The first, *Pakachere* ("education under a kachere tree"), offers a common rural forum for sharing ideas. The second, *Banja la Msogolo* (meaning a dream family) is an HIV/AIDS talk show. The two programs are supplemented by a myriad of faith-based, joint television and radio programs. One such program is a radio/television drama called *Tikuferanji?* ("Why are we dying unnecessarily?"). Programs that fall under this umbrella are particularly aimed at behavior change in the wake of research findings that point to how vulnerable people 14 to 49 years of age are to HIV/AIDS (Soko, 2010).

The interventions described in this chapter have been complemented by what the government has termed mainstreaming HIV and AIDS. This approach calls for budgeting for HIV/AIDS and related activities. The activities in question have included the production of HIV/AIDS workplace policies that have embedded within them programs for the prevention and treatment of AIDS. Since 1994, mainstreaming HIV and AIDS has extended to non-governmental organizations and faith organizations.

Tuberculosis is frequently depicted in Malawi as just one of the opportunistic diseases affecting the population. Because of this, comprehensive programs designed to address tuberculosis-specific issues have not been forthcoming. The little effort that has been made in this respect has been restricted to providing the guardians of tuberculosis patients with information prior to the commencement of home-based treatment sessions. Joint television and radio programs such as *Za umoyo* (health issues) also include information on tuberculosis.

Interventions through Faith and Community Groupings

April 23 is the day set for the annual general meeting of the Interfaith AIDS Association of Malawi (Malawi Broadcasting Corporation Radio 1, 2010). The association claims to have played a crucial role in reducing the HIV/AIDS prevalence rate by 5% from 17% of the population in 2008 to 12% in 2009. The forum claims that its success, in this respect, was because it avoided the "fire-fighting" strategies that the Malawian government and its cooperating non-governmental organizations normally deploy. Every faith organization runs an independent HIV/AIDS intervention. One example is the Livingstonia Synod AIDS/HIV Support Group (LISAP), which was established in 1994 to respond to the threats HIV/AIDS was likely to pose to the church and the communities it serves (LISAP Coordinator of Ekwendeni Hospital, personal communication, May 19, 2010). LISAP uses a wide range of training modes. These include workshops, peer education, drama performances, and information, education, and communication resources.

Because Africa has so many young people who are not in school, most of the interventions in HIV/AIDS, along with other initiatives aimed at disseminating information on health issues, do not reach this sector of the population. Sporadic efforts are being made by volunteer village councilors or *anankungwi* (literally aunts or uncles) to reach out to these young people.

There are many other door-to-door interventions, including one interesting and isolated example. A bishop in a parish in the northern city of Mzuzu has succeeded in winning over large numbers of alcoholics, hemp smokers, and bar-mongers by joining them in drinking sprees. After a few successive visits, the bishop discusses the ills of excessive drinking, smoking hemp, and lingering around bars. The discussions have resulted, over the last few years, in observable behavior changes in the communities in the bishop's parish. Also, and even though they are expensive, door-to-door campaigns have proved to be a very cost-effective means of outreach. An additional advantage is that frequent follow-up visits are possible.

Despite the still prevalent imbalance between in-school and out-of-school young people, MOEST continues to partner with international non-governmental organizations to build capacity in various fields of human health, including HIV/AIDS. An example is Theatre for a Change (2008), which is based in the United Kingdom and currently working in Ghana and Malawi. Theatre for a Change is a pre-service teacher education program, the central objectives of which are behavior change, advocacy, and capacity building.

PROGRESS AND CHALLENGES

Official statements made jointly by government, Interfaith AIDS Association of Malawi, faith organizations, and other non-governmental organizations indicate that Malawi has taken many strides forward in its fight against HIV/AIDS. Major indicators of success in this regard are:

- Mobilization of communities to respond positively to expert advice on the disease;
- Successful training of home-based caregivers who work in home-based care clinics;
- A substantial reduction in hospital admissions;
- A substantial reduction in the HIV/AIDS prevalence rate, which currently stands at 12% of the population;
- A substantial reduction in the school dropout rate of girls (LISAP coordinator of Ekwendeni Hospital, personal communication, May 19, 2010).

Despite this progress, many challenges remain. These include social inertia, inadequate funding, and some cultural practices.

With respect to the first of these challenges, social inertia, the Constitution of Malawi grants all citizens and other persons living in the country freedom of worship. Unfortunately, there are many religious sects across the countries that shun health services on the pretext that they are earthly and ungodly. Because of this belief, many avoidable deaths continue to be registered among communities that are staunch members of such sects. The mortality rates are particularly high among children under five years of age and the elderly, whose immunity is low. What is true of ordinary diseases also applies to HIV/AIDS and tuberculosis because affected communities either simply ignore any form of expert advice on the disease or they literally flee to areas where they cannot be reached.

Inadequate funding is another major challenge, as most of the interventions discussed in this chapter are donor driven. Over time, donor fatigue has impinged negatively on most, if not all, of the interventions. As a consequence, the majority of community members, especially those young people who are the most vulnerable, are not being reached. Furthermore, because few programs are countrywide, the likelihood of programs not reaching large regions of the country is amplified.

Finally, challenges to enhanced health outcomes in Malawi are posed by some cultural practices. For example, the Government of Malawi recently attempted to enact a law to make polygamy illegal. An appropriate Bill for the legal process could not be passed because chiefs and other leaders throughout the country opposed it during consultation meetings prior to tabling. The rejection of the Bill is a symptom of a bigger problem, namely, cultural practices that act as catalysts for the spread of HIV/AIDS continuing to be upheld across the country. Such practices are obstructing the efforts of government, IAAM, faith organizations, and other non-governmental organizations to fight HIV/AIDS.

The cultural practices that pose the greatest threat to health education include wife inheritance, *kuhara chokolo*, in the northern region, and cleansing of evil spirits (*kulowa kufa*) in the southern region districts of Chikhwawa and Nsanje. In the first case, a widow is inherited by a brother, cousin, or any other eligible man in the village, to prevent her leaving the village where she was married. In the case of *kulowa kufa*, a similar practice is followed, but the motive is different. Here, the motive is to drive away evil spirits from the village, thus preventing further deaths. Intergenerational marriages can also contribute to health problems. For example, when younger men or women marry older people, they run the risk of indulging in extramarital sex in the later stages of their marriages as they search for sexual gratification. This poses a great threat to combating the spread of HIV/AIDS because the affected younger men or women establish sexual relationships with multiple partners. Given this situation, it is likely that the official statements concerning substantial reductions in HIV/AIDS prevalence rates may not be accurate.

CONCLUSION AND PROSPECTS

The challenges discussed in this chapter are surmountable but only if deliberate efforts are made to change the mindsets of the people who matter in society, namely, opinion leaders such as chiefs and law enforcers. These people are sporadically caught up in clandestine activities with sex workers in the course of carrying out clean-up exercises in drinking establishments. Although prostitution is illegal in Malawi, there are no appropriate laws in the country's penal code that courts can apply to curb it.

Government too needs to be frank about issues if any headway is to be made in health education. Recently, there have been revelations suggesting not all is well regarding the publicized success in health delivery services in the country. The revelations have serious implications for the fight against HIV/AIDS and tuberculosis and are centered on the rampant outbreaks of measles, which have recently prompted MOHP to move quickly to carry out a fresh immunization campaign targeting all persons between 9 months and 15 years of age. This situation implies that the publicized successes in the country's extended programs of immunization might be merely window dressing. It is likely that these programs, on which successes should have been based, might not have been truly functional over the past 15 years. This conclusion is not a far-fetched one given the inverse correlation between the availability of good health care and related services and the education needs of the rural masses.

REFERENCES

Banda, M. (2004, March 23). Water: Friend or foe? *The Nation*, p. 11.

Blackie, M. J., Conroy, A. C., Malewezi, J. C., Sachs, J. D., & Whiteside, A. (Eds.). (2006). *Poverty, AIDS, and hunger: Breaking the poverty trap in Malawi*. New York: Palgrave Macmillan.

Chavula, J. (2009, October 15). SMS improves children's health delivery. *The Nation*, p. 3.

Chitosi, I. (1999, December 3). Positive approach to AIDS fight—WHO. *The Nation National*, p. 3.

Friends of Malawi. (2004). *Healthcare: Friends of Malawi learn about Malawi*. Retrieved from http://www.friendsofmalawi.org/learn_about_malawi/institutions/healthcare.html.

Kaunda, G. (2009, October 25). CHAM students to lose places. *The Nation National*, p. 2.

Koffi Annan calls on governments of UNO member states to fight HIV/AIDS as a health issue, a political issue, an economic issue and a social issue. (1999, December 1). *The Daily Times National*, p. 9.

Last, M., & Chavunduka, G. L. (1988). *The professionalization of African medicine*. Manchester, UK: Manchester University Press.

Malawi Broadcasting Corporation Radio 1. (2010, July 10). *Malawi observes HIV / AIDS candle memorial ceremony*. Lilongwe, Malawi: Author.

Malawi Economic Justice Network (MEJN). (2003). *Service delivery satisfaction survey*. Lilongwe, Malawi: MEJN.

Malawi Interfaith AIDS Association. (2010, February 25). 2010 interfaith HIV/AIDS prayers. *Salima Advertising*, pp. 4–5.

National Aids Commission of Malawi. (2000). *HIV/AIDS Strategic plan - 2000 to 2004*. Lilongwe, Malawi.

National Statistical Office. (2008, September). *Population and housing census preliminary report*. Zomba, Malawi: Author.

Sekeleza, G. (2010, October 10). Ministry of Health receives vehicles from extended program of immunization (EPI) and Global Alliance and Vaccines (GAVI). *The Nation*, p. 4.

Soko, M. (2010). *Brief outline of David Gordon Memorial Hospital Primary Health Care community activities planned for the year 2010*. PHC Directorate, Gordon Memorial Hospital, Livingstonia, Malawi.

Theatre for a Change. (2008). *Mzuzu University needs assessment report*. Lilongwe, Malawi: Author.

Twea, B. (2010, October 29). Habitat for Humanity eliminates homelessness in Mzuzu and Blantyre. *The Nation National*, p. 6.

Zere, E., Moeti, M., Kirigia, J., Mwase, T., & Kataika, E. (2007). Equity in health and healthcare in Malawi: Analysis of trends. *Bio Medical Center of Public Health, 7*, 78.

Zodiak Broadcasting Station. (2010, March 4). *Malawi still using the wait and see, reactive approach to respond to natural and man-induced disasters*. Lilongwe, Malawi: News anchor.

Zodiak Broadcasting Station. (2010, May 30). *The Center for Human Rights and Rehabilitation Executive Secretary, Undule Mwakasungula, backs Bingu wa Muthalika's pardon of the gay couple*. Lilongwe, Malawi: News Anchor.

Gilbert R. Phiri
Mzuzu University
Malawi
Africa
email: gr_phiri@yahoo.co.uk

FRANCESCA CONRADIE

11. MEDICAL RESEARCH IN SOUTH AFRICA

Education and Ethics

BACKGROUND

South Africa "boasts" the highest number of HIV-infected persons living in one country, with approximately 1 in 10 individuals infected. In 2010, estimates put the number of infected at 5.8 million. It is not within the purview of this article to describe the drivers of the epidemic. In South Africa, HIV (the human immunodeficiency virus) is a generalized epidemic with no identifiable risk groups, and the virus is spread mainly through heterosexual intercourse. The incidence of intravenous drug abuse is low. Those who are infected are not marginalized.

HIV infection causes an insidious decline in immune function. When the damage to the immune system is advanced, infected persons develop AIDS (acquired immune deficiency syndrome.) The infected person is susceptible to a broad range of infections, as well as cancers. Tuberculosis is the most common co-infection with HIV (King & Ahuja, 2006). A number of organisms—viruses, bacteria, and even fungi—that normally do not cause disease can afflict those infected with HIV. These infections are termed opportunistic.

The time from which a person living in South Africa is infected with HIV to the time he or she becomes severely ill or dies is, on average, about 8 to 10 years. In South Africa, about 750 people die every day from AIDS. The brunt of the epidemic is borne by young women between the ages of 15 and 24 (Harrison, Richter, & Desmond, 2007). This is a very grim state of affairs. However, since the advent of antiretroviral therapy, the disease can be halted and the damage done to the immune system reversed almost completely. While there is no cure for HIV infection and, in my opinion, never will be, it has become a chronic and thus manageable disease.

Medication for HIV consists of between two to five or more tablets per day, and a person taking this medicine must do so for the rest of his or her life. South Africa has a national antiretroviral program that supplies over one million patients with these life-saving medications. While the program still falls short of meeting the need, it is nonetheless impressive and is a testament to many hard-working, dedicated, and brave health-care workers.

The first medication that received registration for the treatment of AIDS in 1987 was zidovudine (AZT). Originally a drug developed as a cancer chemotherapeutic agent, it was found to slow down the progress of HIV infection. In time, a number of newer agents were discovered and put through the rigorous clinical trial

N. Taylor, F. Quinn, M. Littledyke and R.K. Coll (eds.), Health Education in Context, 99–106.

procedure. In 1995, the use of a combination therapy of at least three antiretroviral medications changed the face of HIV infection forever. These combinations are also termed "highly active antiretroviral therapy" (HAART) (Rabkin & Chesney, 2002). What originally was a death sentence is now a long-term treatable illness not unlike diabetes or hypertension. According to the best available information, a person, once on HAART, can expect to live for 20 to 25 years, provided that he or she continues to take the drugs (Rabkin & Chesney, 2002).

A key part of the development of these medications is research in the form of clinical trials. The trials are scientifically controlled studies of the safety and effectiveness of a therapeutic agent (such as a drug or vaccine), and they are carried out on consenting human subjects.

ETHICS OF CLINICAL TRIALS

Established ethics governing clinical trials are guided by the principles of autonomy, beneficence, and justice. In order to make an autonomous decision about whether or not to participate in these trials, potential participants need to be presented with all available information about the trial and its purpose. This information includes the potential risks and benefits of the new medication, what current treatment is available, what additional procedures are involved (e.g., electrocardiograms, CAT scans, and extra blood-draws), and how many times participants will have to visit the clinic. Participants are also made well aware that their participation is voluntary. This process is called informed consent; there should be no hint of coercion. All of these details must be explained in the language of choice of the potential participants and must be communicated in a manner appropriate to their level of education and understanding.

For a drug to reach the level of a clinical trial, there must be good evidence, based on animal studies and pre-clinical trials, that the medicine will have the desired benefit and will not harm participants. The adage here is, first, do no harm (non-maleficence), and then do good (beneficence). Finally, if the drug is registered, then the community where the research is conducted should be able to access the medication should it prove to be beneficial. It would not be ethical to conduct a trial in an underprivileged community and then market the trial drug at an excessive price. An appropriate term for research done only to benefit the sponsor is "mosquito research," where what is needed is taken and nothing is given back.

When practicing what is called evidence-based medicine, the health care provider aims to apply the best available evidence, gained from scientific method, during medical decisionmaking. Health care providers may be individual practitioners, health management organizations, regional and national departments of health, and the World Health Organization.

The level of the evidence obtained from the trial process is ranked. Level IV evidence, which is obtained from case studies, is also termed "expert opinion." In contrast, Level I evidence is obtained from a systematic review of all trials employing random sampling of participants and employing control measures (e.g., one group of participants receives the medication, the other—the control group—does not). The necessary regulatory bodies, including the Food and Drug Administration, European Medicines Agency, and (in South Africa) the Medical Control Council, will not register new treatments or medications unless knowledge about their clinical effects is based on evidence obtained from at least one well-designed randomized controlled trial.

The many challenges to conducting clinical trials in South Africa and other nations of Sub-Saharan Africa beg the question, should this work be done at all? Emotive words such as "guinea pig" come to mind. There have been a number of books and movies made about avaricious drug companies out to make a dollar at the expense of individuals in poorer countries. This situation highlights the critical role that sensitive and appropriately targeted education about the relevant issues can play in protecting vulnerable people from exploitation. I strongly urge the conducting of clinical trials in Sub-Saharan Africa.

In the rest of this chapter, I draw on my own experiences as a medical doctor working in South Africa to explain why it should and how it can be done. First, however, I would like to briefly describe the challenges typically involved with conducting clinical trials in this and other nations of Sub-Saharan Africa.

CHALLENGES OF CONDUCTING CLINICAL TRIALS

Those of us conducting clinical trials and attempting to educate participants about what their involvement in these trails means for them typically have to address and accommodate complex issues. I work at a site in Johannesburg where we have over 15,000 HIV-infected patients on HAART. The level of unemployment is high, and the average level of education is only primary school. In South Africa, like most African countries, there is a perception that doctors are all knowing and all powerful. The "average" patient is female and is between 32 and 36 years of age.

There may well be a cultural divide between the potential participant and the health care provider—a divide that encompasses language. Even gender roles come into play. These concerns are pervasive in the health care system, but are made more cogent in clinical trials because of the ethical considerations. Participants tend to be reluctant to question what health care professionals say, although the health care system is working to change this paradigm.

These issues characterize the difficult situation within which I and my colleagues at the Clinical HIV Research Unit of the University of Witwatersrand conduct clinical trials. In the next two sections of this chapter, I describe the steps that we have found useful when endeavoring to provide appropriate education for the community and individuals involved in drug trials.

THE DEVELOPMENT OF COMMUNITY EDUCATION

The first step involves establishing a community advisory board, responsible for facilitating community education. This board should consist of a social worker, a counselor, a community leader, a spiritual leader, a doctor who is not involved in the research, someone with legal knowledge, and lay members of the community. Often the lay members of the board have the particular disease that is under study. Anyone wanting to conduct research must consult with the board before a research protocol can even be considered.

In our unit, this board meets every quarter, and ad hoc meetings can also be called. The board represents the voices of the community at large. When a new research idea is being put forward, it is presented at one of these meetings. The first question asked is, "Will the proposed research be useful to the community?" For example, if HIV is a major health issue in the community, doing a study on an obscure metabolic disease will be of no value to that community. Board members are then asked if they foresee any challenges.

One challenge that the board frequently brings up is the fear that many people with HIV have of disclosure of their illness. To resolve this, at least in part, our clinic appointment cards do not mention HIV, we answer our phones with the introduction "Clinical Trial Unit," and we never identify ourselves as health care workers when we call our patients. Another fear that we address is the concern that, should medication need to be refrigerated, the bottles stored in the fridge will alert family members who are not aware of the participant's status.

INDIVIDUAL EDUCATION

At this point, I would like to define some terms that we commonly use during our clinical trials. I will then describe how we explain them to our patients.

An *investigational agent* is the term used to describe the new medication that is being tested. Because we do not know if this medication will be safe and efficacious, we need to explain the risk to benefit ratio. If we know that the drug will definitely work, a trial is not necessary. If there is *equipoise*—a term used in clinical research to describe a situation where there is genuine uncertainty over whether a treatment will work or not—we can commence the trial. Because there is a balance between not knowing and knowing the outcome of a medication, we use images of a seesaw to explain the concept of equipoise.

Placebo is a medication that looks the same as the active drug but is inert. Trials that include a placebo are today very rare. If there is an accepted treatment for the condition, patients cannot be given a placebo. Instead, they receive whatever is the current accepted treatment.

Randomization is the process whereby the treatment is allocated randomly to participants. This means that all participants have an equal chance of receiving or not receiving the medication. We use various systems to prevent anyone predicting what will be given and received, but when talking with participants we explain this process as akin to flipping a coin. Sometimes we use an actual coin to demonstrate this concept. Because soccer is a very popular sport in South Africa, people understand the reason for flipping a coin, which takes place just before kick-off. Randomization also prevents both investigator and participant bias.

In a *double-blinded trial*, which we conduct, neither the doctor nor the participant can tell which medication is being given or received. Here we use the image of a blindfold to help educate people about this concept. We tell our patients that if they know they are receiving the new medication, they may "blame" subsequent events and symptoms on it. For example, if a person normally suffers from headaches, he or she might still be inclined to blame the trial drug for any headaches experienced during it.

Because we need to measure the response to the treatment and any adverse events, there needs to be a standard to measure against. This is called a *control*. But what happens in the situation when the potential participant has such a low level of education that they cannot grasp these concepts. In South Africa, there are 11 official languages. Not everyone can speak English. Should these people not be allowed to participate? If not, discrimination against the least-empowered members of society continues. To overcome this problem, we bring in an impartial witness, ideally a family member. However, lay counselors and patient advocates who are not involved with the research are also enlisted. These witnesses oversee the process. If they believe the understanding of the patient is adequate, they will sign a statement attesting to this. These procedures, designed to adequately educate participants about the risks, the benefits, and the processes of clinical trials, are time consuming. It can take three or more hours to complete the process. However, it is essential for the ethical conduct of medical research that we work through it. I wholeheartedly endorse it.

ONGOING AND FUTURE CONSIDERATIONS

Why is there a need to continue with medical research programs and their co-requisite educational agendas? Do we not have the answers? In some cases, yes. But even in these instances, better knowledge and understanding can lead to better options than those currently available. Think of the features that were installed in a 1969 Volkswagen beetle. Compare that to a new car off the shelf today, with its safety features—inertia seat belts, ABS braking, air bags, crumple zones—along with luxuries such as built-in GPS, central locking, and a CD shuttle. These are features that were probably not even imagined in 1969. Developments in medicine follow a similar pattern.

The first HAART regimen, for example, consisted of over 12 pills, some that needed to be taken on a full stomach and some on an empty stomach. Today, the most commonly prescribed regimen in the developed world is one tablet only, to be taken at night. Also, when we first began using HAART, we were hopeful that a cure would eventuate. This hope proved to be unfounded. The longer the "older" medications were used, the more apparent it was that there were adverse side-effects that had not been predicted. This situation is not confined to HAART but is evident with other medications, such as an anti-inflammatory that was found to increase the incidence of heart attacks, and the drug thalidomide, which caused birth defects.

We need better, safer, and easier-to-take drugs for AIDS sufferers, and they are being developed. Most years, a new drug is registered; some of those newly registered drugs require new medication regimes and some are improvements on what we already have. This situation raises another role for education, namely, informing people about the latest developments in HIV/AIDS treatment and how best to adopt innovative treatment regimes. This education is needed at the level of individuals, communities, and public health policymakers.

Almost all new drugs are developed by pharmaceutical companies, and most trials are initially conducted in Europe and the USA. When reading papers in medical journals about these drugs, I am surprised to find that the study population is generally made up of Caucasian males whereas my patients are predominantly black women. What this means is that we are using medications on one population group and/or gender that were mainly trialed with a different population group and/or gender. We know that men and women metabolize drugs differently, and that different races have different genetic make-ups; these differences can determine what side-effects of the medicine will manifest in a population.

Take, as an example, nevirapine (NVP), which was registered as an antiretroviral in 1996 and first used in clinical practice in 1999. A number of women were given this medication in South Africa. Three of them died from liver failure (Huff, 2001). This outcome has not been seen elsewhere, but its occurrence resulted in a change in the information included in the medicine's packet. The change advised that use of the drug should be restricted in some circumstances. If this research had not been done in Sub-Saharan Africa, NVP would have been given more widely and there would have been more deaths.

Different subtypes of HIV are evident in different geographical areas. South Africans are usually infected with subtype C, while subtype B is most common in Europe (Renjifo & Essex, 2002). The subtypes are like cousins—from similar stock but each with its own quirks. If resistance to HIV medication develops in subtype C—and resistance to medication will occur if people do not take it correctly—that resistance will differ from that occurring in subtype B. In short, because we have different population groups and different viruses, we need to engage in ongoing research. Such research, moreover, must involve well-designed, robust clinical trials, conducted on relevant study populations, as well as ethically grounded well-targeted education of these populations, the members of which are potential participants in trials and end-users of the research products.

REFERENCES

Harrison, D., Richter L., & Desmond, C. (2007, September). *Changing perceptions of opportunities: Hope for young people in high HIV-risk environments.* Paper presented at the 3rd Global Conference on Hope: Probing the Boundaries, Mansfield College, Oxford, UK.

Huff, W. (2001). Sex differences in nevirapine rash and hepatitis. *The Body: The Complete HIV/AIDS Resource* [website]. Retrieved from http://www.thebody.com/content/ art13572.html.

King, L., & Ahuja, S. (2006). TB and HIV coinfection: Current trends, diagnosis and treatment update. *Physicians' Research Network* [website]. Retrieved from http://www.prn.org/ index.php/ coinfections/article/tb_hiv_coinfection_treatment_80.

Rabkin, J. G., & Chesney, M. (2002). Treatment adherence to HIV medications: The Achilles heel of the new therapeutics. In D. G. Ostrow & S. C. Kalichman (Eds.), Psychosocial and public health impacts of new HIV therapies (pp. 61–82). New York: Kluwer Academic Publishers.

Renjifo, B., & Essex, M. (2002). HIV-1 subtypes and recombinants. In M. Essex, S. Mboup, P. Kanki, & R. Marlink (Eds.), *AIDS in Africa* (pp. 263–279). New York: Kluwer Academic Publishers.

Francesca Conradie
University of Witwatersrand
Pretoria
South Africa
email: fconradie@witshealth.co.za

12. THE DEVELOPMENT OF THE SCHOOL HEALTH POLICY AND CURRICULUM IN NIGERIA

BACKGROUND

The Federal Republic of Nigeria was a British colony until October 1960 when it gained independence. The country is located on the west coast of Africa, with the Atlantic Ocean to the south, and bordered by Niger and Chad to the north, Benin to the west, and Cameroon to the east. Nigeria has 36 autonomous states, but practices a federal system of government. The federal capital city of Abuja is home to about 2.6 million residents. The approximately 250 ethnic groups who live in Nigeria speak diverse languages and dialects, but the official language is English, which is the mode of instruction at all educational levels. At state and local government levels, and except for official meetings, day-to-day communication in offices is usually in local languages and dialects. The population of the country is around 15 million (Central Intelligence Agency, 2011), making it the most populous country in Africa and one of the fastest growing countries on the continent.

Because of its large land mass (923,000 square kilometers), Nigeria's citizens usually refer to their country as the Giant of Africa. The country also has a coastline of 853 kilometers and territorial waters that extend 12 nautical miles out to sea. The country belongs to many sub-regional, regional, and world-based organizations, including the African Union, British Commonwealth, World Health Organization (WHO), and the Economic Community of West African States.

Political leaders, especially at federal state levels, regard education as a tool that can accommodate the ethnic, cultural, and religious diversity of the country and thereby enhance societal development and transformation. The southern states are more educationally developed than the northern states, a situation that has its origins in the position of the southern states along the coastal areas, which gave them more early contact with white Christian missionaries.

THE HEALTH SITUATION IN NIGERIA

Despite more than 50 years as a nation with abundant human and natural resources, Nigeria is still bedeviled with a high prevalence of communicable diseases due to poverty, ignorance, and poor sanitation. The country has also been experiencing an increase in non-communicable diseases because of the adoption of poor lifestyle habits. The health situation in Nigeria is particularly dire because of poor environmental sanitation resulting from limited potable water and ineffective disposal of human wastes. The hitherto uncommon non-communicable diseases such as diabetes, cancer, kidney dysfunction, and cardiovascular ailments are a

N. Taylor, F. Quinn, M. Littledyke and R.K. Coll (eds.), Health Education in Context, 107–114.

burden for the populace in general and health care providers in particular (Lucas, 2002).

At present, Nigeria's health indicators place the country at the same level as countries suffering from civil unrest, overwhelming HIV/AIDS infection, and ongoing war. Nigeria's infant mortality rate (98 per 1,000 births) is higher than that of the Congo (81 per 1,000) and almost double Ghana's (50 per 1,000). These statistics are particularly worrying when it is realized that Nigeria and Ghana have an identical gross national annual income of $320 per capita (Kayode, Owoaje, & Omotade, 2007). Equally abysmally low are immunization rates, especially when compared with those of other countries. In addition, the government budgets only about US$2.00 per head of population for health, despite the above concerns and despite the fact that harmful sociocultural practices inimical to people's health still exist in Nigeria (Kayode et al., 2007).

Records show that Nigeria is lagging significantly behind in terms of meeting the eight millennium development goals, promulgated internationally (Grange, 2008). This lag is especially worrying given that the goals focus on child and young people's rights and thus tie in with amelioration of poverty and hunger, provision of universal primary education, gender equality and empowerment of women, lessening of child mortality, improved maternal health, declining rates of HIV/AIDS, environmental sustainability, and inter-sectorial collaboration. The generally poor outlook for the health of Nigerian children and adolescents makes imperative the contribution that school health education offers their physical and mental wellbeing and their education outcomes. Health education is also important with respect to addressing the health problems of the wider community. This is because health education within schools tends to diffuse into the community at large.

HEALTH EDUCATION AND SCHOOL HEALTH EDUCATION

Health education is the process by which people acquire knowledge, attitudes, and behaviors that promote their health and help them make decisions directed at solving personal, family, and community health problems (Moronkola, 2007). The focus of health education is on helping people appreciate and know how to take the actions they need to in order to enjoy good health (Fabiyi, 2001). Health education is not, of course, peculiar with respect to achieving the needed changes in the health of Nigerians; it has the same relevance for people worldwide (Ajala, 2005).

As Moronkola (2002) explains, health education can be seen as a concept, discipline, course of study, approach, or method through which accredited health information is made available to people with the aim of simultaneously stimulating positive health-related attitudes and practices that promote personal and community health. Moronkola also observes that there are many forms of health education, including school health education and community health education. School health education, he argues, should be a well-planned sequential program of in- and out-of-the classroom health instruction on health topics designed to inform and stimulate desirable health attitudes and behavior among learners within the school setting. According to Tamir et al. (1987), school-based health education is the cheapest and most effective approach to achieving these aims, and it can be applied in most countries. Schools also offer easy and systematic access to the majority of children, all over the world.

In Nigeria, the National Policy on Education of 1981 barely recognized let alone provided for teaching health education in Nigeria. Udoh (1996) later lamented that the instructional health-related programs then evident in public primary schools was incidental learning that could not realize the goals that health education should seek to achieve. At the junior secondary school, health education was being typically integrated with physical education, while at the senior secondary school level—and even though health science was being offered in these schools—many people did not appreciate its value, either as an academic subject or for its lifetime value.

Worldwide, various national governments and international organizations have put in place school health initiatives. These include, for example, the following, the first three of which were instigated by WHO:

- Global School Health;
- Health-Promoting Schools;
- Life Skills;
- Child-Friendly Schools;
- Skill-Based Health Education;
- Focusing Resources on Effective School Health; and
- Home-Grown School Feeding and Health Program.

These initiatives have the overall objectives of making the school environment child-friendly and ensuring collaboration and partnership with all stakeholders so as to harness all available resources for effective implementation of the programs. In related vein, they also encourage schools and their communities to take ownership of the programs in order to ensure their sustainability.

During the earlier part of the last decade, the Nigerian Federal Ministry of Health and Federal Ministry of Education, in collaboration with WHO, conducted a rapid assessment of the school health system throughout Nigeria. This revealed several health problems among learners, including a lack of health and sanitation facilities in schools, and thus the need for urgent action with respect to improving school health. In 2006, the Ministry of Education, along with all other stakeholders of line ministries, Nigeria's Civil Society Organisation, and several international development partners, issued a national school health policy. When writing the acknowledgement section of the policy, Akpam (2006) noted that promoting the health of learners in schools is a critical step toward quality achievement in education and that successful implementation of a school health program was critical to realizing not only the goals of the school health policy but also Nigeria's National Policy on Education.

The Federal Ministry of Education (2006) stated that the vision of the National School Health Policy was to promote the health of learners, such that the country could achieve "Education for All" and "Health for All." The policy's mission statement focused on the need to put in place adequate facilities, resources, and programs. This development, it was noted, would guarantee physical and mental health, social wellbeing, and the safety and security of the school community, outcomes that would, in turn, enhance children's learning.

More specifically, the goals of the National School Health Policy were to "enhance the quality of health in the school community ... [and to] create an enabling environment for inter-sectorial partnership in the promotion of a child friendly school environment, for teaching and learning and health development." The objectives of the policy were listed as follows.

- Provide the necessary legal framework for mobilization of support for the implementation of the School Health Programme;
- Set up machinery for the co-ordination of community efforts with those of government and non-governmental organizations, in order to promote child-friendly school environments;
- Guide the provision of appropriate professional services in schools by stakeholders as part of implementation of the School Health Programme;
- Promote the teaching of skill-based health education;
- Facilitate effective monitoring and evaluation of the School Health Programme; and
- Set up modalities for the sustaining the School Health Programme.

The implementation guidelines for the National School Health Programme were also published in December 2006. Oyinloye (2006) notes that the guidelines were established alongside the National School Health Policy and that the process used to do this was a participatory one involving relevant stakeholders, in recognition that successful development of the policy, program, and guidelines relied on all such stakeholders striving to promote healthy learning environments in Nigerian schools. These documents guided the curriculum contents of health education for primary and post-primary schools in Nigeria. This content was combined with physical education at the primary school level and presented as a separate school subject at the senior secondary school level.

Recently, there has been an awakening recognition of the value of health education in Nigerian schools. The recent adoption of nine-year basic education in Nigeria took care, to some extent, of the disconnection between most subjects at primary school level and at the junior secondary school level. The new curriculum for basic education has heeded the targets of the values of re-orientation, eradication of poverty, job creation, and wealth generation inherent in Nigeria's National Economic Empowerment Development Strategy.

Because of the many subjects that children have to learn during their lower-basic (Primaries 1 to 3) and middle-level basic (Primaries 4 to 6) education, the following themes (with various topics) related to health education have been incorporated into various subjects at all levels of primary school. The themes include first aid and safety education, personal health care, and food and nutrition.

Children engaged in upper basic education (Junior Secondary School 1 to 3) experience the Junior Secondary School Physical and Health Education Curriculum, which covers the following themes (with various topics): first aid and safety education; personal, school, and community health; food, nutrition, and health; and pathogens, diseases, and their prevention. The children also have opportunity to engage in other health-related topics and activities relevant to the curriculum: recreation, leisure, and dance; issues and challenges in physical and health education; career guidance in physical and health education; and physical fitness and body conditioning (Nigerian Educational Research and Development Council, 2007).

At the senior secondary school level, students now study health education, a change in name (brought in by the Nigerian Educational Research and Development Council) from the previously titled health science. The health education curriculum is skills-based, and its philosophy is one of providing students with the necessary skills and competence to take appropriate actions in matters relating not only to their health but also to the health of others. The curriculum also focuses on encouraging students to appreciate the need for a healthy environment. The specific objectives of the curriculum are as follows:

- Enable students to acquire basic knowledge of the body and necessary skills for maintaining health;
- Encourage students to acquire and practice positive health habits in the community;
- Enable students to appreciate the ecological relationship between humans and their environment;
- Give students the ability to observe and draw inferences from practical experiences that have implications for their health; and
- Prepare students for professional training in health-related careers.

The developers of the secondary school health education curriculum adopted a thematic approach, which included spiral development of curriculum contents. The themes covered are:

- History and development of health education;
- Human anatomy and physiology;
- Personal health;
- Environmental health;
- Community health;
- Food and nutrition;
- Safety education and first aid;
- Drug, alcohol, and tobacco education;
- Consumer health;
- Communicable and non-communicable diseases.

To ensure the effectiveness of the School Health Programme in Nigeria, which incorporates school health education, the Federal Ministry of Education, in conjunction with relevant stakeholders from ministries and academia, developed and implemented a monitoring and evaluation checklist.

The United Nations Children's Fund (UNICEF) has played an invaluable role in building the health-education-related capacity of relevant stakeholders, including teachers and what are known as school health-education desk officers, at both the federal and state levels. Their work has helped actualize the vision and mission of the National School Health Policy. UNICEF, together with the Federal Ministry of Education, also facilitated the development and production of the *Skill-Based Health Education Teachers' Manual* and the *Training Manual for Short Courses on the School Health Programme*, among other resources. These resources offer an important means of enhancing the skills and understandings of teachers throughout the education and health sectors. Unfortunately, many health education lecturers, education officers, and health teachers are not aware of them, a situation that is partly a product of the piecemeal distribution of these resources and the piecemeal implementation of the advice and approaches that they advocate.

Another problem is that although many qualified health education teachers exist, few are employed. Also, state governments still accord little importance to health education as a separate teaching subject in schools, even though the potential benefits to learners, parents, and the entire community, especially in terms of lowering the cost of health care to individuals and government, are obvious. Government agencies—federal, state, and local—need to embrace the vision and objectives of the National Health Policy and the School Health Programme. Providing in-service training on new curriculum contents and modes of delivery for teachers, whether dedicated health education teachers or teachers who teach health topics as part of other subjects, is just one action that government agencies need to take. There is also a need for the Department of Human Kinetics and Health Education at the University of Ibadan to conduct a general studies course for tertiary students in colleges of education and polytechnics on health matters. Such a course would ideally focus on general health issues and the pedagogy of health education, and include a component covering contemporary health issues for young people.

CONCLUSION

The Nigerian Government must not be satisfied with the "crisis" health education curriculum provided in too many schools by non-governmental organizations. This curriculum typically focuses on sexuality issues only, especially HIV/AIDS. Instead, the government must ensure that teachers are employed who can teach health education (preferably as a separate subject) that aligns with the recently developed health education policy and curriculum. There is an ongoing need for pre-service and in-service teacher education directed at teaching health education. There is also a need to put in place mechanisms that will sustain and build on the short-term projects implemented by the non-governmental agencies in order to improve the health of Nigerians. Tertiary institution students must also be educated on such issues as drug misuse and abuse, unsafe premarital sex, clandestine abortion, teenage pregnancy, sexual violence, sexually transmitted infections, and HIV/AIDS. As with all health education curricula throughout Nigeria's education system, these courses must be ones that are appropriate to the age and stage of the learners to whom they are directed.

REFERENCES

Ajala, J. A. (2005). *Health education in wellness and sickness: This day, this age*. Inaugural lecture delivered to the university community and other attendees at the University of Ibadan, Ibadan, Nigeria.

Akpam, S. N. (2006). Acknowledgement. In *National school health policy*. Abuja, Nigeria: Federal Ministry of Education Nigeria.

Central Intelligence Agency. (2011). Nigeria. In *World factbook*. Retrieved from https://www.cia.gov/library/ publications/the-world-factbook/geos/ni.html.

Fabiyi, A. K. (2001). *Introduction to health*. Ile-Ife, Nigeria: Obafemi Awolowo University Press.

Federal Ministry of Education Nigeria. (2006). *National School Health Policy*. Abuja, Nigeria: Author.

Grange, A. (2008). *Child health in Nigeria*. Ibadan, Nigeria: Archives of Ibadan Medicine.

Hochbaum, G. M. (1982). Health education as a profession: Reality or illusion? *Health Education*, 4–7.

Kayode, C. M., Owoaje, E. T., & Omotade, O. O. (2007). Social-cultural issues in child health care. *Nigeria Archives of Ibadan Medicine*, 8(2), 55–67.

Lucas, A. O. (2002). Public health in Nigeria. *Archives of Ibadan Medicine*, 3(2), 41–43.

Moronkola, O. A. (2002). Health education or health promotion: What is in a name? In Z. A. Ademuwagun, J. A. Ajala, E. A. Oke, O. A. Moronkola, & A. S. Jegede (Eds.), *Health education and health promotion* (pp. 1–7). Ibadan, Nigeria: Royal People Nigeria Ltd.

Moronkola, O. A. (2007). Multicultural health education curriculum for social transformation of young people in multi-ethnic Nigeria. In I. A. Nwazuoke, E. A. Okediran, & O. A. Moronkola (Eds.), *Education for social transformation* (pp. 88–97). Ibadan, Nigeria: Faculty of Education, University of Ibadan.

Nigerian Educational Research and Development Council. (2007). *Physical and Health Education Curriculum (PHE) for JSS 1–3*. Sheda, Nigeria: Author.

Oyinloye, E. M. (2006). Development process. In *Implementation guidelines on the National School Health Programme*. Abuja, Nigeria: Federal Ministry of Education Nigeria.

Tamir, D., Cohen, S., Edelstein, P., Tor, E., Haflon, S. T., Palti, H., & Reshef, A. (1987). Health education in Jerusalem schools. *Hygiene*, 4, 15–18.

Udoh, C. O. (1996). *The collage that is health education*. Inaugural lecture delivered to the university community and other attendees at the University of Ibadan, Ibadan, Nigeria.

Olawale A. Moronkola
University of Ibadan
Ibadan
Nigeria
email: walemoronkola@yahoo.com

13. THE CHILD-TO-CHILD CURRICULUM IN EAST AFRICA (KENYA AND TANZANIA)

Strengths, Challenges, and Weaknesses

INTRODUCTION

According to Waljee and Hawes (2004), the child-to-child curriculum is a program that teaches and encourages children to concern themselves with the health and welfare of others in their communities. The program can target learners within a school and/or a community, and so involve family members, relatives, and neighbors in the place where the children live.

Under this program, children are encouraged to examine and reflect on their health and welfare and the health and welfare of their younger siblings and other children at school and in the community as a whole (Waljee & Hawes, 2004). The child-to-child curriculum encourages the holistic development of a child as a member of a school community as well as a member of the community in which his or her school is situated. The curriculum is a way of encouraging conscious development among learners not just as future scholars, but also as important participants in the affairs and activities of their communities (Freire, 1996).

In Kenya, public health workers train children in how to educate others to implement this curriculum. The Ministry of Public Health thus collaborates with the Ministry of Education and works through early childhood education structures. But this collaboration is not confined to the two ministries alone. It involves all stakeholders, including non-governmental organizations (NGOs) and community- based organizations (CBOs). In Tanzania, multilateral organizations, such as the United Nations Children's Education Fund (UNICEF), are also involved.

The curriculum is currently being implemented in early childhood development education (ECDE) centers and primary schools in Kenya and Tanzania. The target group is mainly children 6 to 10 years of age. The children are taught about the most common diseases in their locality and how to detect the symptoms through observation of signs displayed or manifesting in a patient (Dan Andanje, personal communication, May 2010). Other lessons include how to avoid contracting diseases by, for example, washing hands after visiting a toilet and before and after eating food. This simple practice helps limit the contraction and spread of, for example, diarrhea, cholera, and typhoid, most of which are waterborne diseases. Children are also taught about the importance of sleeping under a net to avoid

N. Taylor, F. Quinn, M. Littledyke and R.K. Coll (eds.), Health Education in Context, 115–122.

mosquito bites, which can cause malaria. This teaching occurs mainly through the Malaria is Unacceptable (*Malaria Haikubaliki*) campaign presently taking place in our countries.

Teaching strategies include song, dance, drama, role-play and storytelling about the common diseases, and simulation games about the dangers associated with them. Those trained (peer educators) are encouraged to spread the message to others and to report signs of diseases identified in their locality to health workers, teachers, and community elders. The curriculum has been very effective where it is implemented. This success confirms what a number of educationists argue is one of the best ways of educating children to be productive members of the community (Freire, 1996; Gravett, 2004; Waljee & Hawes, 2004; Wanyama, 2009).

Although the child-to-child curriculum has shown much potential in preparing children to become more active participants in most community activities affecting them and others, it continues to encounter a number of challenges, which we consider in this chapter. But first, we want to discuss the strengths of the child-to-child curriculum in Kenya and Tanzania.

STRENGTHS OF THE CHILD-TO-CHILD CURRICULUM IN KENYA AND TANZANIA

One of the strengths of the child-to-child curriculum is the confidence that children develop as they undergo the learning process promoted through the program. The different strategies and skills that the children learn drive this confidence— confidence that facilitates a meaningful partnership between learners and educators (Takanishi & Bogard, 2007). Takanishi and Bogard (2007) also argue that when educators and learners collaborate in the learning process, learners are better able to draw meaning from what they are taught, which often relates to real-life situations. For example, in the Kitale district in the North Western Rift Valley, Kenya, public health workers and selected teachers in lower-primary school classes meet once a week to educate selected youth from local schools on the detection and prevention of diseases. These meetings are organized by district education officials and sponsored by a number of local NGOs as well as by the Kitale Anglican Diocese. The young people selected work with public health workers and teachers in camps, during which they experience a range of the methods referred to above. They support one another and are instrumental in spearheading campaigns that include, amongst others, *Malaria Haikubaliki* (mentioned earlier) and the campaign to combat measles.

Peer educators have thus become an integral part of education and public health activity implementation strategies in Kitale. Their role and the significance of their work recently received recognition from the local district administration, recognition that was perceived as a big honor for the individuals and groups working toward the betterment and wellbeing of the people of Kitale.

The collaborative process by which teachers and educators construe meaning from the child-to-child curriculum enables them to constructively reflect on and challenge lore that might otherwise be taken for granted as truth. Reflection allows learners to consider and present different views and perspectives on the ideas they encounter through their engagement with the curriculum. This kind of curriculum encourages more experiential learning activities that enable learners to deepen their understanding about new concepts such as diseases and their causes and, at the same time, learn new skills, such as problem-solving.

For instance, learners learn how to detect symptoms of a disease in a patient through observation and simple reasoning (Torkington & Foundation, 1992). In Kenya, the aforementioned camps for peer educators are hosted in malaria-prone areas such as Nandi, Uasin Gishu, Lugari, Bungoma, and Kitale. The young people involved learn away from traditional classroom settings. They also learn, in line with the collaborative approach, in groups, which enables them to learn about new things and to learn from one another as they play and participate in activities prepared by their mentors (i.e., public health officers and teachers).

Collaborative learning is deemed a particularly effective way of learning for young people because it gives them opportunity to challenge one another about misconceptions and misinformation relating to everyday occurrences in their society. It also teaches them how to listen to one another, to appreciate diverse views, and to solve problems as a group (Gravett, 2004; Wanyama, 2009).

The child-to-child curriculum has the potential to encourage a close working relationship between the school and the community in which the school is located. This relationship enables learners to understand their role in the community from an early age, thus preparing them to be productive members of their respective communities (Wanyama, 2009). During the process, young people learn skills and develop roles related to environmental sustainability, good hygiene, avoidance of risky situations, and maintenance of a healthy lifestyle. They also learn how to explain emerging problems to others, and how to transfer and adapt their skills and knowledge to new situations encountered in adult life. A curriculum that creates such opportunity for learners is worthwhile and progressive, and different from one where learners are expected to be passive participants in the learning process, receiving, as Freire (1996) would put it, "banked" (memorized) knowledge brought out for tests and examinations.

In Tanzania, according to O-saki (2004), the child-to-child curriculum complements already existing local methods of learning in which boys of a certain age are taught about medicine and medicinal plants and herbs by their local elders. These children then pass the knowledge on to other children. A curriculum that is meaningful to learners is one that enables them to learn skills, knowledge, and values that they can use for solving problems in their locality and beyond. Also, as Takanishi and Bogard (2007) observe, the curriculum promotes a number of outcomes among learners, including cognitive advances, social competence, and self-regulation—skills that are critical for productive engagement of children when they become adults in their communities.

The curriculum is, however, yet to be fully implemented in the two countries, and much needs to be done before it can realize its full potential. In the next section, we consider the various challenges that the child-to-child curriculum faces in Kenya and Tanzania.

CHALLENGES TO THE IMPLEMENTATION OF THE CHILD-TO-CHILD
CURRICULUM

In this section, we discuss two major groups of challenge. The first group relates to the internal contradictions between the approach underpinning the child-to-child curriculum and the approach underpinning the current public-school curriculum in the two countries. The second group relates to the lack of a unified, collaborative approach by policymakers, educators, and educational institutions with respect to determining what learning processes should be implemented in schools.

Kenya

In Kenya, the challenges inhibiting implementation of the child-to-child curriculum can be viewed from three perspectives: the low or poor level of education that most educators in early childhood education and primary school education possess; the lack of formal recognition of any curriculum other than the national one, which is examination oriented; and the barely existent tradition of collaboration among different stakeholders with respect to how education should be conducted.

In Kenya, ECDE teachers and teacher educators usually have little in the way of formal educational qualifications (D. Andanje, personal communication, May 2010). Few have formal training in this area. Often those teaching in ECDE settings and primary schools are there because they were unable to secure "better" employment. For them, delivering a curriculum that requires a lot of interaction is extremely difficult because they want to prove that they are better than their learners in subject knowledge, and they are afraid to be challenged on matters of which they may have little knowledge (Takanishi & Bogard, 2007). They thus constrain the implementation of the curriculum instead of promoting it. Also, the public health workers who assist implementation of the child-to-child curriculum in health education have not been trained as educators and so do not know the best way of working with younger learners, especially in terms of creating opportunities for exploring knowledge and developing skills. Lacking co-learning awareness skills, these educators generally resort to the show-and-tell method of teaching instead of letting learners find out by themselves.

This situation is perhaps made worse by a lack of recognition of curricula other than the curriculum implemented by the national governments, which are geared toward achieving national examination goals. The examination framework favored by the Ministry of Education in Kenya does not take into consideration activities outside the prescribed curriculum, no matter how useful they might be in enhancing learners' cognitive and social skills. The current child-to-child curriculum does not have a "formal" structure (i.e., one that allows for examination or testing of skills) that is recognized by the Ministry of Education. Because of this, most of the activities favored by the child-to-child curriculum are offered on an ad hoc basis, and that offering is typically determined by the interest, innovation skills, and proactivity of teachers and public health officers.

The child-to-child curriculum is therefore not sustainable as an education program under Kenya's current educational ethos. Takanishi and Bogard (2007), using examples drawn from South East Asia, argue that this lack of recognition of the importance that activities encompassed within curricula such as the child-to-child have for children's modes of learning discourages those involved in working with children. It also discourages the children themselves, who feel that society attaches little value to what they learn, how they learn, and the activities in which they are involved.

The lack of collaboration among stakeholders such as educators, NGOs, public health officers, and others in the education process and activities is a product of the traditional view that Kenya, along with Tanzania and many other countries, has of teaching and who should teach. In Kenya, teaching is for teachers who are trained to teach (Wanyama, 2009). Other stakeholders in the education process either provide resources or attend meetings called by head teachers. The child-to-child curriculum challenges the traditional perception of teaching and learning (Freire, 1996; Gravett, 2004; Wanyama, 2009), which helps explain why it is not well supported.

As Torkington and Foundation (1992) observe, a curriculum such as the child-to-child allows children to interact freely during learning, to be creative, to be taught through a variety of methods. Such a curriculum, they continue, also enables children to imagine and to engage in learning activities that are tailored to their individual needs. Such learners must be given the opportunity to explore new ways of looking at the world, while teachers need to appreciate the importance of applying innovative and new ways of teaching. However, say Torkington and Foundation, educators currently facilitating the child-to-child curriculum engage in what the two authors describe as self-perpetuity, meaning that the teachers stick to what they know and use the methods that were used to teach them. Not surprisingly, these teachers avoid new and unfamiliar ways of teaching and learning.

Given this situation, there is a real danger that this dynamic curriculum may fail to be promoted and popularized in Kenya. That, in turn, would mean the loss of a vital opportunity to have children become considerably more involved in solving local health-related and other problems.

Tanzania

Tanzania, like Kenya, also has very limited teacher education and training provision, to the extent that very few schools have ECDE teachers who have gone beyond primary school themselves (O-saki, 2007). The Education and Training Policy of the United Republic of Tanzania (URT, 1995) requires all public primary schools to have a preschool stream attached to it. However, the country has only one teacher training college that trains preschool teachers, and its graduates usually teach Grades 1 and 2 as well as the preschool class. Most teachers trained as preschool teachers refuse to teach the preschool class because they feel it is "beneath them." Hence, most preschool children are taught by school-leavers who are not trained teachers, let alone skilled in ECDE techniques. With the exception of a few élite and privately run preschools, which have graduate teachers, most preschools attached to primary schools experience poor pedagogy. Although some universities are now producing ECDE graduates, few of them elect to teach in public preschools.

ECDE teachers, whether formally trained or not, do not have available to them well-designed and trialed curriculum materials. Such resources, especially those offering instructional advice, would immensely benefit the many poorly trained or inexperienced ECDE teachers. More work must be done in this area to research and trial child-centered programs and curriculum materials.

As in Kenya, Tanzanian health workers receive little, if any, training in ECDE techniques; most of these workers simply "tell" children what to do instead of helping them to think and be innovative. There is also little collaboration between the Ministry of Health, the Ministry of Community Development, Gender, and Children, and the Ministry of Education and Vocational Training. Each ministry prefers to run its own affairs without reference to the work of like ministries. Except for sporadic radio-based health campaigns, there is no unified approach at governmental level to health-based programs.

Steps Taken to Address Challenges Identified in Kenya and Tanzania

In Kenya, there is closer collaboration than in Tanzania between the Ministries of Education and Health with respect to implementing the child-to-child curriculum. Through this collaboration, the Kenyan Government may begin to alleviate some of the problems associated with making this curriculum a reality, especially if it pays strong heed to addressing inadequate or non-existent resources and to bringing a coherent and consistent structure to the curriculum nationwide. Another step in the right direction is encouraging and training more ECDE teachers so as to de-stigmatize the work that they do. Incentives such as better salaries would attract more qualified teachers to both this area of educational provision and to the primary schools. Encouraging NGOs to work closely with schools and government so that the different stakeholders bring a collaborative approach to implementation of the curriculum is also needed.

In Tanzania, more ECDE degree programs are being established in higher learning institutions. At present, the Universities of Dodoma, Mzumbe, and Dar es Salaam offer such programs, as does the Aga Khan University. Although enrolment in these programs is still low, it is another good step forward. Also heartening is the drafting of an early childhood policy that will hopefully delineate the structures necessary to develop quality early childhood education. We are also seeing more senior primary school teachers undertaking degree training, and some are doing research and postgraduate education in the field. Their endeavor might produce the much needed early childhood curriculum innovations that will give the teachers the support they need. The Ministry of Health has become more vigorously involved in health education campaigns, especially those targeting killer diseases such as malaria as well as HIV/AIDS and other sexually transmitted diseases. The ministry is also now working to raise awareness about teenage pregnancy and family health. Their work is furthermore giving increasing recognition to the role of children in health education, which is perhaps one of the most encouraging advances to date.

CONCLUSION

There is no doubt that the child-to-child curriculum could not only revolutionize how children learn and teachers teach but also enable learners to participate in problem-solving activities in their locality. It is particularly important that we foster knowledgeable and skilled teachers and learners at a time when so many health and other social problems face our two countries. However, whether this aim succeeds will depend on how active a role all stakeholders play in encouraging and popularizing the child-to-child curriculum. The greater the number of trained ECDE and other teachers, the more likely it is that the popularity and effectiveness of the child-to-child curriculum will grow. Encouraging more collaboration between stakeholders in the learning process would also go a long way toward ensuring that peer educators are properly utilized among learners, and that schools become important centers where the social and health problems facing the community are discussed and solutions found. Learners, particularly younger learners such as those currently targeted by the child-to-child curriculum in Kenya and Tanzania, have a large and important role to play in this endeavor.

REFERENCES

Freire, P. (1996). *Pedagogy of the oppressed*. New York: Continuum.

Gravett, S. (2004). Teaching and learning: Establishing communities of inquiry and interpretation. In S. Gravett & H. Geyser (Eds.), *Teaching and learning in higher education* (pp. 22–31). Pretoria, South Africa: Van Schaik Publishers.

O-saki, K. M. (2004). Reflections on the state of science education in Tanzania. In K. O-saki, K. Hosea, & W. Ottevanger (Eds.), *Reforming science and mathematics education in Sub-Saharan Africa: Obstacles and opportunities*. Dar es Salaam, Tanzania: Teaching of Mathematics and Science (TEAMS).

O-saki, K. M. (2007). Science and mathematics teacher preparation in Tanzania, 1966–2006: Lessons from teacher improvement projects in Tanzania, 1965–2006. *International Journal of Education, 2*, 51–64.

Takanishi, R., & Bogard, K. L. (2007). Effective education programs for young children: What we need to know. *Society for Research in Child Development, 1*(1), 40–45.

Torkington, K., & Foundation, B. V. L. (1992). *Experiential learning in action: Early childhood counts. Programming resources for early childhood care and development*. Washington DC: The Consultative Group on ECCD, World Bank.

United Republic of Tanzania (URT). (1995). *Tanzania: Education and Training Policy*. Dar es Salaam, Tanzania: Government Press.

Waljee, A., & Hawes, H. (Eds.) (2004). *Not just a cold*. Kuala Lumpur, Malaysia: Longman.

Wanyama, H. S. (2009). *School environmental education programmes and their application to local communities' socio-economic development and conservation issues (South Africa, Tanzania)*. Unpublished doctoral thesis, University of Johannesburg, Johannesburg, South Africa.

Henry Sammy Wanyama
University of Johannesburg
Johannesburg
South Africa
email: kangaihs@gmail.com

Kalafunja Mlang`a O-saki
University of Dodoma
Dodoma
Tanzania
email: kalafunja@yahoo.com

14. HEALTH EDUCATION IN ETHIOPIA

Practices, Challenges, and Prospects

THE CONTEXT: ETHIOPIA AND ITS HEALTH EDUCATION SYSTEM

Ethiopia is one of the least developed countries in eastern Africa, although it has been showing economic progress in recent years. One consequence of this poorly developed economy is the poor health conditions of its people. Ethiopians experience many health problems, particularly infectious diseases, because of sub-standard sanitary conditions, nutritional deficiencies, harmful health practices, and so forth (Ministry of Health, 2003). The Government of Ethiopia recognizes that common poverty-related diseases, including malaria, tuberculosis, childhood illnesses, and HIV/AIDS, continue to cut short the lives of Ethiopians (Ministry of Health, 2003). The relatively poor health status of Ethiopian people, in turn, constrains their enjoyment of life, their productivity, and efforts to reduce poverty.

Global studies indicate that the major determinants of health are people's knowledge about health, their health-related beliefs, attitudes, and practices, and the desire they have to bring about positive behavioral change in their lives (Glanz, Rimer, & Viswanath, 2008). In line with this understanding, the Government of Ethiopia considers that health education is the best way to positively change individuals' beliefs and practices in a way that will help them control many of the health problems in their communities. Health education includes disease prevention, fostering optimal health, and detecting illness. It also treatment and long-term care, spans infectious and chronic diseases, and takes account of environmental issues.

Our aim in this chapter is to describe current issues facing health education in Ethiopia as well as future challenges and prospects. In order to report on these matters, we drew on information and opinion from informal interviews conducted with selected health professionals in Ethiopia. We also used other sources of information, including published and unpublished documents.

POLICY SUPPORT AND IMPLEMENTATION STRATEGIES

In almost all sectors of Ethiopian society, policy-driven programs do not have a long history. The country had no clear health policy until the 1950s. From then until 1974, Ethiopia adopted a comprehensive health services policy, brought into the country through the initiatives of the World Health Organization. However, because of the downfall of the Imperial regime in 1974, the policy was not

N. Taylor, F. Quinn, M. Littledyke and R.K. Coll (eds.), Health Education in Context, 123–132.

implemented in practice (Transitional Government of Ethiopia (TGE), 1993). The Dergue (military) regime that replaced the Imperial regime "formulated a more elaborate health policy that gave emphasis to disease prevention and control, priority to rural areas in health service and promotion of self-reliance and community involvement" (TGE, 1993, p. 1). After the overthrow of the Dergue regime in May 1991, the present government made the following claim:

… in both of the previous regimes there was no meeting ground between declaration of intent and demonstrable performance. Furthermore, the health administration apparatus contributed its own share to the perpetuation of backwardness in health development because, like the rest of the tightly centralized bureaucracy, it was unresponsive, self-serving and impervious to change. (TGE, 1993, p. 2)

On the basis of these premises, the government formulated a new health policy in 1993, and it has been taking different measures to implement the policy since. The preamble to the new policy sets out the government's thinking:

… the Government believes that health policy cannot be considered in isolation from policies addressing population dynamics, food availability, acceptable living conditions and other requisites essential for health improvement and shall therefore develop effective inter-sectorally for the comprehensive betterment of life. (TGE, 1993, p. 3)

According to the policy:

… health education shall be strengthened generally and for specific target populations through the mass media, community leaders, religious and cultural leaders, professional associations, schools and other social organizations for:

- Inculcating attitudes of responsibility for self-care in health and assurance of a safe environment;
- Encouraging the awareness and development of health promoting life-styles and attention to personal hygiene and a healthy environment;
- Enhancing awareness of common communicable and nutritional diseases and the means for their prevention;
- Inculcating attitudes of participation in community health development;
- Identifying and discouraging harmful traditional practices while encouraging their beneficial aspects;
- Discouraging the acquisition of harmful habits such as cigarette smoking, alcohol consumption, drug abuse and irresponsible sexual behavior;
- Creating awareness in the population about the rational use of drugs (TGE, 1993, p. 7).

Determined to develop a major mechanism for putting this policy into practice, and mindful of the existing health issues, the present Ethiopian Government initiated a 20-year rolling Health Sector Development Program (HSDP) in 1997/1998. This program specifies long-term goals for the health sector and the means to attain them throughout a series of phases. The strategy takes into account the call inherent in the United Nations' millennium development goals to improve "health service delivery, capacity building and development of preventive health care and equal access to health services" (United Nations Economic Commission for Africa, 2007).

HSDP was launched with the purpose of increasing the coverage and improving the quality of health services (Italian Development Cooperation in Ethiopia, 2004). Improving the health status of Ethiopian people and achieving the United Nations' millennium development goals are the stated goals of HSDP, according to the Ministry of Health (2010a). HSDP aims to develop a health system that provides comprehensive and integrated primary care services, primarily based in community-level health facilities. It focuses on communicable and non-communicable disease prevention and control, common nutritional disorders, environmental health and hygiene, reproductive health care, maternal and child health, immunization, and the treatment and control of infectious diseases such as upper-respiratory tract infections (Ministry of Health, 2010a). It also focuses on health care administrative issues, including the establishment of quality health care, human resource management, and financial resource mobilization.

The first and second phases of HSDP were completed in 2001 and 2005, respectively (Ministry of Health, 2005). The third phase of HSDP, covering the period 2005/2006–2009/2010 has just been completed. During these years, the program has been continually reviewed and evaluated (Ministry of Health 2010a).

Our informal discussion with health focal persons in the federal health offices of Ethiopia revealed that these professionals consider that the Ministry of Health has been formulating inspiring strategies, guidelines, and policies that have brought profound positive impacts in the areas of information dissemination, awareness and capacity-building, and community mobilization. However, the informants stress, much still needs to be done to fully implement policies and strategies at the grassroots level.

PRESENT HEALTH EDUCATION PRACTICES

Health education is one of the health sector programs that is being accorded priority in terms of helping the community develop knowledge, self-reliance, and competence, and thereby solve their health problems through their own initiatives. Health education can be implemented in all manner of settings. It can be promoted via mass media and the internet, in government health departments, and in "universities, schools, hospitals, pharmacies, grocery stores and shopping centers, recreation settings, community organizations, voluntary health agencies, worksites, churches, prisons, health maintenance organizations, and migrant labor camps" (Glanz et al., 2008, p. 9; Ministry of Health, 2003).

One of the program components receiving particular attention within the HSDP is information, education, and communication (IEC). The earlier national health policy actually foregrounded the degree of priority given to IEC by making it the first strategy for achieving a better standard of health in the country, an aim that led the government to establish the Health Extension Education Center in 1995

(Ministry of Health, 2004). IEC is seen as a cost-effective approach to mobilizing communities into making life-saving behavioral changes in their daily health and sanitation practices (Ministry of Health, 2010b). Certainly, the IEC has been instrumental in facilitating the following:

- Knowledge, attitudes, and practice about personal and environmental hygiene and common illnesses and their causes;
- What is known as behavioral change communication; and
- The promotion of political and community support for preventive health services by educating and influencing planners, policymakers, managers, women's groups, and potential collaborators (Ministry of Health, 2010b).

The IEC has played a core role in establishing training programs and manuals for health extension workers. A set of guidelines was recently implemented for health workers on "community conversation". This social mobilization tool has demonstrated success in engaging community members as agents for behavioral change. Community conversation was very successful in curtailing discrimination against patients with HIV/AIDS (Ministry of Health, 2010b).

IEC activities at the federal level have more recently been gaining momentum, especially in the domains of print and audiovisual media. For example, more than 1,000 radio and 140 television health programs have been developed by the Health Extension Education Center. These have been broadcast across the country in five local languages. A manual setting out the health education program has been produced in order to help extension workers accelerate the implementation of all programs through dynamic person-to-person communication. The manual focuses on the following major components:

- Health education, its meaning, principles, and objectives;
- Health education (message) communication methods;
- Health program planning, implementation and evaluation;
- Communication skills;
- Problems related to health education communication processes; and
- Ethics and principles that health extension worker should follow (Ministry of Health, 2003).

Experts in the field whom we interviewed noted that the traditional method of implementing health education uses the mass media (mainly radio, television, and printed materials) for communication, but it has not achieved the desired results and needs to be supported by the person-to-person communication method. This generally means that health extension workers need to carry out their work in the community, discussing health issues and persuading communities "to solve their health problems through their own involvement and action" (Ministry of Health, 2003).

According to the interviewees, the Health Extension Education Center, established during the previous regime and responsible for managing, training, producing, and disseminating health-related materials at a federal level, has recently been dismantled due to government restructuring. This has left only the production unit. The remaining employees are disengaged and demoralized.

However, the present regional offices are autonomous, and health experts are comfortable with the new business model of government functioning because it has reduced the long bureaucratic chain from federal to regions to *woreda* (districts). In addition, federal initiatives are no longer directly imposed on the regions but are contextualized and localized by the regions. Thus, regional offices are empowered and are responsible for disseminating health materials. Over 40,000 health extension workers have received training from their respective regional offices. Of these, 8,000 are in urban areas. Two health workers are assigned to and are responsible for one health post, where they carry out their activities. Each pair is accountable to the respective *kebele* (health post).

Respondents who favored the present practices stressed particular gains:

- The profound impact that the health extension workers' involvement in dissemination information has had in helping combat communicable and preventable diseases;
- Behavioral changes in the community with respect to hygiene and sanitation (but there is still resistance to the use of condoms);
- The decision that all health workers should be female, because women are more acceptable than men to the local communities. The women receive training in the 16 health packages and are employed by the government. Training is carried out over one year in technical and vocational education and training facilities as well as nursing schools; and
- The presence of a health education department at Jimma University. This has strengthened workers' professional competence and acceptance by the community.

All informants, however, unanimously expressed the view that there is a lack of inter-ministerial collaboration between various government agencies, such as the Ministry of Health, the Ministry of Education, and the Ministry of Agriculture. Although there were attempts several years ago to improve this situation, there was no tangible success. This lack of inter-ministerial collaboration partly explains the absence of a concrete health education curriculum in the formal sector of primary and secondary schools.

Another notable ongoing project in Ethiopia is the Ethiopia Public Health Training Initiative (EPHTI), which was launched in 1997 by the Carter Center (established by former US President Jimmy Carter and First Lady Rosalynn Carter in Atlanta, Georgia, USA) in partnership with the Government of Ethiopia. The project is attempting to improve the delivery of health care throughout Ethiopia by enhancing the quality of pre-service training for health staff, such as nurses and trainers of health workers. The institute is also working to strengthen the teaching skills of university faculty so that they can better instruct the health professionals they train (Carter Center, 2010).

According to EPHTI, the main factor contributing to the poor health of Ethiopians is lack of access to trained health personnel. To address this challenge, EPHTI creates opportunities whereby Ethiopian university teaching staff can work side by side with international experts to develop curricula and learning materials based on local experience. Teachers and academics at seven Ethiopian universities use these materials to train health students. The students, in turn, train and manage community health workers. EPHTI has developed and produced several instruction manuals, nearly 70 specific training modules, and over 150 sets of lecture notes covering a range of health related topics (Carter Center, 2010).

EPHTI has grown to include seven Ethiopian universities as partners, namely, Addis Ababa University, Defense University, Gondar University, Haramaya University, Hawassa University, Jimma University, and Mekelle University. Of particular note is Jimma University, established through the merger of Jimma College and the Jimma Institute of Health Sciences. It was founded in 1999 as a community-oriented educational institution for higher learning. Jimma's community-based education initiative is directed at providing education relevant to community needs and implementing community-oriented education programs. The initiative consists of learning activities that take place within the community. Extensive use is thus made of the community as a learning environment. Not only students but also teachers and members of the community and other sectors are actively engaged in these experiences (Jimma University, 2009).

In order to achieve its community-based education aims, Jimma carries out its work through three programs:

- *Community-Based Training Program:* for at least three weeks every academic year, students go into the community in a group to participate in the learning activities. The same group of students is assigned to the same locality each year. The students' growing familiarity with the locality and the members of the community and other stakeholders with whom they work means that they gain a good understanding of the problems in the community, which helps them make a true difference to the health status of its members.
- *Team Training Program:* under this initiative, graduating students from different health categories are posted as a team (each team consists of 20 to 30 students) in one of six different health centers. The aim of the program is to enable each student to work as a member of a health team intent on solving community health problems by applying the knowledge and skills of the health profession and integrating these with the knowledge and skills of other members of the team. This approach also helps students familiarize themselves with the primary health care units.
- *Student Research Program:* here, each student designs, conducts a piece of research, and writes a research report. All degree-program students from all faculties of the university are required to carry out an independent research project. The intent behind this requirement is for students to develop critical thinking capacity and problem-solving skills.

DISCUSSION AND THE WAY FORWARD

As mentioned earlier, our objective in this chapter was to describe the practices, challenges, and prospects of health education in Ethiopia. Using as our basis what we learned from the informal interviews we conducted with selected health professionals in Ethiopia and the information we procured from secondary sources, we offer the following reflections.

We generally applaud the effort made in Ethiopia to address health education by providing policy support and implementing it through the nationwide Health Sector Development Program (HSDP). However, the system has relied mainly on non-formal approaches, with limited effort being made to implement health education in the formal education sector (i.e., primary and general secondary schools). The absence of a health education curriculum within the formal education system has undermined many aspects of the health of Ethiopians. For instance, it is recognized that a considerable number of school adolescents start pre-marital sexual activity that might predispose them to different sexual and reproductive health problems (Abebe & Mitikie, 2009). Abebe and Mitikie found that students who have sexual experience are less likely to undertake voluntary counseling about sexually transmitted diseases and to be tested for presence of these diseases.

As an outcome of their assessment of the training experienced by the first intake of health extension workers in 10 of the 11 health training centers in the country, Kitaw, Ye-Ebiyo, Said, Desta, and Teklehaimanot (2007) identified a number of deficiencies. They noted, in particular, that technical and vocational education and training institutes lack adequate facilities for accommodating workers. This lack encompasses classrooms, libraries, information and communication technologies, water, and latrines.

With regard to human resource development, Girma et al. (2007) noted a shortage of different groups of health professionals in Ethiopia, such as medical doctors, health officers, nurses, and general health workers. They also highlighted the inequitable distribution of professionals across regions, between urban and rural settings, and within governmental and non-governmental/private organizations. They furthermore pointed out that Ethiopia has no policy or proper mechanism for effective management of the existing health workforce.

The health experts that we interviewed stressed the importance of communicating closely with individuals and communities and of respecting their opinions. They emphasized that health education messages need to be clear and concise, and delivered in a language that the target audience easily understands.

We believe that the good practices of the Carter Center and Jimma University should be strengthened and scaled up to involve other tertiary education institutions, including teacher training colleges. The Ministry of Health, in collaboration with other ministries, needs to offer a more coordinated approach to health education. A strategy has to be developed that can appropriately target the different educational, ethnic, age, and gender groups, and effectively communicate health-related information in a way that will have an appropriate impact on the long-term health-related behaviors of Ethiopians.

We support the conception of health defined by the World Health Organization as "complete physical, mental, and social well-being, and not merely freedom from disease or infirmity" (Rash, 2010, p. 7). This definition, we believe, gives impetus to the primary aim of health education, namely, the intelligent self-direction of health behavior. Thus, we also agree that, "health education, in both schools and community organizations, is an essential educational concern no less important than the fundamental processes of calculating and communicating" (Willgoose, 2010, p. 21).

It is difficult to take a position on the question of whether health education in schools should be offered either as a multidisciplinary or as a single subject. Both approaches have their own philosophical positions and strengths. In this regard, Willgoose (2010) argues as follows:

> Obviously, the health education effort will always be a multidisciplinary endeavor ... the health dimension in a school could be nicely handled by dividing it up among science, physical education, and social studies personnel ... However, research over the years has demonstrated that health education is poorly handled in isolated and single-topic fashion. It requires direct attention in the classroom with full subject matter status. This is chiefly because the topic of health and wellness is both subtle and dramatic, both obvious and hidden, and means many things to many people, which requires an in-depth treatment. (p. 23)

At classroom level, we believe that relying only on the expertise of the teachers may not be sufficient to achieve the intended health outcomes for the nation. Experts in various national and international organizations and their programs can and must be utilized. Ethiopia can particularly benefit from this approach because the country is the seat of the African Union, the Economic Commission for Africa, and many other United Nations and bilateral organizations, including UNESCO and its International Institute for Capacity Building in Africa (IICBA). The experts in these organizations can also be considered as guests, able to share their health-related special areas with the school communities. For instance, UNESCO-IICBA has developed two electronic resources on HIV/AIDS. One is titled *Innovative HIV/AIDS Curriculum: A Companion for Math and Science Lessons*, and the other is UNESCO's course on education, planning, and management in a world affected by HIV and AIDS. These interactive resources are available for free and can be used, in any school, on any computer that has a CD-ROM drive.

REFERENCES

Abebe, A., & Mitikie, G. (2009). Perception of high school students towards voluntary HIV counselling and testing, using a health belief model in Butajira, SNNPR. *Ethiopian Journal of Health Development, 23*(2), 148–153.

Carter Center (2010). *The Carter Center Ethiopia Public Health Training Initiative.* Retrieved from http://www.cartercenter.org/health/ephti/index.html.

Girma, S., Yohannes, A., Kitaw, Y., Ye-Ebiyo, Y., Seyoum, A., Desta, H., & Teklehaimanot, A. (2007). Human resource development for health in Ethiopia: Challenges of achieving the Millennium Development Goals. *Ethiopian Journal of Health Development, 21*(3), 216–231.

Glanz, K., Rimer, B. K., & Viswanath, K. (2008). *Health behavior and health education: Theory, research and practice.* San Francisco, CA: Jossey-Bass.

Italian Development Cooperation in Ethiopia (IDCE). (2004). *Italian contribution to the Health Sector Development Program in Ethiopia: 2003–04 report.* Retrieved from http://www.itacaddis.org/italy/images/uploaded_pictures/HSDP%202003-04%20Report1.pdf.

Jimma University. (2009). *Community-based education (CBE)*. Jimma, Ethiopia: Author. Retrieved from http://www.ju.edu.et/?q=node/10.

Kitaw, Y., Ye-Ebiyo, Y., Said, A., Desta, H., & Teklehaimanot, A. (2007). Assessment of the training of the first intake of health extension workers. *Ethiopian Journal of Health Development, 21*(3), 232–239.

Ministry of Health. (2003). *Health education and communication methods manual: Health extension package*. Addis Ababa, Ethiopia: Author.

Ministry of Health. (2004). *National Health Communication Strategy*. Addis Ababa, Ethiopia: Africa Printing.

Ministry of Health. (2005). *Health Sector Strategic Plan (HSDP III): 2005/6–2009/10*. Unpublished document, Ministry of Health, Addis Ababa, Ethiopia.

Ministry of Health. (2010a). *Health Sector Development Program*. Addis Ababa, Ethiopia: Author. Retrieved from http://moh.gov.et/index.php?option=com_content&view=article&id= 84&Itemid =148.

Ministry of Health. (2010b). *Information, communication and education (IEC)*. Addis Ababa, Ethiopia: Author. Retrieved from http://moh.gov.et/index.php?option=com_content&view=article&id= 84&Itemid=148.

Rash, J. K. E. (2010). Philosophical bases for health education. In J. M. Black, S. Furney, H. M. Graf, & A. E. Nolte (Eds.), *Philosophical foundations of health education* (pp. 7–10). San Francisco, CA: Jossey-Bass.

Transitional Government of Ethiopia. (1993). *Health policy of the Transitional Government of Ethiopia*. Addis Ababa, Ethiopia: Author.

United Nations Economic Commission for Africa. (2007). *Health Sector Development Program (HSDP)—Ethiopia: Country experiences*. Paper presented at the ECOSOC Annual Ministerial Review.

Willgoose, C. A. E. (2010). Health education as a basic. In J. M. Black, S. Furney, H. M. Graf, & A. E. Nolte (Eds.), *Philosophical foundations of health education* (pp. 17–28). San Francisco, CA: Jossey-Bass.

Frehiwot Wubshet
World Vision International/Ethiopia
Ethiopia

Temechegn Engida
UNESCO-IICBA
Ethiopia
email: temechegn@gmail.com

CHOSHI D. KASANDA, MARIA CHARLOTTE KEYTER AND
DONOVAN ZEALAND

15. THE STATUS OF HEALTH EDUCATION
IN NAMIBIAN SCHOOLS

INTRODUCTION

Namibia faces many challenges in its development as a democratic society. Improving the current situation will include tackling several interrelated issues pertaining to youth and education (UNICEF, 1995). Namibia has a young population, many of whom live in rural areas (National Planning Commission, 2001). Namibian youth are an integral part of the social changes that have accompanied the transition from colonialism to post-colonialism. They can be seen as agents of this transition from authoritarianism to democracy and from a racially divided society to a more integrated nation. Reconstructing education from what it has been to a system that brings equity of educational opportunity for all children is just one of the urgent challenges facing the Namibian government.

Since achieving independence 20 years ago, Namibia has achieved its goal of more children in school and more children receiving basic education. However, HIV/AIDS, sexually transmitted infections, teenage pregnancies, alcohol and substance abuse, and debilitating illnesses such as malaria prevent the youth of Namibia from fulfilling their personal development and therefore their potential to contribute to national development (National Planning Commission, 2001). Many of the health issues in Namibia are interrelated with social issues—often stemming from poverty—such as high rates of family mobility, abuse of drugs and alcohol, and crime.

As in most post-colonial societies, poverty is a reflection of the power relationships that have disadvantaged particular groups in a society. Even when these power relationships change in terms of the legal and political system, the process of changing the economic realities of daily living for the poorest of the poor takes a very long time. Poverty and poor educational opportunities often reinforce one another. For example, living under conditions of poverty can lead to certain learning difficulties. Learning needs may be neglected, a situation that ultimately results in lower levels of qualification for work, thus promoting more poverty in a negative cycle of cause and effect (Donald, Lazarus, & Lolwana, 2002). It is important to begin to turn the negative cycle into a positive one. Interventions need to be considered at all levels of the education system, from the individual student, through to the classroom, whole-school development, school–community collaboration, and (ultimately) the wider issues of social transformation.

In her speech to the second roundtable at the Millennium Development Goals Summit, Margaret Chan (2010) of the World Health Organization (WHO)

N. Taylor, F. Quinn, M. Littledyke and R.K. Coll (eds.), Health Education in Context, 133–144.

indicated that education is a powerful tool for breaking the cycle of poverty. She stated that if health issues amongst children and adolescents are not addressed sufficiently, they can destabilize investment in education. She noted that some diseases could prevent children from attending school or force them to leave school early to take care of younger siblings.

THE NAMIBIAN HEALTH CARE SYSTEM

After independence, the government reformed the previously segregated health system of Namibia, changing its focus to that of primary health care. Primary health care is concerned with realizing the following aims (amongst others):

- Promoting proper and safe nutrition;
- Ensuring an adequate supply and utilization of safe water;
- Addressing reproductive health, including maternal health, child care, and family planning;
- Implementing education and training focused on prevailing health and social problems in the communities and the methods of preventing and controlling them; and
- Promoting and maintaining oral and mental health (Ministry of Health and Social Services, 2009).

Another important focus, additional to these aims, is the prevention of HIV/AIDS and care of people living with these conditions.

As has been the case in all other sectors of public management in Namibia, many policies have been drafted and implemented. Several policies with relevance to health education in Namibian schools are:

- Community-based health care;
- Namibia orphans and vulnerable children;
- Food and nutrition;
- Namibian food-based dietary guidelines; and
- Infant and child feeding policy. (For details, see Ministry of Health and Social Services, 2009.)

No policy document exists to guide health education in Namibian schools. However, the Government of Namibia recently signaled its intention to develop a health promotion policy for the country. Whether this new policy will also focus on schools as part of the community is uncertain.

NAMIBIAN EDUCATION SYSTEM

Prior to independence in 1990, the Namibian education system was patterned after the Bantu education system in South Africa. The Bantu education system assigned no importance to learning science and mathematics for the majority of black learners, because they were to be prepared for the menial work assigned to them by the apartheid government. The apartheid view of education for the majority of Namibians underwent a dramatic change during the education reform of the early

1990s, which sought to reflect the needs, aspirations, and requirements of the new state (Angula, 1993). Among the many developments that took place were teaching methods, which changed from teacher centered to learner centered (Ministry of Education and Culture, 1993; National Institute for Educational Development, 2003). This change drew on the constructivist theory of learning, which now underpins teaching throughout the country and is accompanied by inclusion of continuous assessment in all subjects.

Namibia currently uses a 1-7-3-2 education system. The seven years of primary education (four years lower primary and three years upper primary) are followed by three years of junior secondary and two years of senior secondary education. Learners sit for phased leaving examinations in specific subjects at Grades 7, 10, and 12. Learners who successfully pass the Namibia Senior Secondary Certificate examination are eligible for entry to tertiary education institutions.

Normally, learners start primary school at the age of seven and complete senior secondary school at the age of 18. At the lower-primary level (Grades 1 to 3), learners are taught in their mother tongue or a language that is commonly used within a particular locality. They may also be taught in English, depending on the mix of the community. From Grade 4 onwards, English is the medium of instruction in state schools (Ministry of Basic Education, Sport, and Culture, 2003).

HEALTH EDUCATION IN NAMIBIAN SCHOOLS

In 2005, a major review of the education sector in Namibia was undertaken with technical assistance from the World Bank (Marope, 2005). The review formed the basis for the development of the Education and Training Sector Improvement Programme (ETSIP) (Government of the Republic of Namibia, 2007a). ETSIP has is serving as a road map for improving the quality of education in Namibia over the 15 years subsequent to 2007. While HIV/AIDS features prominently in the program, no reference is made to health and physical education in either it or the review, and nutrition education is only referred to in guidelines for the school-feeding program for orphans and vulnerable children.

Health Education in the Curriculum

Every five years, a review of the National Curriculum for Basic Education takes place. The latest version was approved and published in 2009. In contrast to ETSIP, this curriculum includes broader health-related education, the aim of which is to develop a healthy Namibian society where people:

> ... live a healthy lifestyle with highest level of responsible behaviour practices that eliminate STI's, HIV infection and alcohol and substance abuse. Preventable diseases including Foetal Alcohol Disorder (FAS) and HIV and AIDS, and curable diseases are reduced to a minimum. People have a balanced diet. People are empowered physically and mentally to meet the continuing demands of making an effective contribution to development

processes. There is a long life expectancy. (National Institute for Educational Development, 2009, p. 7)

In addition to the key learning areas and core skills in the National Curriculum for Basic Education, there are five cross-curricular learning themes: HIV/AIDS, health and wellness education, human rights and democracy education, information and communication technologies, and environmental learning. These themes are placed as topics or sub-topics in subjects across the curriculum and across the phases of education (National Institute for Educational Development, 2009). Table 1 sets out the health education competencies within the key learning areas.

Table 1. Health education competencies across the key learning areas of the Namibian National Curriculum for Basic Education

Phase	Key learning area	Competencies
Pre-primary	Environmental studies	• Learners are aware of the importance of their own basic health and nutrition.
	Physical education	• Learners participate to the best of their abilities in a variety of physical activities that promote movement and motor development.
Lower primary	Natural science	• Learners look after their own health and nutrition.
	Physical education	• Learners participate to the best of their abilities in a variety of games, sport, and physical activities.
Upper primary	Natural sciences	• Learners relate the implications of scientific understanding to their personal and social health.
	Physical education	• Learners develop co-operative activity and games skills, monitor their own progress and achievements, and explain why continued physical activity is important for health and wellness.
Junior secondary	Natural sciences	• Learners have the skills and knowledge to maintain a safe and healthy lifestyle.
	Physical education	• Learners evaluate their ability to contribute to teamwork in games, and their individual motivation and attitude for, and effort in, different games and sporting activities. They explain what physical activities are optimal for health and wellness in different phases of life, and why.
Senior secondary	Natural science	• No specific competency given.
	Physical education	• Learners evaluate their fitness, strength, and endurance. They demonstrate basic instructions or refereeing in selected games or sports. They draw up a plan with a rationale and targets for their own health-related physical activities during the different phases of their lives.

Source: National Institute for Educational Development (2009, pp. 20–23)

It is clear that, at the national level, health and physical education are priorities. However, different curriculum panels are assigned to design the different syllabuses within the curriculum, and there is a clear gap between what is happening in the Ministry of Health and the Ministry of Education. The piecemeal design of syllabuses produces problems and inconsistencies related to interpretation of the competencies and the extent to which health education is based on current data and research in Namibia. This situation also calls into question whether this form of educational provision is clearly focused on health behavior outcomes that will help individuals meet the goals of the nation set down in Vision 2030. Vision 2030 is Namibia's "perception of the future … The goal … is to improve the quality of life of the people of Namibia to the level of their counterparts in the developed world, by 2030" (Government of the Republic of Namibia, 2004, p. 9).

Although health and physical education are a priority, health education still receives little classroom time in comparison to the time given over to other topic areas. HIV/AIDS topics are very prominent, however. During the senior secondary phase, health education is not even compulsory, except for life skills, which in general does not cover major health education concepts. Life skills periods are also used for other activities, and for most teachers it is an additional subject for which they are not trained (Ministry of Education, 2006). Nutritional education is also limited; what content there is uses the South African rather than the Namibian food group system and does not address some current nutritional concerns in Namibia, such as iron and Vitamin A deficiencies. Comprehensive inclusion of health issues beyond HIV/AIDS in the school curriculum requires someone or some agency to champion it.

In Grades 1 to 4, health education content is student centered, balanced, sequential, and progressive in nature, but the same cannot be said of the later phases of the national curriculum. Most of the competencies listed in the individual syllabuses do not go beyond "list, state, define, describe, and discuss." A question therefore remains unanswered: how can a syllabus based on mainly knowledge and facts help to improve healthy behavior in learners and contribute to a lifelong healthy living attitude?

Given the current explosion of health information, it is evident that school curricula cannot focus only on teaching scientific facts and increasing learners' knowledge. A clear shift to functional health education is vital; personal values likely to support healthy behavior amongst individuals as well as amongst groups and communities should be shaped, and skills and practices designed to sharpen health-related decisionmaking skills practiced.

Health Promoting Schools Initiative

Namibia has signed up for the health promoting schools initiative of the United Nations. The Namibian government recognizes that promoting health is more than just health education and that it involves the whole school. This recognition saw several relevant workshops held in 2004, along with dissemination of a survey called the Global School-Based Student Health Survey. Of the nine possible areas recommended for inclusion in the survey, Namibia chose to collect data on all but one—dietary behavior. The areas covered were alcohol, tobacco, and drug use; hygiene; mental health; physical activity; protective factors; sexual behaviors that contribute to HIV infection and other sexually-transmitted infections; unintended pregnancy; and violence and unintentional injury.

The results showed that Namibia indeed had problems in several health-related areas in schools (Ministry of Health and Social Services, 2004). However, effort to remedy these deficits is currently dormant not only because of the lack of co-ordination between the Ministries of Education and Health but also because no one person or agency has responsibility for driving this process through curriculum development, school implementation, and teacher involvement. Perhaps the ministries could use the same contact people involved with HIV/AIDS education to drive general health education issues. This approach might also prevent further fragmentation of health education in Namibian schools.

School-Feeding Program

Health education in schools involves more than just teaching in the classroom. In many countries, health education includes feeding programs as well as policies regarding food sold at schools. The Ministry of Education in Namibia runs a school-feeding program in primary schools. This initiative was initially sponsored by the World Food Programme, but is now solely sponsored by the Namibian Ministry of Education. In 2006, almost 110,000 orphans and vulnerable children received nutritional support through the education system, but a large number of learners are still not reached through this scheme. One of the major obstacles limiting the success of the program is that it operates only during week days and school terms.

The program provides children with a fortified, yellow-maize-based porridge during break times at school. During the cooking process, the cooks add additional oil to the porridge, which provides a third of children's daily kilojoule needs. Very often, the porridge is the only food that the children receive. The supply and delivery of this program is contracted out; parents or school community members typically prepare the food and receive some meals in return (Government of the Republic of Namibia, 2007b). There have been many calls from the community to make this program available to all children in Namibian schools, not just orphans and vulnerable children.

EDUCATION ABOUT HIV/AIDS AND RISKY BEHAVIORS

Data from the National Sentinel Survey (Ministry of Health and Social Services, 2007, p. 11) reveal an overall HIV prevalence rate of just under 20%. Prevalence rates vary from a low of almost 8% in Opuwo to a high of 39.4% in Katima Mulilo. Infection rates climb from 10.2% among 15- to 19-year-old women to 16.4% among women 20 to 24 years of age, just under 30% among women 25 to 29 years of age, and up to 29.5% among 30- to 34-year-old women. One implication of these figures is the need for a better understanding of specific groups and how their prevalence rates link in with specific living conditions and sexual behavior patterns.

It is anticipated that one impact of HIV/AIDS on the Namibian school system will be an increase in the number of children without caregivers at home, a situation that will, in turn, reduce enrolments and increase learner and teacher absenteeism. Against this background, government policy has called for an information dissemination campaign conducted as a collaboration among relevant ministries and agencies and directed at reducing the spread of HIV and AIDS infections amongst learners, teachers, and other stakeholders. Both the formal school curriculum and existing and new co-curricular activities at schools will be used as vehicles for transmitting these awareness campaigns (see also, in this regard, the National Planning Commission, 2001).

Namibia has made some progress in this area. All primary and secondary schools now have in place HIV/AIDS programs that provide young people with facts about sexual health and reproduction, pregnancy, and sexually transmitted infections, including HIV/AIDS. In addition to covering the relevant topics in the curriculum, schools also offer extracurricular programs. These include Windows of Hope (primary school students, 8 to 13 years of age), My Future My Choice (secondary school students, ages 14 to 18), and Let's Talk (out-of-school youth and parents). A number of community organizations are also targeting the school population with programs such as Stepping Stones and True Love Waits, along with the Feeling Yes, Feeling No program that is run by Lifeline and Childline and targets pre-primary and junior-primary children (Government of the Republic of Namibia, 2007a; Ndjozo-Ojo & Kandjii-Murangi, 2001).

Chinsembu (2011) notes that the majority of learners in six regions thought My Future My Choice was effective in making them more aware of the impacts of HIV/AIDS infections. The program also addressed the behavior changes deemed necessary to reduce learners' HIV risk behaviors. In the schools where these programs are active, learners' sexual risk behaviors seem to have decreased and the early sexual debut that places many learners at risk of HIV infection appears to be less prevalent. These programs are thus slowly reducing new HIV infections amongst school learners in the country (Government of the Republic of Namibia, 2008). However, Chinsembu (2011) notes that even though these programs emphasize behavior change, learners in the six regions still appear to be adhering to norms and practices that predispose them to HIV infection.

In 2001, Ndjozo-Ojo and Kandjii-Murangi recommended that HIV and AIDS programs should be integrated into the school curriculum and that key persons in schools and regions should be identified to champion this cause. Their recommendations were acted on, so much so that students now complain that the same content is repeated over and over from primary school onwards. It seems that some kind of knowledge fatigue is starting to set in, which is an issue of potential concern for educators.

However, there are still some areas that are not covered, for example, the importance of adhering to the antiretroviral drug regimen. Educating learners about food security and safety for individuals living with HIV and AIDS is also important in order to ensure that good quality food is prepared and handled hygienically, thereby reducing the chance of inducing sickness in people whose immunity is already compromised by HIV infection.

It is worth noting that when nutritional management was included in the HIV and AIDS programs of first-year classes at the University of Namibia, the students said that this was the first time they had received a more positive message about HIV/AIDS. They stated that healthy nutrition was something practical they could do with respect to HIV and AIDS.

PHYSICAL ACTIVITIES AND FITNESS EDUCATION

The rationale behind having a well-planned and extensive physical education curriculum in Namibian schools is that the subject is an integral part of the general education process, a primary aim of which is to provide children and young people with holistic development. The main thrust of physical education in Namibia must therefore be part of this aim of educating each student as a total entity. Knowledge of how to maintain a healthy lifestyle is an important component of ability to function effectively in society.

During 1999, the Presidential Commission on Education, Culture, and Training established by His Excellency, the President of the Republic of Namibia, focused on identifying areas wherein education could be used to address the problems of Namibian society. One of the commission's recommendations was that physical education should be taught in all schools in accordance with curriculum requirements. School principals, teachers, and inspectors were asked to ensure that this recommendation was fully implemented. However, the commission found that although the subject is compulsory in all Namibian schools, the time allocated to it is often used for teaching other academic subjects or is used as a free period (Presidential Commission on Education, Culture, and Training, 1999).

This is certainly the case in most of the historically black schools, and especially those situated in the rural areas. In these schools, physical education is not taught regularly or is not taught at all, even though it forms part of the National School Curriculum for Basic Education and appears on school timetables. In most cases, as the commission found, teaching time is used to teach other academic subjects, or students are left sitting around doing little that is constructive. However, in most formerly white schools in Namibia, physical education *is* taught regularly, and most of the teachers in these schools are qualified to teach the subject.

The non-examination status of physical education in the school curriculum makes it possible for teachers to ignore its importance and contribution to developing a healthy nation. As is the case in other parts of the world, including the African continent, the subject tends to be neglected, misunderstood, perceived as being of little importance, and regarded as inferior when compared to other subjects in the school curriculum (Zealand, 2006).

Although the Namibian government recognizes the importance of physical education, the impact of this subject in terms of its contribution to the goals of basic education appears to be minimal (Presidential Commission on Education,

Culture, and Training, 1999). To many Namibians, physical education is seen as useless, serving no purpose and wasting time. In this regard, educators have failed to elevate the status of the subject and to relate it to the needs and challenges of the present-day world.

Many of the current difficulties facing the subject could be because those of us who are educators have, like our students, mainly judged success or failure in physical education in terms of performance. Many of our lessons have failed to instill positive feelings of self-worth and achievement in young people, resulting in many thinking they are "no good" at physical education. Yet, as we all know, it is not possible to be "good" or "bad" at the subject. Physical education is a process of learning designed to enable young people to develop physical competence, knowledge, skills, and understanding through a balanced program of activities appropriate to the age and stage of each student. The benefits of participation in physical activity are well documented. Studies have found that participation in physical activity can increase young people's self-esteem, reduce anxiety and stress, and promote a healthy lifestyle. Sport and physical activity programs have demonstrated their potential to introduce young people to skills such as teamwork, self-discipline, sportsmanship, leadership, and effective socialization (Zealand, 2006).

Participation in physical activity and recreation also appears particularly promising in modifying health risk factors. A considerable body of research has found positive benefits with respect to psychological health, physical health, family interactions, peer influence, academic performance, community development, and other lifestyle behaviors. Participation can furthermore cultivate protective factors, that is, factors that help children develop individual resilience, so making them less likely to participate in at-risk activities. Resilience can be developed by creating opportunities for all children to be successful, by helping them learn how to set realistic and manageable goals for themselves, and by supporting their efforts to solve problems. Resilience also comes from opportunity to learn in an atmosphere of trust rather than in an atmosphere that engenders stress (Parks and Recreation Ontario, 1999).

Children thus need to be taught about the health benefits and principles of health-related physical fitness in physical education programs. Such programs should include cognitive objectives that emphasize students' appreciation of health and physical activity. Certainly, a major goal of the health-related physical fitness component of the physical education curriculum in Namibia is to provide students with knowledge, positive attitudes, and skills that will allow them to develop healthy lifetime habits (Zealand, 2006).

The key to excellence in any form of education is the teacher. Although costly facilities and equipment are nice to have, the teacher is the indispensable part of the educational process. The outstanding teacher is one who nurtures students to develop body awareness and movement skills whether the class is being held in a spacious, beautiful gymnasium or on a piece of open—albeit safe—ground. Attitudes toward physical education are instilled at school, and these may be either positive or negative. Therefore, the future of the subject in Namibia lies in the hands of its teachers. They are at the grassroots level, face to face with the children. *What* they do and *how* they do it are absolutely crucial in improving the physical and broader health education of the youth of Namibia.

CONCLUSION

Like many other countries, Namibia acknowledges that school can have a major effect on the health of children and future generations by promoting health and healthy behaviors among learners. School can also be the place where specific health problems such as malaria and HIV/AIDS and risky behaviors such as abusing alcohol and drugs can be addressed, since children spend more time at school than at home or anywhere else. Despite skeptics in Namibian society questioning the need for and utility of health (including physical) education, it is widely accepted that this form of education enhances the overall development of children and young people and that it is therefore amongst the most cost-effective means of preventing early school-leaving and absenteeism.

Even though efforts are being made to ensure a healthy school community in Namibia, challenges still exist. A number of students remain at risk, especially with respect to contracting HIV/AIDS. The feeding system needs to be rolled out to all schools, and physical education needs to be given an appropriate and assured place in the school calendar. Unless education and health are viewed as indistinguishable partners engaged in eradicating poverty and developing opportunities for the citizens of Namibia to reach their full human potential, Namibia is unlikely to realize its Vision 2030 as an industrialized and knowledge-based economy.

REFERENCES

Angula, N. (1993). Senior secondary education in Independent Namibia: Policy issues. In Ministry of Education and Culture (Ed.), *Proceedings of the National Conference on IGCSE and IGCSE* (pp. 14–17). Windhoek, Namibia: Ministry of Education and Culture.

Chan, M. (2010). *Education and health go hand in hand.* Retrieved from http://www.who.int/speeches/2010/education and health_20100920/en/.

Chinsembu, K. C. (2011). *HIV/AIDS and science education in Namibian secondary schools: Impacts, risk factors, knowledge gaps and implications for curriculum and education policy reforms.* Unpublished doctoral dissertation, University of Namibia, Windhoek.

Donald, D., Lazarus, S., & Lolwana, P. (2002*). Educational psychology in social context: Challenges of development. Social issues and special needs in Southern Africa.* Cape Town, South Africa: Oxford University Press.

Government of the Republic of Namibia. (2004). *Namibia Vision 2030: Policy framework for long-term national development.* Windhoek, Namibia: Office of the President.

Government of the Republic of Namibia. (2007a). *Education and Training Sector Improvement Programme: Planning for a learning nation.* Windhoek, Namibia: Author.

Government of the Republic of Namibia. (2007b). *Namibia National Plan of Action for Orphans and Vulnerable Children: Volume One.* Windhoek, Namibia: Ministry of Gender Equality and Child Welfare.

Government of the Republic of Namibia. (2008). *Report of the 2008 National HIV Sentinel Survey.* Windhoek, Namibia: Ministry of Health and Social Sciences.

Marope, M. T. (2005). *Namibia human capital and knowledge for economic growth and equity.* Windhoek, South Africa: The World Bank.

Ministry of Basic Education, Sport, and Culture. (2003). *The language policy for schools in Namibia: A discussion document.* Windhoek, Namibia: Author.

Ministry of Education. (2006). *Upper primary phase: Natural science and health education syllabus, Grades 5–7.* Okahandja, Namibia: National Institute for Educational Development.

Ministry of Education and Culture. (1993). *Toward education for all.* Windhoek, Namibia: Gamsberg Macmillan.

Ministry of Health and Social Services. (2004). *Global School-Based Student Health Survey: 2004 fact sheet Namibia.* Atlanta, GA: Centers for Disease Control and Prevention.

Ministry of Health and Social Services. (2007). *Report of the 2006 National HIV Sentinel Survey: HIV prevalence rate in pregnant women, biannual surveys 1992–2006.* Windhoek, Namibia: Author.

Ministry of Health and Social Services. (2009). *Ministry of Health and Social Services* [website]. Retrieved from http://healthnet.org.na/.

National Institute for Educational Development. (2003). *Learner-centred education in the Namibian context: A conceptual framework.* Windhoek, Namibia: John Meinert Printing.

National Institute for Educational Development. (2009). *The National Curriculum for Basic Education.* Okahandja, Namibia: Author.

National Planning Commission. (2001). *NDP2: Draft National Development Plan* (Vol. 1). Windhoek, Namibia: Author.

Ndjozo-Ojo, B., & Kandjii-Murangi, I. (2001). *An impact accessment survey of the school-based HIV/AIDs programmes in Namibia.* Windhoek, Namibia.

Parks and Recreation Ontario. (1999). *Together with youth: Planning recreation services for youth at risk.* Toronto, Ontario, Canada: Parks and Recreation Ontario.

Presidential Commission on Education, Culture, and Training. (1999). *Draft report: Conference report.* Windhoek, Namibia: Ministry of Basic Education, Sport, and Culture.

United Nations Children's Fund (UNICEF). (1995). *Children in Namibia: Heading toward the rights of children.* Windhoek, Namibia: UNICEF/Legal Assistance Centre.

Zealand, D. (2006). *Current issues and developments in physical education in Namibia.* Paper presented at a workshop on the use of physical education, sport and traditional games to address HIV/AIDS through the Zambian education sector in Lusaka, Zambia, February 2006.

Choshi D. Kasanda, Margaret Charlotte Keyter and Donovan Zealand
University of Namibia
Windhoek
Namibia
email: ckasanda@unam.na

JOSIAH O. AJIBOYE AND FOLASHADE AFOLABI

16. ENVIRONMENTAL PROBLEMS AND THEIR IMPACT ON PEOPLE'S HEALTH

The Nigerian Context

BACKGROUND

Nigeria, located in West Africa, has a population of 140,431,790, comprised of diverse ethnic groups and about 71 million males and 69 million females (Federal Republic of Nigeria, 2009a). The major ethnic groups are Yoruba, Hausa, and Igbo. The official language of communication is English because the country was colonized by the British in the 19th and 20th centuries. Colonization imposed the objectives of Western values and lifestyles on the socioeconomic, political, and environmental structures of the nation ("Tourism," 2002).

The Nigerian environment is blessed with many scenic riches, ranging from the wide ocean coastline, through verdant swamp and moist forest vegetation to lush savanna, culminating in the country's Sahel savannah. These diverse environments are interspersed by rivers, lakes, streams, caves, valleys, and mountains, and enlivened by many birds and animals.

In this chapter, we examine the health and environmental problems facing the people of the Baruten Local Government Area, especially the school-age children. We also consider the school health education curriculum and instructional strategies that teachers could adopt in order to make the curriculum more relevant to people's lives. The chapter is informed by recent research, the findings of which show that use of appropriate instructional strategies, such as entertainment education, inculcates healthy behaviors and attitudes and promotes understanding of health and environmental concepts. These developments are ones that help people apply the knowledge acquired to their real-life situations.

ENVIRONMENTAL AND HEALTH ISSUES FACING BARUTEN

Health and environmental issues are closely related in Baruten, a typical Nigerian community that has experienced little development. Baruten is situated in the northern part of Kwara State, which is located along the middle belt of Nigeria. Kwara has a population of about two million people, just over 200,000 of whom live in Baruten (Federal Republic of Nigeria, 2009a).

Baruten is a largely agrarian community that prides itself on producing food and cash crops. In addition to coping with the poverty that is evident in such communities in Nigeria, Baruten faces indiscriminate sewage disposal, which has

N. Taylor, F. Quinn, M. Littledyke and R.K. Coll (eds.), Health Education in Context, 145–152.

resulted in waterborne diseases, among others, and has claimed many lives, generally those of school-age children. As a response to this situation, the government developed a health education curriculum for school students. The curriculum is designed not only to inculcate healthy behaviors and attitudes but also to provide children with strategies that they can apply to real-life situations. The overall aim is to change the lifestyle of people living in this area for the better. However, it appears that the curriculum is not being taught appropriately, and attention has now turned to how it and the way in which it is taught can be made more relevant to the lives, realities, and practices of local people.

The improper disposal of human, domestic, agricultural, and industrial waste has contaminated the underground water system in Baruten (Ahiakwo, 1998). Agu (2000) and Okebukola (1995) note that underground water contamination continues to be a major environmental problem throughout Nigeria and especially in communities such as Baruten. The Federal Government of Nigeria joined the global crusade against environmental degradation when, in 1992, toxic waste was imported into Nigeria and dumped into the country's waterways and onto the land. This event gave impetus to the establishment of Nigeria's Federal Environmental Protection Agency. It also led to the government commissioning the Nigeria Educational Research and Development Council to develop a curriculum for environmental education, using the infusion approach. The government duly approved the curriculum for use in all states in Nigeria.

Another government (both federal and state) initiative, conducted in collaboration with international non-governmental organizations, involved a series of workshops set up to identify and inventory Nigeria's various environmental problems. One outcome, at the state level, involved encouraging various environmental agencies to promote separation of waste materials at the point where they were being generated so as to avoid contamination of stream and river water. Another was the requirement for schools to organize school conservation clubs so that children could gain a better understanding of their environment and take a more active part in resolving the problems affecting it.

These developments were much needed in Baruten, where no one had scientifically tested water purity and where water was being used without concern for waterborne diseases. In general, the people of the area believed that polluted water is harmless. People walked through streams when coming from farms, threw refuse into the waterways, and even washed in them, not minding that the same streams were serving the community's drinking water. Sickness from waterborne diseases was attributed to the gods seeking to punish people, including children, for violating their laws (Petters, 1995). People's efforts to appease the gods by offering sacrifices pointed to the need for both environmental and health education—and enlightenment.

According to the Pulitzer Center (2010), just over 900 million people worldwide lack reliable access to water that is free from disease and industrial waste, and 40% of the world's population does not have access to adequate sanitation facilities. These figures denote one of the world's greatest public health crises; an estimated 4,500 children die daily from waterborne diseases. More specifically, diarrhea kills an estimated 1.5 million people a year in the developing world (Pulitzer Center,

2010). In Nigeria, according to the National Bureau of Statistics (Federal Republic of Nigeria, 2009b), there were 6,330 reported cases of cholera throughout the country during 2008. In Kwara State, where the study presented in this chapter took place, there were 1,321 reported cases of cholera, 19,347 cases of diarrhea, and 5,035 cases of diarrhea dysentery within the same period. The Bureau of Statistics data also show the reported deaths from cholera in Kwara State across a number of years: 2002 (478), 2003 (112), 2004 (149), 2005 (284), 2006 (387), 2007 (180), and 2008 (429). These figures make clear the endemic nature of water-related diseases in this area.

RECENT DEVELOPMENTS IN ENVIRONMENTAL AND HEALTH EDUCATION

In Nigeria, environmental and health education curricula occur in both formal and informal settings, but their content, methods, and emphasis unfortunately are not equal to the challenges that Nigeria faces (Noibi, 1990). Although both curricula are supposed to communicate the nature and magnitude of Nigeria's environmental and health problems, and the array of alternatives available for their solution, the way in which they are taught means that these aims are rarely achieved (Lawal, 1998). Teaching approaches that are interactive in nature are needed. The pedagogy associated with entertainment education, which is highly activity based, offers one way forward.

Tufte (2001) has defined entertainment education as the process of purposively designing and implementing a media message that simultaneously entertains and educates. During the 1970s, groups in the UK, USA, and Latin America began to use what became known as "edutainment" to address health and social issues, generally with considerable success as Adeleke (1991) and Abiona (2009) point out. The approach, which is now used in many other parts of the world, is successful not only because the "audience's" knowledge of an issue increases but also because their attitudes and behavior with respect to that issue change for the better. Given the success of this approach, it was anticipated that if it were adopted in Baruten, the curriculum would be appropriately imparted and the attitude of the community toward their environment and, more importantly, health issues would change in the intended direction.

Entertainment education/edutainment or, as it is now more commonly known, enter-education, can be grouped into two basic types—the old and the modern. The first type (old) includes such activities as parables, fables, riddles, jokes, moonlight stories, songs, dance, drama, gesticulations, and excursions. The second type involves playing cards, ludo, and video and computer games, doing puzzles, listening to music and radio programs, watching films and television, engaging in in-class skits, developing PowerPoint presentations, making and/or watching animated cartoons, and taking part in situation comedy. Street theatre, exhibitions, internet and mobile phone games, agricultural shows, and a host of other activities also feature.

The enter-educate strategy is informed by two major learning theories—incremental learning and distributed learning. Ahove (2001), Olagunju (1998), and Schmidhuber (2003) are all at the forefront of research on incremental learning theory. Schmidhuber, for instance, was the first to show empirically that bringing incremental learning practices into the classroom makes for much faster learning.

Dweck (1999) provided a useful account of what is meant by incremental learning in his account of two theories—one being entity, the other incremental—that tend to underpin people's views of intelligence. People who ascribe (not necessarily knowingly, of course) to entity theory consider their intelligence to be a fixed trait—the amount of intelligence that they have does not change. Those who perceive intelligence not as a fixed entity but as something they can "cultivate" through ongoing learning fall into the incremental theory group. The implication of incremental leaning theory for environmental and health education as well as the use of enter-educate is based on the understanding that because intelligence can be cultivated through personal effort, learners will want to learn more and more in order to increase their intelligence.

Fossard and Launder (2008) described distributed learning theory in terms of a learning situation in which different people learn in different ways over different periods of time. Because of this diversity, information needs to be presented in different ways so that people can absorb it. This thinking is the same as that under-pinning the enter-educate strategy. Hence, teachers engaged in enter-education impart information through media that both entertain and educate, such as games, dancing, music, outdoor recreation, movies and theater, posters, community celebrations, home-based electronic information and communication technologies, and the like.

In the remainder of this chapter, we report a recent study carried out according to the following objectives:

- To investigate the effect of the entertainment education strategy on students' cognitive achievement in the environmental and health education curricula;
- To determine the influence of gender (male and female) on students' cognitive achievement in environmental and health education after being taught with entertainment education strategies; and
- To enable curriculum developers to include appropriate environmental and health education teaching strategies, such as entertainment education, in the curricula in order to impart better environmental and health attitudes and practices to students.

THE RESEARCH PROJECT

Purpose and Method

The research project adopted a pre-test/post-test, control group quasi-experimental design with an intervention based on entertainment education. Participants were 188 primary school students from four co-educational primary schools within the Baruten Local Government Area of Kwara State, Nigeria. A purposive sampling technique was used to select primary schools. Schools were required to have:

1. At least one National Certificate in Education science graduate teacher and one university graduate science teacher with a minimum of three years' teaching experience;

2. A well-equipped and functional science laboratory; and
3. Candidates for the school-leaving certificate.

Seven primary schools met these criteria, but only four of them were randomly selected for participation. Two of the schools were then assigned to the experimental group and two to the control group.

Two instruments, the Entertainment Education Achievement Test (EEAT) and the Entertainment Education Attitude Questionnaire (EEAQ), were used to gather data for the study. The EEAT consists of 30 multiple-choice items relevant to environmental and health education curricula. It was used to determine the participating students' achievement in curricular content. Each correct answer received a score of two marks. The EEAQ consists of 20 statements, each with a four-point Likert response format.

Two environmental educators and two secondary school science teachers validated the initial drafts of these instruments. Some items were deleted while others were modified according to the assessors' suggestions. The reliability of the two instruments was ascertained by conducting a trial test on a group of 40 students using a test–retest approach. Science teachers in each school served as research assistants. They were all briefed on the objectives of the study and the procedure for administering the research instruments. They also received relevant training with respect to the specified health and environmental education content and were provided with lesson plans.

The science teachers in the two experimental schools used entertainment education to teach the content over a period of six weeks. The science teachers in the control schools taught the content over the six weeks using their usual teaching methods. Students in all four schools were administered the EEAT and the EEAQ both before and after completion of the specified content. The students' scores on each were averaged, and the pre- and post-test means were then analyzed for statistical significance, using an analysis of covariance.

The intervention involved the following steps:

1. Teacher provided students with media-based instruction on the specified topic. Instruction was in the form of video clips showing the health-related consequences of poor environmental conditions.
2. Students interacted with the media-based instruction.
3. Teacher led media-based discussion.
4. Students identified various types of entertainment media with respect to the issue discussed.
5. Students participated in drama and poem recitations in the classroom.
6. Teacher summarized the main points and ideas arising from the discussion and interaction with the media-based instruction.
7. Teacher evaluated the media-based instruction and students' level of mastery.
8. Teacher gave out an assignment.

More specifically, the enter-educate strategy adopted in this study included a short play written and presented by the students to their peers. The title of the play was "Whose Responsibility?" The students tried, through the play, to demonstrate the prevalence of waterborne diseases in the local community, and to show how unconcerned some members of that community were about keeping their surroundings clean and maintaining a healthy living style. The students also endeavored to demonstrate the apathy of the community in responding to the environmental and health challenges they all faced, and to demonstrate the importance of a communal response to those challenges. In addition to working on the play, the students were asked to document the lessons learned from it and then to discuss these in class. The enter-educate strategy thus provided a different approach to the normal classroom practices of the school.

Findings and Discussion

The results of the project showed a statistically significant positive change across time in the experimental students' average environmental knowledge and attitude scores ($p < 0.5$). No such change across time was observed for the control group students. Students taught using entertainment education performed significantly better on the achievement and attitudinal instruments than the students who experienced conventional teaching. No significant difference was apparent, however, between the achievement of the males and females in both the experimental and the control groups.

 Before the intervention, a majority of the students (both experimental and control) demonstrated poor knowledge of the environmental- and health-related issues evident in the content that they were to be taught. The issues included water pollution, air pollution, deforestation, and the impact of these on the health of the people in the community, especially in terms of waterborne diseases. The fact that the experimental group showed advances in both knowledge *and* attitudes after completing the course suggests an interrelationship between the two, with improved knowledge aligned with improved attitudes.

The achievement findings align with the findings of Singhal and Rogers (1999), who carried out studies under the auspices of the United Nations Fund for Population Activities in Africa, Asia, and Latin America. The two researchers showed that the entertainment education teaching strategy not only helped to entertain, educate, and increase the various audiences' knowledge about educational issues but also their attitudes and behaviors relative to those issues. The lack of a significant difference between the achievement of male and female students taught using the entertainment education learning strategy in the current study accords with research carried out by Akinbobola (2006) and Akinbobola and Afolabi (2010). They found that gender had no significant effect on the academic achievement of students taught with entertainment education techniques. These findings suggest that entertainment education appeals to the learning needs of both genders.

The very positive outcomes for the experimental students may be because entertainment education allows people to learn through all their senses. Moreover, because the learning is fun, they are also likely to be more relaxed and therefore more receptive to absorbing information. Certainly, Afolabi (2009) found that when students experience learning that engages all their senses, learning is enhanced and achievement is improved. In terms of environmental and health education, the entertainment education strategy contains some inherent communication and behavior change tools that allow learners to connect what they learn with the current environmental and health realties in their communities. Learners thus have ample opportunity to explore and learn and to have fun while doing so.

CONCLUSION

The findings of this study in association with findings from other like research suggest that entertainment education is an effective instructional strategy, use of which could enhance students' achievement in environmental and health education curricula. Students taught using an entertainment education strategy performed significantly better than those taught using conventional methods. There was no significant difference between the achievement of male and female students taught using the entertainment education learning strategy.

The health challenges facing people in most African countries make the issue of how best to manage our environment a very critical one. Over the years, people have not taken seriously the nexus between the environment and their health, a circumstance that highlights the need for community-based and school-based education directed at attitudinal and behavioral change. However, just how that education is imparted needs to be carefully considered if it is to have effective outcomes. As has been demonstrated here, pedagogical strategies that entertain appear to engage learners in ways not evident in conventional teaching practice. We commend these strategies as ones likely to bring about positive changes to both the environment and health challenges facing our communities.

We also, given the findings of this study, offer several other, more specific, recommendations. In order to reduce environmental and health problems among the people of Baruten, we consider that an entertainment education learning strategy should be made mandatory for teaching environmental and health education curricula in schools. We also recommend that curriculum planners include entertainment education as an instructional strategy for teaching other subjects. Both government and non-governmental organizations should not limit efforts to enlighten people about health and environmental issues to schools alone but should extend this work to public places such as markets and religious venues. Seminars and workshops should be organized regularly for teachers so that they can become acquainted with more innovative learning strategies, while schools should be provided with multimedia technologies that enhance effective use of the entertainment education learning strategy.

REFERENCES

Abiona, O. F. (2009). *Impact of three life skill strategies on students' environmental learning outcomes in sewage disposal and water treatment in biology.* Unpublished doctoral post-field seminar paper, University of Ibadan, Nigeria.
Adeleke, O. A. (1991). *Promoting population/family life education concepts through the enter-education approach.* Paper presented at the training workshop for lecturers at Alvan Ikoku College of Education, Owerri, Nigeria.

Afolabi, F. (2009). The effects of inquiry-based and competitive learning strategies on academic performance of senior secondary school students in physics. *International Journal of Social and Management Sciences*, 2(2), 4–10.

Agu, E. (2000, June 5). Recipe for solid waste management. *Business Times*, p. 23.

Ahiakwo, M. J. (1998). Teaching chemical aspects of waste water pollution in strategies for environmental education: Focus on water pollution. *Environmental Education Series: Science Teachers Association of Nigeria, 7*, 196–202.

Ahove, M. A. N. (2001). *Environmental management and education: An introduction.* Lagos, Nigeria: Goldenpen Books.

Akinbobola, A. O. (2006). Effects of team teaching on students' academic achievement in senior secondary school physics. *The Architects: Interdisciplinary Journal of Academic Architects in Nigeria, 3*(1), 57–72.

Akinbobola, A. O., & Afolabi, F. (2010). Analysis of science process skills in West African senior secondary school certificate physics practical examinations in Nigeria. *Bulgarian Journal of Science Education Policy, 4*(1), 32–47.

Dweck, C. S. (1999). *Self-theories: Their role in motivation, personality and development.* Philadelphia, PA: Taylor and Francis.

Federal Republic of Nigeria. (2009a). *Official gazette of the 2006 Nigeria population census.* Abuja, Nigeria: Government Printers.

Federal Republic of Nigeria. (2009b). *Social statistics in Nigeria.* Abuja, Nigeria: National Bureau of Statistics.

Fossard, E. D., & Launder, R. (2008). *The Info Project Center for Communication Programs.* Baltimore, MD: John Hopkins University.

Lawal, M. B. (1998). Teaching water pollution using the value clarification. In P. A. O. Okebukola & B. Akpan (Eds.), *Strategies for environmental education: Focus on water pollution* (Series 2, pp. 63–73). Abuja, Nigeria: Science Teachers Association of Nigeria (STAN) EE.

Noibi, A. S. (1990). Challenges of environmental education in Nigerian schools. *EE Workshop and Seminar Proceedings, 1,* 16–26.

Okebukola, P. A. O. (1995). *Instructional strategies for sustaining the development of environmental education among science students.* Unpublished manuscript, Lagos State.

Olagunju, A. M. (1998). *The impact of two curriculum packages in environmental education in biology on learners' performance, problem-solving abilities and environmental attitudes.* Unpublished doctoral thesis, University of Ibadan, Ibadan, Nigeria.

Petters, S. W. (1995). Natural and manmade hazards. In S. S. Peters (Ed.), *Environmental education* (pp. 110–114). Lagos, Nigeria: Macmillan.

Pulitzer Center. (2010). *Diarrhea kills 1.5 million a year in developing world.* Retrieved from http://pulitzercenter.org/education/student-report/diarrhea-kills-1.5-million-year-developing-world-bronx-has-problems-too.

Schmidhuber, J. (2003). *The incremental self-improvement paradigm.* Retrieved from http://www.wfp.org/stories/bangladesh-nutrition-magicians-keeps-kids-spellbound.

Singhal, A., & Rogers E. M. (1999). *Entertainment education: A communication strategy for social change.* Mahwah NJ: Lawrence Erlbaum Associates.

Tourism: A global industry. (2002, February 8). *Awake*, pp. 12–15.

Tufte, T. (2001). Entertainment education and participation: Assessing the communication strategy of Soul City. *Journal of International Communication, 2*(3), 45–58.

Josiah O. Ajiboye and Folashade Afolabi
University of Ibadan,
Ibadan
Nigeria
email: josiah.ajiboye@gmail.com

WENDY R. HOLMES AND JENNIFER JOSEPH

17. PROMOTING HEALTHY AGEING

Experience from Tea Estate Communities in Sri Lanka

INTRODUCTION

The population of the world is ageing. There is growing awareness of this in developed countries, but less awareness that the pace of population ageing is much faster in poorer countries than in richer ones. It took a century in developed countries for the proportion of people over 60 years of age to double from 7% to 14%; many Asian countries are making the same demographic transition in fewer than 25 years. By 2020, it is predicted that 67% of the global population over 60 years of age will be living in developing countries (Shrestha, 2000).

The change in the age structure of populations, as societies develop, is the result of a fall in high death rates, followed, after a lag, by a fall in fertility rates. Death and birth rates then tend to stabilize at lower rates, and population growth slows. The proportion of older people increases. This transition is also happening at a time of other major social changes, including migration, modern social and technological influences, smaller families, with commensurate changes in traditional roles, and women working outside the home—all of which are influenced by and influence globalization and urbanization.

The ageing of populations has many benefits. Older people make significant social, cultural, and economic contributions to their families and communities. They undertake childcare, domestic and agricultural work, guide young people, and influence reproductive, maternal, and child health choices. However, their ability to contribute is often undermined by chronic health conditions, poor nutrition, and preventable disability. These conditions often lead to financial hardship and loss of productivity for the families of elders and for health care services. Promotion of healthy ageing therefore has the potential to contribute to poverty alleviation. Issues associated with ageing of the population particularly affect women, not only because women have longer life expectancies than men but also because women are the ones who tend to care for dependent elders in the family.

The rapid increase, within low-income settings, in non-communicable diseases, especially cardiovascular disease, cancers, respiratory diseases, and diabetes, is now receiving increasing attention on the international health agenda. But considerations relating to *healthy* ageing on the one hand and to the chronic conditions that predominantly affect quality of life on the other remain relatively neglected. These conditions include muscular-skeletal problems, urinary

N. Taylor, F. Quinn, M. Littledyke and R.K. Coll (eds.), Health Education in Context, 153–162.

incontinence, blindness, falls, nutritional deficiencies, tuberculosis, violence or neglect, and mental health problems such as dementia and depression. The risk factors of high-fat, high-salt diets, lack of exercise, smoking and alcohol use also come into play (World Health Organization, 2010). Although there is strong evidence that social isolation is as significant a risk factor for premature mortality and morbidity as the other conditions cited (Holt-Lunstad, Smith, & Layton, 2010), this factor is one that receives even less attention than the physical concerns. There is an urgent need to re-orient primary health care and health promotion toward healthy ageing.

Sri Lanka has one of the fastest ageing populations in the world (Siddhisena, 2000). It also has a strong primary health care system. Since 2004, the Burnet Institute (an Australian medical and public health research institute) and a local non-government organization (NGO), the PALM Foundation (a community-driven development organization working toward the social empowerment of tea plantation communities), have collaborated on a community-based project in the district of Nuwara Eliya. The project aims to improve the health and wellbeing of older people in the tea estate sector, to promote traditional values of respect, and to teach lessons that will be useful for health care of the elderly throughout Sri Lanka and other nations in the region.

CONTEXT

The Democratic Socialist Republic of Sri Lanka is a small South Asian lower-middle-income island nation with a population of about 20 million. The decades-long civil war ended in 2009. The population is ethnically and culturally diverse: about 74% are Sinhalese (mostly Buddhist), 18% Tamil (mostly Hindu), and 5% Muslim. The remaining percentage is made up of Burghers and Malays. The proportion of the population aged over 60 years is currently about 12%, projected to increase to 18% by 2020.

The cool and damp district of Nuwara Eliya district is in the hill country of the Central Province. Here, 56% of the population work on tea estates and are predominantly Tamils of Indian origin; their ancestors were brought by the British in the 19th century to work on the tea plantations. Because mortality and birth rates did not decline in the estate sector until the 1980s, the rate of ageing has been slower than elsewhere in Sri Lanka; about 7.5% in the district are over 60 years of age (Department of Census and Statistics, 2010).

In 2005, we undertook a baseline survey of a random sample of households in a "project-designated" area of Nuwara Eliya district. We found that nearly all elders were living with relatives; only five percent were living alone. About 70% of the women and 34% of the men were illiterate, and 32% of respondents reported their health as "bad" or "very bad." About 60% of the men had experienced prostate symptoms. About 44% of the respondents had experienced some degree of urinary incontinence, with similar proportions of men and women suffering symptoms. The women elders had had a mean of 5.6 live births. Almost 10% of the elders reported being blind and 9% reported poor hearing. Almost a third (32%) said they were missing more than half of their teeth, and 17% reported that they had no teeth left.

About 84% of women and 69% of men reported chewing betel, and 57% of men and 18% of women said they were smokers. These retired tea estate workers had little or no income, were living in poor, cold, and crowded conditions, and had limited access to health and other services. Barriers to accessing appropriate health care included transport costs, the cost of drugs, lack of mobility due to disability or lack of transport, long waiting times, and health care providers showing lack of respect and warmth. Sometimes older people were unaware that their condition could be treated, or considered that trying to access care was not worthwhile because they were too old. Many were reported by others to be apathetic and less socially engaged than before their retirement.

THE ELDERS' CLUB STRATEGY

PALM Foundation and the Burnet Institute, in line with their participatory approach to health care, planned a care strategy that centered on establishing Elders' Clubs. A participatory evaluation found that the strategy was successful, had produced a wider range of benefits than anticipated, and facilitated other project objectives.

Members of the Albion Elders' Club.

Today, establishment of clubs follows a pre-determined strategy. First, PALM community mobilisers make a list of older people in their estate communities and consult them about forming a club. At the first meeting, the elders map their communities, identifying households where elders—including those who are bedridden or disabled—live. Club members elect two leaders, a woman and a man, and meet monthly.

Evaluation shows that activities such as playing music, dance, sports, oral history, and excursions provide greater social contact, an increase in self-esteem, and better relationships within families. The elders often request visits to temples and religious sites. Opportunities to practice their religious rituals are often especially important to these older people. Ritual provides meaning, a sense of familiarity, belonging and continuity, opportunity to meet regularly with others, and motivation.

Soon after the establishment of a club, elders typically begin to organize their own activities, including providing social support, such as visiting sick or bereaved peers, and setting up or offering savings and small loan schemes. Elders' Club meetings and the records they produce and archive have made it easier to gather health data, and have facilitated greater access to services for club members, including obtaining identity cards, securing access to welfare entitlements, and organizing eye-health screening, along with referrals for cataract surgery. The availability of screening data have made advocating for government services for the elderly much easier. Treatment for cataract blindness again provides an important example. Circumventing preventable blindness has had a great emotional, social, and economic impact on the communities concerned.

Leadership skills training and intergenerational activities with young people have resulted in greater community participation and respect for elders. More youth and children are helping elders—to water vegetable gardens, for example, along with repairing latrines, accompanying elders to the hospital for cataract surgery, and preparing and serve tea at club meetings. Elders now have greater visibility in such areas as estate management, and the community-based organizations are recognizing and responding to their needs. Through their clubs, the elders now have a collective voice to influence politicians and government services. The clubs have grown in strength and independence; whenever a new one is set up, its members soon take over managing it.

However, taking on leadership is not without its challenges and conflicts, particularly in relation to savings and small loans schemes. These concerns led to the setting up of monthly regional meeting of leaders so that members can support and learn from one another. Clubs are vulnerable to illness, death, and migration of leaders and members, and some members have domestic commitments or jobs that limit their involvement. In response to these concerns, club leaders have helped develop their own evaluation criteria to identify weak clubs, which are invited to visit and learn from stronger clubs, with good results. Some clubs have merged in order to become stronger.

The clubs have also, as noted earlier, set up their own savings schemes and opened bank accounts, allowing them to apply successfully for government registration, which then entitles them to certain benefits. The registration of the clubs has increased their status, and club meetings and events are now often attended by the Grama Niladari (community government representative) and members of estate management. There has been steady progress toward sustainability, with many stories demonstrating increasing strength and independence.

The success of these efforts to encourage greater social participation by elders was assisted by the familiarity that PALM Foundation workers have with their own communities. They understand the social and political dynamics and have been able to suggest new ways ahead when problems occur. The partnership with Burnet Institute has enabled the contribution of new ideas from outside, including technical expertise and the benefit of experiences from other countries. Our experience has also shown the valuable role that local NGOs can play in linking with different government sectors to provide more appropriate services and in assisting older people to access services.

The international NGO, HelpAge International, has also had successful experiences, including a range of health and social outcomes, through its establishment of Older People's Associations in varied settings across South and South-East Asia (HelpAge International, 2009). Older people generally have more time than younger adults to participate in social activities, and often have the interest, skills, and wisdom to contribute to organizing and managing their clubs or associations.

Recent research is providing a better understanding of the mechanisms by which social participation, such as that evident in the Elder Clubs and the Older People's Associations, protects against chronic diseases (Grant, Hamer, & Steptoe, 2000; Suttajit et al., 2010; Troxel et al., 2010).

HEALTH EDUCATION STRATEGIES

Another advantage of the Elders' Clubs is that they make it easier to organize interactive health promotion sessions, hence improving knowledge and care-seeking behavior. Studies in developed countries have shown that, even in old age, health education efforts can have a measurable impact on health behaviors, such as physical exercise, with concomitant improvements in health (Kaczorowski et al., 2011; Kerse, Flicker, Jolley, Arroll, & Young, 1999; Vetter & Ford, 1990). But this education needs to be sustained if it is to be effective (Cupples & McKnight, 1999).

While older people may have more time for and interest in health education, those planning health education strategies need to take into account low literacy levels, potential cognitive deficits, and poor hearing or sight. In estates and villages, life can be relatively monotonous. If visitors are entertaining, they are more likely to engage attention, and messages are more likely to be remembered, and stimulating discussion is more likely to lead to behavior change.

With these considerations in mind, we prepared a health education kit containing two identical sets of picture cards to enable discussion of healthy behaviors, suggestions for facilitators, and a set of key messages (see text box on page 159–160). The cards can be used in a variety of flexible and entertaining ways. They can be used within a single household with a single older person, with his or her family, or in small groups supported by a facilitator. Simple card games such as "Snap!" and "Memory" provide opportunities to stop the game to discuss a health behavior triggered by the picture on the card. The group might tell a story that features the picture on a card, which the facilitator and group members then discuss. At the end of the discussion, the health educator summarizes the main points that have been made—and also gets the group to agree on how they plan to use the information for the benefit of their own health. When used within the context of small-group discussions, the cards can also be used to gather information relevant to elders' health or to convey information and stimulate wider community discussion about elders' health issues.

It is important to think about the effect of behavior change messages from the perspective of older people. For example, it is important to encourage less salt in the diet, but we should reach men with these messages rather than simply addressing women, often older women, who cook for their husbands and families. We need to take into account that older women may find it difficult to reduce the amount of salt they add when cooking. For women, making tasty meals is important—they naturally want approval, and may have reason to fear disapproval.

Sometimes, a harm-reduction approach is more appropriate than a "zero tolerance" approach. Smoking tobacco is so obviously dangerous to health that we recommend not smoking at all. The widespread habit of chewing betel is much less likely than smoking tobacco to cause oral cancer (Ariyawardana et al., 2007). Chewing betel is an important pleasure for older people in settings where there may be few pleasures, and this practice also plays a social role. Instead of simply telling people to give up chewing betel, we suggest to them that they reduce harm by not mixing betel with tobacco, limiting the amount of lime added, not leaving it in their mouth for long periods, and especially not sleeping with betel in their mouths. Older people may follow traditional beliefs, such as those relating to food taboos, more closely than younger people do. For these reasons, it is important to explore cultural beliefs before developing and conveying messages and producing and utilizing pre-test materials and other research-related resources and methods.

When providing information about chronic conditions in a group situation, we need to remember that some problems are associated with stigma or shame. We also need to be aware that someone in the group may be affected by one of the conditions being discussed. At the same time, it is important not to avoid topics that may be embarrassing, such as promoting pelvic floor exercises to prevent urinary incontinence, or discussing sexual health.

We also need to remember that older people may have little control over relevant aspects of their lives, such as visiting health care providers for early detection of illness, or eating more nutritious foods. Health education efforts should include reaching out to family members and others who care for older people, and giving them the same messages.

As is the case with young people, we have found that peer education is effective with older people. For example, many blind older people are fearful of having cataract surgery to restore their sight, but are reassured when they meet and hear about the operation from those who have experienced it. Information and support from peers can also improve self-management of chronic conditions such as diabetes (MoPoTyso Patient Information Centre, n. d.).

SOME KEY HEALTH PROMOTION MESSAGES FOR OLDER PEOPLE

What can you do to help yourself to stay healthy? There are some things we cannot change—such as illnesses we might inherit through our family, or the weather. But there are many things we can do to help us to stay healthy and happy.

Eat in a healthy way
- Eating rice, roti, and vegetables is healthy
- Try to eat lentils, beans, or cowpeas every day
- Try to eat more green leafy vegetables and fresh fruit
- Try to eat an egg, some fish, or some meat, more than once a week
- Tea with sugar is healthy—but try to avoid drinking tea at mealtimes.

Try to add less salt to your food. Instead, use chilies and spices to flavor your food. Salty food increases the risk of high blood pressure.

If you are thin, try to eat more often.

If you are overweight, try to eat less food, especially less fried and sweet food.

Remain active
After retirement, some older people find that they are much less active. Lack of activity increases the risk of aches and pains from arthritis, and can cause you to gain weight. Your general health and wellbeing will be better if you stay active. It is never too late for exercise to make a difference.

It is good to take exercise with friends—go for a walk, play some sport, even dance! Kick a ball with your grandchildren.

Protect yourself from getting chilled
When the weather is cold and damp, it is easy to become chilled. If you become chilled, you are more likely to become ill. If you are caught in the rain, try to change into dry clothes as soon as possible. Wearing socks when inside, a hat on your head and a scarf is one way to keep your body warmer.

Look after your mental health
Life is difficult, and as we grow older we have to deal with the death of our family members and friends. Family problems can also make us feel sad. But older people have a very important role in their family and in the community. Older people are wise from the experiences of their life and can give good advice to younger people. Try to keep in touch with friends and family members. Ask them to visit, and spend time talking with them, walking together, watching TV, listening to the radio, or playing games.

Sometimes when we feel sad, we feel like drinking to forget. Alcohol is a dangerous and addictive drug. If you like to have a drink, try to drink less. If you find your alcohol drinking is causing problems for yourself or your family, try to discuss this with a friend or health worker and get some support to cut down on your drinking.

Betel chewing

Chewing betel causes little harm for most people. But in a few people, especially those who also smoke and drink alcohol, it can result in mouth cancer. You can reduce this risk.

- If you like to chew betel, try to chew for a shorter time and less often
- Never sleep with betel in your mouth
- Do not add tobacco to the mix when you chew betel
- Use less lime in the mix
- Clean your teeth every day with a brush or stick
- When you visit the doctor or dentist, ask them to check your mouth for white patches
- If you have diabetes, do not chew betel; it may make the diabetes worse.

Don't smoke

Smoking beedis or cigarettes causes cancer and heart disease. Smoking near children harms their health, too.

If you are a smoker, try to cut down your smoking and then stop. The nicotine in beedis and cigarettes is very addictive—that means you may crave for a smoke when you try to stop smoking.

You might find it easier to stop smoking if you can stop with a friend, or a group of friends. Then, when you feel tempted to smoke, you can talk to your friend and receive encouragement to stay strong. Even if you have failed to stop smoking before, it is worth trying to stop again. Sometimes it takes several attempts before you succeed. Your reward is that you will feel healthier and you will have more money to spend on other things.

Get regular health checks

It is useful to have your health checked twice a year. Make sure that your blood pressure and blood sugar are checked, as well as your teeth and your sight.

Older people often care for young children, influence the reproductive decisions of women and the care of their infants, and have a good relationship with young people. Older people may be key to promoting health in the broader community, and should therefore be included in broader health education efforts related to sexual and reproductive health, hygiene behavior, and infant nutrition. Preparation for healthy ageing is an important concept, and health education efforts should also aim to reach those in middle age, before they retire.

CONCLUSION

As Chiva and Stears (2001) point out, it is important, when promoting healthy ageing, not to introduce vertical interventions that address a particular disease or behavior. Integrated and participatory strategies are needed that encourage an enabling environment for behavior change at community and health-service levels and that address social, emotional, and economic determinants of health. There is a danger that current efforts to analyze the cost-effectiveness of specific interventions to prevent "non-communicable diseases" may result in these narrow vertical programs (Ha & Chisholm, 2010).

Our experience in the tea estate communities of one region of Sri Lanka highlights the important role that local non-government and community-based organizations can play in forming links between older people and their families and government services, and in advocating with government officials across sectors. Religious leaders and organizations are also important partners. Older people, once given support to become organized, are able to contribute to their communities. Intergenerational activities are especially important because they benefit both young people and older people. Above all, we should recognize the significance of social participation, both as a protective factor in preventing a range of chronic conditions and as a means of improving self-management of these conditions.

ACKNOWLEDGEMENTS

We thank the leaders and members of the Elders' Clubs and the PALM Foundation community mobilisers and project staff, including Sarawanaluxmi Kitnasamy, Praba Selladurai, Christina Christopher, Ashok Kumar, and Matilda Jesudasan. The project is funded by the Australian Agency for International Development.

REFERENCES

Ariyawardana, A., Sitheeque, M. A., Ranasinghe, A. W., Perera, I., Tilakaratne, W.M., Amaratunga, E. A., Yang, Y. H., & Warnakulasuriya, S. (2007). Prevalence of oral cancer and pre-cancer and associated risk factors among tea estate workers in central Sri Lanka. *Journal of Oral Pathology and Medicine, 36*(10), 581–587.

Chiva A., & Stears, D (2001). *Promoting the health of older people: The next step in health generation.* Buckingham, UK: Open University Press.

Cupples M. E., & McKnight A. (1999). Five year follow up of patients at high cardiovascular risk who took part in randomised controlled trial of health promotion. *British Medical Journal, 319*, 687–688.

Department of Census and Statistics. (2010). *Sri Lanka: Statistical abstract 2010.* Retrieved from http://www.statistics.gov.lk/abstract2010/Pages/chap2.htm.

Grant, N., Hamer, M., & Steptoe, A. (2000). Social isolation and stress-related cardiovascular, lipid, and cortisol responses. *Annals of Behavioral Medicine, 37*(1), 29–37.

Ha, D. A., & Chisholm, D. (2010). Cost-effectiveness analysis of interventions to prevent cardiovascular disease in Vietnam. *Health Policy and Planning*, doi: 10.1093/heapol/czq045 Sep 15 [Epub ahead of print].

HelpAge International. (2009). *Older people in community development: The role of Older People's Associations in enhancing local development.* Chiang Mai, Thailand: HelpAge International East Asia/Pacific Regional Development Centre. Retrieved from http://www.helpage.org/resources/publications/.

Holt-Lunstad, J., Smith, T. B., & Layton, J. B. (2010). Social relationships and mortality risk: A meta-analytic review. *PLoS Medicine, 7*(7), e1000316.

Kaczorowski, J., Chambers, L. W., Dolovich, L., Paterson, J. M., Karwalajtys, T., Gierman, T., Farrell, B., & Sabaldt, R. J. (2011). Improving cardiovascular health at population level: 39 community cluster randomised trial of Cardiovascular Health Awareness Program (CHAP). *British Medical Journal, 342*, d442. doi:10.1136/bmj.d442.

Kerse, N. M., Flicker L., Jolley D., Arroll, B., & Young D. (1999). Improving the health behaviours of elderly people: Randomised controlled trial of a general practice education programme. *British Medical Journal, 319*, 683–687.

MoPoTsyo Patient Information Centre. (n. d.). *Peer education*. Retrieved from http://www.mopotsyo. org/peereducation.html.

Shrestha, L. B. (2000). Population ageing in developing countries. *Health Affairs, 19*(3), 204–212.

Siddhisena, K. A. P. (2000). Mortality trends, determinants and implications in Sri Lanka: Retrospect and prospect. In K. A. P. Siddhisena (Ed.), *Demography of Sri Lanka: Issues and challenges* (pp. 119–131). Colombo, Sri Lanka: Department of Demography, University of Colombo.

Suttajit, S., Punpuing, S., Jirapramukpitak, T., Tangchonlatip, K., Darawuttimaprakorn, N., Stewart, R., Dewey, M. E., & Abas, M.A. (2010). Impairment, disability, social support and depression among older parents in rural Thailand. *Psychological Medicine, 40*(10), 1711–1721.

Troxel, W. M., Buysse, D. J., Hall, M., Kamarck, T. W., Strollo, P. J., Owens J. F., Reis, S. E., & Matthews, K. A. (2010). Social integration, social contacts, and blood pressure dipping in African-Americans and whites. *Journal of Hypertension, 28*(2), 265–271.

Vetter, N. J., & Ford, D. (1990). Smoking prevention among people aged 60 and over: A randomized controlled trial. *Age and Ageing, 19*(3), 164–168.

World Health Organization (WHO). (2010). *Package of essential non-communicable (PEN) disease interventions for primary health care in low-resource settings.* Geneva, Switzerland: WHO. Available online at W84.6.whqlibdoc.who.int/publications/2010/9789241598996_eng.pdf.

Wendy R. Holmes
Burnet Institute
Melbourne
Australia
email: holmes@burnet.edu.au

Jennifer Joseph
PALM Foundation
Hawa Eliya
Nuwara Eliya
Sri Lanka

SHYAMALA MANI, D. K. BANERJEE, DIVYA PANT,
PRIYANKA PORWAL AND SHEFALI GODURA

18. EDUCATING INDIAN CHILDREN ABOUT THE IMPACT OF CLIMATE CHANGE ON HEALTH

There is increasing agreement that greenhouse gas emissions generated by human activity are responsible for global climate change (International Panel on Climate Change, 2007). There has been an observed 0.5°C rise in average global temperatures since the mid-1970s, a change that the international panel attributes partly to these anthropogenic emissions. It is also believed that these changes will have, in many parts of the world, adverse health effects ranging from heat-stroke and injury from extreme weather events to hunger and infectious diseases.

As Smith and Ezzati (2005) point out, societies tend to sweep environmental health problems out of the house and into the community during the first stages of development and then out from the community to the general global environment during later stages. This shifting of risk by the affluent has put the poor and vulnerable at the receiving end of the transmission. The rate of infectious diseases increases with malnourishment, lack of access to clean resources, indoor smoke, and unsafe sex and are thought to be intimately connected with age and sanitation. When health risks are analyzed according to mortality rates and age, as occurs with respect to the World Health Organization's global burden of disease (Lopez, Mathers, Ezzati, Jamison, & Murray, 2006a), it becomes evident that rates of infectious diseases are often highest amongst the very young, and that mortality from such diseases is highest amongst infants and children below the age of five, even in developed countries. As countries address basic environmental and sanitation issues and infant mortality reduces, deaths from chronic diseases appear to take over. Deaths from unintended injury (accidents) and intentional violence appear to remain constant (Lopez, Mathers, Ezzati, Jamison, & Murray, 2006b).

Thus, if global warming causes extreme weather events or an increase in infectious disease-causing organisms and their vectors, it will be the very young (under five) and the vulnerable who are primarily affected. This situation will be amplified amongst those who do not have access to safe and clean resources, nutrition, and healthcare, a lack that is especially evident in the poor and developing countries. As McMichael, Woodruff, and Hales (2006) explain, health effects due to climate change have hitherto spanned mostly thermal stress, problems from extreme weather events, and infectious diseases, but there is now increasing evidence of a wider spectrum of health risks associated with the social, demographic, and economic disruptions of climate change. McMichael and colleagues emphasize that evidence of adverse health effects should strengthen

N. Taylor, F. Quinn, M. Littledyke and R.K. Coll (eds.), Health Education in Context, 163–170.
© *2012 Sense Publishers. All rights reserved.*

pre-emptive policies and guide priorities for planned adaptive strategies. Therefore, we need to focus on adaptation to climate change.

EFFECTS ON HUMAN HEALTH

Several diseases and threats to human health can be directly or indirectly attributed to climate change. Extreme temperatures can lead to loss of life, while climate-related disturbances in ecological systems, such as changes in the range of infective parasites, influence the incidence of serious infectious diseases. In addition, higher temperatures affect air and water quality, which may, in turn, be detrimental to human health. Human health is also strongly affected by social, political, economic, environmental, and technological factors, including urbanization, affluence, scientific developments, individual behavior, and individual vulnerability (e.g., genetic makeup, nutritional status, emotional wellbeing, age, gender, and economic status) (Environmental Protection Agency, 2010). Human beings are exposed to climate change through changing weather patterns (e.g., more intense and frequent extreme weather events), thermal stress, and infectious diseases. The extent to which human health is affected by climate change depends on:

- How much populations are exposed to climate change and its environmental consequences;
- The sensitivity of populations to that exposure; and
- The ability of affected systems and populations to adapt (World Health Organization, 2008).

India, which can be said to be somewhere in the middle of the development spectrum, is experiencing, with the re-emergence of pathogens due to climate change, a stage where non-communicable and lifestyle-related diseases along with communicable diseases are almost equally responsible for morbidity and mortality, posing a serious challenge. Vector-borne diseases, especially dengue infection, which was earlier restricted to urban areas, are now being widely reported in rural areas. Dengue infection has also spread to areas of the country where it was previously unknown (*South Asia Voice*, 2008). During 2009, many of India's states began reporting widespread incidences of chikungunya, an insect-borne virus of the genus *Alphavirus*, which is transmitted to humans by the *Aedes* mosquito; this, after a long period in which the virus had not been evident. Malaria, which was thought to be controlled, is re-emerging in both rural and urban areas (Narain, 2009). Thus, the effects of climate change on health have already become an issue.

CLIMATE AND HEALTH EDUCATION PACKAGE

The Waste and Resource Management (WaRM) group of the Centre for Environmental Education (an Indian non-governmental organization) recently developed an interactive program designed to heighten students' awareness of the impacts of climate change on human health. The team trialed the program with a group of 40 middle school (Class VIII) students. The program, which includes classroom teaching, a PowerPoint presentation, a quiz, and a game based on the subject, endeavors to explain causes, mitigation of, and adaptation to health effects of climate and environmental change. The WaRM team did extensive work to develop, as part of the program, a booklet that includes appropriate illustrations easily understood by all the children. The booklet was used as base material for developing the PowerPoint presentation, quiz, and game, as well as a pre-test and a post-test used to measure each student's individual knowledge and understanding of the program's subject matter.

The booklet was developed through a number of stages, including group brainstorming, a literature review, readability assessment, independent booklet review, and feedback to authors. All these stages resulted in meaningful input to the booklet, especially in relation to the inclusion of interactive activities. The booklet can be accessed at http://www.paryavaranmitra.in/index.htm.

WaRM trialed the program and booklet in classroom sessions, at the beginning of which the Class VIII students were asked to complete the pre-test. The team then handed out the booklet to the students and gave them time to read it. The team also conducted a teaching session, during which they explained the basics of climate change, the impact of climate change at the regional level, health risks associated with climate change, and the different methods and approaches that are being or can be used to help humans adapt to this process and to mitigate its effects. At the end of the classroom session, students were asked to complete the post-test. The post-testing indicated that students' knowledge and understanding of climate change and health increased after they attended the session.

Program Overview

The program sessions begin with an explanation, via the PowerPoint presentation, of the causes and effects of climate change. Students also see an online film on climate change. To gain a better understanding of the health effects of climate change, groups of students are asked to do some of the activities described in the booklet, such as measuring ambient temperature in the sun, in the shade, and inside a glass jar, and then to discuss what would happen to people experiencing a high temperature inside a closed car. Some of the activities, such as melting ice in a glass and role-playing examples of thermal stress and the health effects of and responses required during and after droughts and floods, are used to elicit discussion of emergency response systems and the skills that everyone needs to develop. Through the quiz, students answer questions in teams. They also play the interactive game called Web of Life and take part in a question and answer session designed to clarify difficult issues.

The importance of strong health systems as a frontline defense for addressing the impacts of climate change is emphasized. Particular attention is paid to preventive public health interventions likely not only to improve health now but also to reduce climate vulnerability in the future. The post-test questionnaire is distributed to the students and their answers recorded. The following section provides further detail on the program's individual components.

Program Components

The PowerPoint presentation. The presentation covers these topics:

- What is climate change?
- Regional effects of climate change.
- Health effects due to climate change.
- Mitigation measures.
- Adaptation measures to climate change.

The presentation highlights that climate change is now a concern for health, wellbeing, and security, rather than being simply an environmental or development issue. The presentation stresses that climate change is already increasing health risks through extreme weather events and changing patterns of vector-borne diseases. It also makes clear that continuing climate changes will further (and directly) exacerbate risks from malnutrition, diarrhea, and cardio-respiratory disease associated with extreme heat and air pollution, and indirectly thorough impacts on socioeconomic development. The presentation stresses the importance of climate change as a dominant theme in international relations and development, with this importance likely to increase in future decades. It also highlights the importance of the efforts that individuals and communities need to take to meet climate change and its associated health challenges. The presentation furthermore includes pictures and short video clips, features that make it truly multimedia and able to accommodate different learning styles. Website links to various presentation topics also feature.

The game. At the end of the classroom session, presenters and students can play the Web of Life game. The activities in this game have been developed to encourage students to observe and explore their environment; to understand relationships in nature, and between humans and nature; and to gain a better appreciation of the fact that humans are an integral part of the intricate web of life. Those of us associated with the WaRM team believe that learning is more fun, for both student and teacher, when it is based on real experiences. Our experience is that students enjoy the game and that it helps them understand that all components of the earth/environment need to work in harmony in order to ensure a greener and healthier environment.

Booklet information. The following is an extract of the information presented in the climate change and health booklet that specifically supports the classroom session.

Heat-stroke. In countries such as India where average temperatures in summer go up to 45°C or more in some places, even a rise in one or two degrees Celsius would cause extreme discomfort or death among people who are compelled to work outdoors or travel long distances in open vehicles for work or business.

Extreme air temperatures contribute directly to deaths from cardiovascular and respiratory disease, particularly among elderly people. Higher temperatures throughout the day are expected to increase the occurrence of heat-related illnesses, such as heat exhaustion and heat-stroke, which exacerbate existing conditions related to circulatory, respiratory and nervous system problems. Prolonged heat exposure may lead to heat exhaustion or heat-stroke.

Respiratory diseases. Diseases such as asthma and allergies are leading causes of mortality in developing countries and one of the most common causes of illness in children of developed countries. There has been a sharp rise in the number of respiratory diseases in the past few years because of dust or particulate matter, micro-fine particles, and other air pollutants. Key air pollutants such as nitrogen dioxide and sulphur dioxide worsen existing cardiovascular and lung diseases. The continued emissions of some greenhouse gases will worsen this kind of air pollution.

Water-borne diseases. Warmer temperatures associated with melting ice will raise the risk of flooding, increasing diarrheal diseases such as typhoid, cholera, and other waterborne illnesses. Heavy rainfall, even without flooding, may increase rates of diarrheal disease as latrines or sewage systems overflow. Floods cause sewage and drinking water systems to mix, and that water, if ingested, can lead to waterborne diseases. A lack of availability of water for personal hygiene and washing of food may also lead to an increase in diarrheal disease and other diseases associated with poor hygiene.

Vector-borne diseases. Climate change may increase the risk of some infectious diseases, particularly those diseases that appear in warm areas and are spread by mosquitoes and other insects. A change in climate will be more favorable to the growth of vector organisms, such as mosquitoes and rodents. Important vector-borne diseases that may increase include malaria, dengue fever, yellow fever and encephalitis.

Malnutrition. A change in temperature and rainfall patterns decreases agricultural productivity by changing the chemical properties of soil. Food production, especially cereal crops, would be severely affected by climate change. Crop pests could find ideal conditions in which to thrive. Food security problems would lead to widespread malnutrition. Malnutrition also makes humans susceptible to a range of other debilitating diseases.

Injuries. Changes in the frequency of extreme weather events such as heat waves, cold spells, hurricanes, cyclones, floods and storms would result in injuries and deaths.

Psychosocial stress. Natural disasters lead not only to destruction but also to displacement. Survivors of such disasters have to cope with physical injuries as well as the pain and stress of losing their family members, homes and livelihood. Witnessing such traumatic events could have a devastating impact on their mental health, sometimes forever.

A-Z tips. Students are encouraged to remember these through a quiz.
What can you do to reduce the health effects due to climate change?

- **A**lways remember to wash hands before you eat, prepare, serve, or pack food.
- **B**eware of unclean water and unsafe food! Beware of dangerous chemicals; beware of dangerous habits! Be safe and don't get injured.
- **C**are for others, carry a handkerchief or tissue if you have a cold and always hold it to your nose when you sneeze or cough.
- **D**on't go to sensitive places such as hospitals or near babies, patients, and very old people when you have a cough, fever, or flu.
- **E**xamine your surroundings and understand it. If it is dangerous in terms of being very dirty or polluted, go away from it and stay away.
- **F**ollow simple steps to eat good, nutritious food; eat balanced food and stay healthy.
- **G**ood living is simple living. Be kind to people, animals and yourself.
- **H**ome is heaven; make your home, room and your surroundings clean and green; do not use unnecessary chemicals to clean or disinfect, as these will harm you in the long run
- **I**mitate nature. Don't use and throw away things; use durable things, which can be safely reused and recycled.
- **J**unk the junk food! Too much cheese and potato can make you fat and ill.
- **K**nowledge is power! Try to learn about the environment and all the ways you can help save it.
- **L**ower the sound of your music system; noise pollution can hurt your ears and the ears of others too.
- **M**inimize wastage. Food, water, air, land and all resources are precious, so be careful not to waste, burn, or dump it.
- **N**ever eat spoilt food or drink water or any other beverage from broken, dirty, unclean, or unsafe containers
- **O**rganize and have a feeling of ownership for the place where you live, play, and visit. Do not spoil or litter roadsides, parks, or marketplaces; ultimately everything will have a bearing on your life,
- **P**ick the right way to do things! Walk or bicycle to the places wherever you can; exercise not only your body, but your choice of the right things; choose eco-friendly things—they are often also healthy
- **Q**uestion blind faith and also pointless criticism of traditions; there may be some good in everything but question, understand, and only then adopt what is useful.
- **R**espect good values and good advice too! Good suggestions always help; be responsible for your actions; don't be reckless now and regret later.

- Support good causes. Surround yourself with good things and always be safe; learn skills that can help people during normal time and in emergencies.
- Travel sustainably. Think before you do anything. Make decisions that will help others, and treat everyone kindly.
- Universal precautions are very important; if you are injured by any sharp object or any blood-containing items, immediately see a doctor and take the necessary precautions and antidotes.
- Verify information before you blindly follow anything or anybody; value your life and the lives of others too. Be vocal when you know something is wrong.
- Wonder at the beauty of nature! Oppose wrong behavior, whether to humans, animals, or plants. Be willing to take up responsibility for at least small tasks in your neighborhood.
- 'Xecute your decisions; just making plans for good health doesn't help; you must execute them. Start today, start now.
- Yearly health check-up is good for everyone in the family; similarly, yearly clean-ups of your things is a good habit. Every year on your birthday, bring happiness to a needy child and share your day of love.
- Zero in on your priorities. Live your life with zest and enthusiasm. Zap it up—let everyone say you have the zing!

As described above, students are taught about general healthy lifestyle choices and adaptive measures beyond those relating to climate change issues. They are also informed about what measures they can take to address these concerns.

CONCLUSION

Health professionals have only now become aware of the immediate health benefits of climate change mitigation, and are yet to implement the adaptive measures urgently required to deal with the challenges that climate change poses for our health. The importance of adaptive measures needs to be explained to students through programs such as the one described in this chapter because many of these measures have benefits beyond those associated with climate change.

The rebuilding and maintaining of public health infrastructure is often viewed as the most important, cost-effective, and urgently needed adaptation strategy. This process needs to include public health training, more effective surveillance, emergency response systems, sustainable prevention, and control programs. Climate-related adaptation strategies must therefore be considered in tandem with other interventions, such as those concerning population growth, poverty, sanitation, health care, nutrition, and environmental degradation that influence a population's vulnerability and capacity to adapt.

Adaptive strategies intended to protect public health will be needed whether or not actions are taken to mitigate climate change. Building capacity is an essential preparatory step. Adapting to climate change requires more than financial resources, technology, and public health infrastructure. Education, awareness-raising, and the creation of legal frameworks, institutions, and an environment that enables people to make and then act on well-informed, long-term, sustainable decisions are all needed. Besides the suggested mitigating and adaptive measures taught in the WaRM classroom sessions, action must be taken to reduce greenhouse gas emissions.

The central message of this chapter is that climate change and health is a global issue affecting billions of people, not just an environmental issue about the plight of polar bears and the extent of deforestation. Children are the decisionmakers of the future. Children therefore need to be aware of the health effects of climate changes so that they can protect themselves by adopting measures, both now and in the future, that are appropriate for them and their communities. If they are made aware of their surroundings and the need to adapt to this major challenge, they will, it is hoped, be able to develop innovative approaches and practices that will protect them in long term.

REFERENCES

Environmental Protection Agency (EPA). (2010). EPA website. Retrieved from http://www.epa.gov/.
International Panel on Climate Change. (2007). *Climate change 2007: Synthesis report.* Retrieved from http://www.ipcc.ch/pdf/assessment-report/ar4/syr/ar4_syr_spm.pdf.
Lopez, A. D., Mathers, C. D, Ezzati, M., Jamison, D. T., & Murray, C. J. L (2006a). Global and regional burden of disease and risk factors, 2001: Systematic analysis of population health data. *The Lancet, 367*, 1747–1757.
Lopez, A. D., Mathers, C. D., Ezzati, M., Jamison, D. T., & Murray, C. J. L. (2006b). *Global burden of disease and risk factors.* Washington DC: Oxford University and World Bank. Retrieved from http://www.dcp2.org/pubs/GBD.
McMichael, A. J., Woodruff, R. E., & Hales, S. (2006). Climate change and human health: Present and future risks. *The Lancet, 367*(9513), 859–869.
Narain, J. P. (2008). *Impact of climate change on communicable diseases.* Communicable Diseases Department, World Health Organization Regional Office for South-East Asia. Retrieved from http://www.searo.who.int/LinkFiles/CDS_cds_SciDev.pdf.
Smith, K. R., & Ezzati, M. (2005). How environmental risks change with development: The epidemiologic and environmental risk transitions revisited. *Annual Review of Environment and Resources, 30*, 291–333.
South Asia Voice: An International Monthly News Magazine. (2008, May). Vol. 1, p. 67. Retrieved from http://www.searo.who.int/en/Section10/Section2537_14458.htm.
World Health Organization (WHO). (2008). *World Health Day kit.* New Delhi, India: World Health Organization, Regional Office for South-East Asia. Retrieved from www.searo.who.int/en/Section260/ Section2468 _13925.htm.

Shyamala Mani, D. K. Banerjee, Divya Pant, Priyanka Porwal and Shefali Godura
Centre for Environment Education
Delhi
India
email: shyamala.mani@ceeindia.org

SADIA MUZAFFAR BHUTTA

19. HEALTH EDUCATION IN PRIMARY SCHOOLS
IN PAKISTAN

Perils and Promises

BACKGROUND

The Islamic Republic of Pakistan is a South Asian country that covers an area of 796,096 square kilometers. The country is bordered by Afghanistan and Iran in the west, India in the east, China in the north, and the Arabian Sea and Gulf of Oman in the south. This federal parliamentary republic is the sixth most populous country in the world, with an estimated population of 176 million inhabitants (UNICEF, 2009). Pakistan is an ethnically and linguistically diverse country. An overwhelming majority of the population (above 95%) is Muslim. They reside with religious minorities that include Christians, Hindus, and Sikhs. Multiple languages are spoken along with the official language, English, and the national language, Urdu.

The geography of Pakistan is similarly varied. It blends landscapes that range from plains and deserts, to forests, hills, and plateaus that extend from the coastal areas of the Arabian Sea in the south to the mountains of the Karakoram Range in the north. The number of people living in urban areas has risen substantially; however, a majority (65%) still lives in rural areas. Agriculture is the single largest sector of Pakistan's economy. It contributes about 24% of the gross national product, directly accounts for about 70% of the country's export earnings, and employs more than 50% of its civilian labor force (Pakistan Water Partnership, 2001).

A general profile of Pakistan across the last five decades demonstrates substantial gains in health, education, and economic status, increased average life expectancy, a reduction in child death rates, improved nutrition programs, as well as better levels of immunization, disease prevention, and school attendance. These improvements have led to an overall reduction in the mortality rate of infants and children under five (Federal Bureau of Statistics, 2009; UNICEF, 2009; WHO, 2009). Since 1990, life expectancy in Pakistan has increased by five years, and the mortality rate for children five years of age and under has improved from 132 to 90 children per 1,000 live births (WHO, 2009).

As more children survive to school age, the number attending primary school has increased. Although the goal of universal access to basic education is still far from being achieved, net primary enrolment ratios have increased. The figures for

N. Taylor, F. Quinn, M. Littledyke and R.K. Coll (eds.), Health Education in Context, 171–182.
© *2012 Sense Publishers. All rights reserved.*

2008 suggest that the proportion of children in Pakistan who completed primary education has reached 70% overall (UNICEF, 2009). While the progress and achievements of the past 50 years have resulted in a reduced mortality rate overall, morbidity remains a concern. Babies who, in the past, would have died in infancy are surviving into childhood, adolescence, and adulthood, but typically experience multiple threats and impairments to their physical, mental, and social health (UNICEF, 2009; WHO, 2009).

Communicable diseases such as malaria, diarrhea, acute respiratory illness, and vaccine-preventable diseases (e.g., measles, hepatitis) still constitute major public health challenges. Pakistan is considered a low-prevalence but high-risk country for HIV/AIDS, especially among injecting drug users. Natural disasters such as the massive earthquake of 2005 and floods of 2010 along with the "war on terror" have put an additional burden on the country's economy in general and health and education in particular. That said, Pakistan is committed to achieving the United Nations Development Programme's Millennium Development Goals as the national agenda for development as well as reducing the burden of poverty and disease. The question that arises here is "How can the people of Pakistan continue to make progress in the face of the emerging problems that are influencing the health and education of children as well as youth?" Part of the answer lies in the role of education. This is because schools can provide a strategic point of entry for the delivery of comprehensive health education.

PRIMARY EDUCATION IN PAKISTAN: A LANDSCAPE

Schooling in Pakistan generally starts at Grade 1, although private schools provide Montessori and kindergarten schooling systems. Schooling continues through to secondary school matriculation or "O" levels and thus encompasses a period of 10 to 13 years. The country also has a parallel secondary school education system which operates through private schools and is based on the curriculum set by the University of Cambridge. The overall literacy rate for Pakistan's population 15 years of age and above is 56%, with 69% literacy amongst males and 44% amongst females (Federal Bureau of Statistics, 2009; UNICEF, 2009).

At primary level, the educational landscape in Pakistan is characterized by the prevalence of government and private schools. There are 156,592 primary schools in Pakistan. The total enrolment at the primary stage is 17.3 million children, of whom 7.5 million (44%) are girls and 9.7 million (56%) are boys. The overall teacher–child ratio is around 1:40 (Ministry of Education, 2009; UNICEF, 2009). The main subjects taught in primary schools are science, mathematics, social studies, and language.

In urban areas, many children attend schools where each grade level has its own teacher. However, there are many multi-grade schools in rural areas in which one teacher instructs more than one grade. Most of the multi-grade schools are one-room schools, where one teacher teaches all grades. A number of non-governmental organizations throughout Pakistan have initiated multi-grade schooling, especially in rural areas, in order to cater for the educational needs of disadvantaged groups, girls in particular.

The minimum requirement to teach at primary level is 10 to 12 years of education plus a one-year professional qualification, the Certificate of Teaching or the Primary Teaching Certificate. However, many teachers join the teaching profession in both urban and rural areas despite not having a pre-service qualification. In some cases, teachers have opportunities to attend in-service training courses to learn pedagogy and enhance their curriculum-content knowledge. It is important to note that there are primary school teachers who have attained higher academic (a Bachelor's or Master's degree) and professional (a Bachelor's or a Master's of Education) qualifications.

In recent years, considerable effort has been spent on improving the quality of education, with this initiative including increased spending on education. Public and private institutions are today striving to contribute to excellence in education through their in-service teacher training courses. In addition, foreign aid targeted at strengthening the education sector has become available. However, investment in education is still inadequate. Low salaries for teachers, a lack of investment in teacher training, mismanagement within education departments, a lack of monitoring of public education, and a lack of research to inform policy and practice are some of the major issues that continue to stymie high-quality education nationwide.

HEALTH EDUCATION IN THE PAKISTANI CURRICULUM

Health education has been positioned as an "emerging trend" and "key issue" that needs to be infused within curricula and learning material (Ministry of Education, 2009). Pakistan's most recent national education policy highlights the importance of developing contextually relevant and culturally sensitive training material for teachers. It also emphasizes the need for relevant departments, including health, environment, and population, to coordinate policy development and implementation at local and national levels in order to improve the three basic pillars of school-based health: school environment, health curriculum, and health services (Ministry of Education, 2009). These coincide with some of the basic elements described in the World Health Organization's health promoting schools framework (WHO, 1996a).

Pakistan's iterations of its national curriculum highlight the long-held importance of health education in schools. Respective curricula have offered health education of the kind deemed essential for meeting the needs of much of the population and that aligns with the core principles of the education system. The curriculum of the 1970s, for example, covered a broad range of health issues: personal hygiene, elimination of certain habits (smoking, spitting), accident prevention, food and nutrition, environmental sanitation, communicable diseases, growth and development, and human physiology. The current curriculum (developed in the 1990s) does not identify health education as a separate theme; however, the different disciplines of the curriculum cover numerous aspects of health education. An analysis[1] of a sample of primary school textbooks conducted in the mid-1990s indicated the substantial amount of health education content available to primary-school children (WHO, 1996b). Table 1 presents a summary of this content.

Although educational policy acknowledges the importance of health education, and curricula offer space to teach health, it is the implementation level that presents significant problems. Health education is not identified as a regular component of classroom teaching, and didactic teaching approaches at primary level make it difficult to provide health education that actively promotes the health of children and their communities. What is needed is a pedagogical approach wherein health education is taught in an interactive manner so that children learn not only facts about health and healthy behaviors but also develop positive attitudes toward promoting their own and their communities' health and wellbeing. Most of the various health education projects implemented with these aims in mind employ variants of a widely used approach to health education called Child-to-Child or CtC.

Table 1: Content of a sample of primary textbooks for health topics—some examples

Subjects	Health-related topics
Science	Food and health, environment, clean and safe water, pollution, germs and disease
Social studies	Environment, our neighborhood, healthy habits, rights and duties, safety from accidents
Islamiat	Cleanliness, prayers and punctuality, values, taking care of others
Mathematics	Measurement—height, weight, volume (making oral rehydration solution using appropriate amounts of salt and sugar)—and graphs (growth charts)
Language	*English*: play, road safety, beneficial plants, food for the family
Urdu: taking care of health, immunization, helping others

The CtC is a rights-based approach and is grounded in the United Nations Convention on the Rights of the Child. It is used worldwide, and evaluations of it show that it has a positive impact on children's health knowledge and self-esteem. This is because the approach emphasizes directly involving children in acquiring health-related knowledge (physical, mental, social) and developing life skills by promoting understanding rather than exercising persuasion. The approach provides a framework within which children can use inquiry-based learning to extend their knowledge and skills. The CtC approach is thus an educational process that links children's learning with taking action directed at promoting their own health, wellbeing, and development as well as that of their families and their communities (Hawes, 1988; Hubley, 1998). Figure 1 presents a brief summary of the CtC step-by-step educational approach.

In Pakistan, various non-governmental agencies and donor organizations have been using the CtC approach since 1990 in order to create awareness about health issues among children and the community. Much of this work has been conducted in camps for Afghan refugees[2] and in less-developed rural areas, and is generally filtered through school and community-based projects (Child-to-Child Trust, 2011). The Health Action Schools (HAS) project, which is housed at the Aga Khan University Institute for Educational Development, provides one such example.

HEALTH ACTION SCHOOLS: AN EXAMPLE OF A SCHOOL HEALTH PROJECT

The Health Action in Schools (HAS) project began as an initial three-year (1998–2001) action research project in partnership with Save the Children UK. The HAS model is based on WHO's health promoting schools initiative (WHO, 1996a). Its linking of school learning with health action in the home encompasses the CtC approach. The five primary schools in which the project was trialed represented different social (low income to high income) and educational (government and private) contexts. The primary objective of the project was to develop prototypes of health promoting schools in different social and educational contexts in Pakistan.

The teachers who participated in HAS at this time were teaching health content either as a separate subject or across the curriculum via other carrier subjects such as science, language, and social studies. On average, they were teaching 30 lessons per year or one lesson per week, given that, under the HAS model (refer Figure 1), health education topics cannot be taught in one lesson but must be taught over a series of steps that link lessons at school with action at home or in the community. The health topics covered in these lessons ranged from biomedical to social, although the former attracted more emphasis than the latter.

More precisely, the health topics taught can be grouped under three main themes (Kassam-Khamis, Shivji, & Bhutta, 2007):

1. Hygiene and disease prevention (e.g., clean, safe hands, immunization, malaria prevention);
2. Environmental and community health (e.g., clean, safe water, prevention of accidents); and
3. Family and social health (e.g., caring for children who are sick, accommodating children with disabilities, HIV/AIDS prevention).

LEARNING AND DOING: LEARNING PLACE AND LIVING PLACE

Class/school   Home/community

Step 1

Understanding the health topic Learning about diarrhoea and dehydration.

Step 2

Finding out more

(1) A survey at home and with neighbours. Who suffers from it? How is it treated?

(2) Discuss findings. Which babies are most at risk? Which local remedies are helpful?

Step 3

Planning and taking action

(1) Plan action (How can children help to prevent and treat diarrhoea?)

(2) Helping mother at home when the baby has diarrhoea. Washing hands after cleaning the baby's bottom. Telling 'what we learnt at school' why this is important.

(3) Making puppets and preparing our play.

(4) Performing the play in the village square.

Step 4

Evaluation

(1) 'What did we do? How well did our show work? Should we change it next time?'

(2) 'Can we remember all we learnt? Can we all make a rehydration drink?'

(3) Carrying on with actions to prevent and treat diarrhoea at home.

Figure 1. The child-to-child four-step approach (adapted from Hawes, 1997, p. 41).

Monitoring of the HAS project showed that it contributed to improving the health knowledge and self-esteem of the children in the target schools (see, for example, Kassam-Khamis & Bhutta, 2006). It also provided a platform for needs-based professional development for teachers (Carnegie & Kassam-Khamis, 2002; Kassam-Khamis & Bhutta, 2006), with that development geared toward providing teachers with interactive methods of teaching.

Since completing the trial phase of the project, HAS has expanded both nationally and regionally (e.g., Afghanistan, Tajikistan). Research detailing the effectiveness of the project has been shared periodically with government and other stakeholders at different forums, and health promotion courses are now a formal component of certificate- and Master's-level courses at the Agha Kahn University Institute of Educational Development. Another major outcome of the project has been the development of a contextually relevant health education curriculum (i.e., SEHAT 1–5) for primary schools, which is offered in English and Urdu (Kassam-Khamis, Shivji, & Bhutta, 2007, 2008).

The project's expansion called for research designed to explore the classroom practices of teachers, given these are vital to ensuring that HAS, and the CtC umbrella under which it shelters, and to provide children with the right sort of educational experiences. CtC is not only about classroom teaching, as depicted in Figure 1, but also about what happens beyond the classroom boundaries. However, it is the classroom that provides opportunities for structured and spontaneous discussions, a platform for planning and practicing community activities, and a place for reflecting on those activities. What follows is a summary of and reflections on the main results of a study carried out by the author (Bhutta, 2006) that aimed to document health education classroom practices within the Pakistani context.

INSIDE HEALTH EDUCATION CLASSROOMS: REFLECTIONS ON AN EMPIRICAL
STUDY OF HAS CLASSROOMS

The prime aim of the study was to describe and compare health education classroom practice in urban and rural primary school settings in the Sindh province of Pakistan. The health education CtC Classroom Profile and an observational measure adapted from a previous study (Bhutta, 2002) were used to conduct this work.

The classroom profile consists of 32 items descriptive of classroom practice in primary schools. Profile items are organized under six categories:

1. Physical set-up;
2. Classroom interaction;
3. Teaching methods and approaches;
4. Children's involvement in decisionmaking;
5. Planning and monitoring; and
6. Structure of health education activities.

The profile's scoring scheme was adopted from a valid and reliable observational measure, the Early Childhood Environment Rating Scale, which researchers worldwide have long used to assess the quality of early childhood settings (Harms & Clifford, 1980). Each item within the profile is accompanied by a seven-point Likert scale, ranging from 1 (inadequate) to 7 (excellent). The profile was used to conduct structured observations of health lessons in 67 primary classrooms randomly chosen from the HAS schools in urban ($n = 32$) and rural ($n = 35$) areas.

One of the major findings of the study was that health education practices were significantly more "participatory" in nature in rural classrooms than in their urban counterparts ($p < 0.01$). However, neither the urban nor the rural classes reached a level that could be described as "good" (5 on the rating scale). Although the rural teachers had taken health education on board and been supported in their efforts by their school management, they still had a long way to go to achieve a balance of active teaching and active learning in their classrooms.

Balance is a key idea underpinning the CtC approach. In practice, it means a close integration of active teaching and active learning. It also means not working within a loose interpretation of "participatory learning," wherein children always take the lead role and responsibility for their learning. Rather, it means seeing participation from the perspective of "balanced practice," where children benefit from teacher-initiated teaching (e.g., whole-class teaching) while simultaneously exploring for themselves through, for example, group work (Klein, 2001; Perry & VandeKamp, 2000; Siraj-Blatchford, 1999; Siraj-Blatchford & Sylva, 2004).

In order to gain a clearer picture of the balanced approach "in action," the study also looked into the extent to which "whole class teaching" and "group work" were evident in the observed classrooms. The findings of this part of the research revealed that most of the teachers in both urban and rural schools were using whole-class teaching as part of classroom processes. However, the implementation of this form of teaching was different across groups. While most of the rural teachers used pictures, storytelling, and questioning to interact with children, the majority of urban teachers relied either on "chalk and talk" or used "activities" such as reading out a picture story and offering little in the way of interaction with the children. When it came to group work, where children are likely to have more autonomy to discuss and share their ideas, the observations revealed that this approach was more commonly used in rural than in urban classrooms.

However, making children sit together in groups does not necessarily lead to children's involvement. It would be interesting to unpack the examples to gain clearer insight into just what was happening in these instances. In some of the classes, group work seemed to have been interpreted as an approach that lessens teachers' responsibility. Observations revealed that the teachers who were more vigilant during whole-class teaching (e.g., asking questions, talking to the children) "relaxed" after asking the children to form groups. They tended to "patrol" the class instead of interact with the children, or they sat behind their desks marking children's work.

It may seem self-evident, but interacting with children is, for teachers, a fundamentally important means of actively presenting content and ideas within whole-class contexts as well as of scaffolding individual children's learning during group work (Siraj-Blatchford, Odada, & Omagor, 1997). Teacher-initiated interaction provides children with a participatory, yet structured, environment in which to develop basic (e.g., literacy and numeracy), generic (e.g., problem-solving, communication, social), and practical (e.g., making things) skills (Hawes, 2003; St Leger, 2001; St Leger & Nutbeam, 2000; WHO, 1993).

Discussion of the results of the study in various forums focused on the need for teachers to enhance their content knowledge and to learn and practice a variety of management skills so that they can effectively initiate and engage in the two types of interaction. The majority of the research participants, it was concluded, thus needed to further their skills in order to bring a balanced approach, in its truest sense, to their classrooms. They could, for example, have presented content in interactive sessions and facilitated children's work in groups by setting age-appropriate challenging tasks, providing opportunities for purposeful interaction, employing purposeful monitoring, and giving feedback. Within the context of classroom processes conducive to participatory health education, classroom teachers needed to develop the skills necessary to give children autonomy whenever they were working on activities. This meant providing choices and allowing children some control over when and what they did. This approach resonates with Paulo Freire's view of the teacher's role as that of "facilitator," a viewpoint that is sometimes misinterpreted as teachers giving up responsibility (Freire & Macedo, 1999).

Consideration of the study's findings in the light of Jerome Bruner's four models of folk pedagogy (Bruner, 1996) suggests that the two perspectives—active teaching and active learning—are complementary. One cannot sensibly propose that skills and the accumulation of factual knowledge are trivial. No sensible critic would deny that children should know that, because the presentation and acquisition of knowledge is mediated by the interests of the individual (whether teacher or child), everyone involved in these processes needs to share and negotiate his or her perspectives (Bruner, 1996).

The importance of a balanced approach to effective learning cannot be overstated, but it is also necessary to note that one should not expect a miracle when replacing "didactic" teaching, which was observed in most of the classrooms in this research, with participatory approaches. Effectively involving children in teaching and learning activities is a gradual process and cannot be achieved overnight. Change in classroom processes will, and must, occur before this involvement is realized. As is the case with implementation of any educational change, teachers and other educational stakeholders must see the enhancement of children's participation as a gradual process (Fullan, 2001).

CONCLUSION

Many factors—family, peers, school, and community—shape the health perspectives of young people. School, however, plays a critical role in this regard because it serves as a system that bridges the other systems of influence (family, peers, community). In Pakistan, educational policymakers seem to have acknowledged, to some extent, this crucial position of the school. The education policy they put forward acknowledges the importance of health education, and the school curriculum certainly offers ample space to teach health. However, there is an "implementation gap."

Various NGOs have introduced school health programs to address this gap. The Health Action Schools (HAS) approach discussed in this chapter provides a distinctive example of a partnership between schools and the tertiary education sector (in this case, the Aga Khan University), a partnership designed to impart effective health education in classrooms throughout Pakistan. Aga Khan University has made health education a mandatory part of its graduate and certificate courses, and has helped develop contextually relevant health education programs for primary schools. However, these efforts will have little rigor unless the government exercises the discipline needed to close the implementation gap. The other major and related issue hindering implementation of school health plans in need of redress is the predominant use of didactic teaching. Teacher education, both pre- and in-service, needs to focus on providing teachers with the knowledge and skills that allow them to offer children interactive and participatory learning experiences.

The CtC approach provides a model for this type of teacher development. Within the context of health education, the CtC approach is likely to develop differently in different physical and sociocultural contexts. However, active teaching and active learning will always remain its central feature.

Enhancing children's participation means changing the way adults traditionally treat children and the way children traditionally treat adults so that the disparity of power between them is reduced. Such change takes time because both adults and children need to learn new ways of thinking and new skills and to feel confident about their new relationship. It is therefore recommended that teachers and teacher education programs work to identify and build on the positive ways in which children are already participating and then slowly increase the amount of autonomy the children have with respect to decisions about their learning. All the while, teachers, acting as facilitators rather than prescribers, will be learning how to let go so that they and the children can work together democratically.

NOTES

[1] The analysis was guided by WHO's broader definition of health as a state of complete physical, mental, emotional, and social wellbeing and not merely as the absence of disease (WHO, 1996b).
[2] The Afghan war in the 1980s forced millions of inhabitants of Afghanistan to take refuge in neighboring countries. Pakistan has been hosting Afghan refugees since that time.

REFERENCES

Bhutta, S. M. (2002). *Developing health education: The child-to-child classroom profile.* Unpublished Master's dissertation, University of Oxford, Oxford, UK.
Bhutta, S. M. (2006). *Health education classroom practice in primary schools in Pakistan.* Unpublished doctoral thesis, Department of Education, University of Oxford, Oxford, UK.
Bruner, J. (1996). *The culture of education.* Cambridge, MA: Harvard University Press.

Carnegie, R., & Kassam-Khamis, T. (2002). *Quest for quality: An evaluation of the Health Action Schools project.* Unpublished report prepared for Save the Children UK. Karachi, Pakistan: Aga Khan University Institute for Educational Development.

Child-to-Child Trust. (2011). *Children changing their lives (CtC worldwide).* Retrieved from www.child-to-child.org.

Federal Bureau of Statistics. (2009). *Pakistan Social and Living Standards Measurement Survey.* Islamabad, Pakistan: Federal Bureau of Statistics, Government of Pakistan.

Freire, P., & Macedo, D. (1999). *Ideology matters.* Lanham, MA: Rowman and Littlefield Publishers.

Fullan, M. G. (2001). *Leading in a culture of change.* San Francisco, CA: Jossey-Bass.

Harms, T., & Clifford, R. (1980). *Early Childhood Environment Rating Scale.* New York: Teachers College Press.

Hawes, H. (1988). *Child-to-Child: Another path to learning.* Hamburg, Germany: UNESCO Institute for Education.

Hawes, H. (1997). *Health promotion in our schools.* London, UK: Child-to-Child.

Hawes, H. (2003). *Skills-based health education: Content and quality in primary schools with examples from India (Maharashtra State), Uganda and Zambia.* London, UK: UNESCO, Child-to-Child.

Hubley, J. (1998). *School health promotion in developing countries: A literature review.* Leeds, UK: Metropolitan University.

Kassam-Khamis, T., & Bhutta, S. M. (2006). Affecting schools through a health education initiative. In I. Farah & B, Jaworski (Eds.), *Partnerships in educational development* (pp. 219–233). Oxford, UK: Symposium Books.

Kassam-Khamis, T., Shivji, F., & Bhutta, S. M. (2007). *Health Education Curriculum for Classes I–5.* Karachi, Pakistan: Aga Khan University Institute for Educational Development.

Kassam-Khamis, T., Shivji, F., & Bhutta, S. M. (2008). *Health Education Curriculum for Classes I–5.* Karachi: Aga Khan University Institute for Educational Development (Urdu version).

Klein, R. (2001). *Citizen by right: Citizenship education in primary schools.* London, UK: Save the Children and Trentham Books.

Ministry of Education. (2009). *National educational policy 2009.* Islamabad, Pakistan: Ministry of Education, Government of Pakistan.

Pakistan Water Partnership. (2001). *Supplement to the framework for action (FFA) for achieving the Pakistan water vision 2025: Civil society response to FFA.* Islamabad, Pakistan: Pakistan Water Partnership.

Perry, N. E., & VandeKamp, K. O. (2000). Creating classroom contexts that support young children's development of self-regulated learning. *International Journal of Educational Research, 33,* 821–843.

Siraj-Blatchford, I. (1999). Early childhood pedagogy: Practice, principles and research. In P. Mortimore (Ed.), *Understanding pedagogy and its impact on learning* (pp. 20–45). London, UK: Paul Chapman.

Siraj-Blatchford, I., Odada, M., & Omagor, M. (1997). *The school improvement project of the Aga Khan Education Service, Uganda: Evaluation report.* Geneva, Switzerland: Aga Khan Foundation.

Siraj-Blatchford, I., & Sylva, K. (2004). Researching pedagogy in English pre-schools. *British Educational Research Journal, 30,* 713–730.

St Leger, L. H. (2001). School, health literacy and public health: Possibilities and challenges. *Health Promotion International, 16,* 197–205.

St Leger, L. H., & Nutbeam, D. (2000). A model for mapping linkages between health and education agencies to improve school health. *Journal of School Health, 70,* 45–50.

United Nations Children's Fund (UNICEF). (2009). *Statistics.* Retrieved from http://www.unicef.org/infobycountry/Pakistan.

World Health Organization (WHO). (1993). *Life skills education for children and adolescents in schools: Introduction and guidelines to facilitate the development and implementation of life skills programmes in schools.* Geneva, Switzerland: Author.

World Health Organization (WHO). (1996a). *School health promotion, Series 5, regional guidelines: Development of health promoting schools. A framework for action*. Manila, the Philippines: Author.
World Health Organization (WHO). (1996b) *The status of school health*. Geneva, Switzerland: Author.
World Health Organization (WHO). (2009). *World health statistics 2009*. Geneva, Switzerland: Author.

Sadia Muzaffar Bhutta
Aga Khan University
Institute for Educational Development
Karachi
Pakistan
email: sadia.bhutta@aku.edu

MALA SHARDA AND MIKE WATTS

20. HEALTH AND SEX EDUCATION IN INDIA

The Collapse of a Policy

INTRODUCTION

India is truly believed to be a land of values, the epitome of culture and traditions. But there are very definitely clashes of culture. In this chapter, we discuss one such clash: the majority of people in India are orthodox in their beliefs and harbor deep-rooted conservative notions about health issues, particularly those that are sex-related, yet ancient Indian culture was commonly very open about sex, as the legendary book on sex literature, the *Kama Sutra*, and the temples of Khajuraho attest. But, over time, as Went (1985) rightly maintains, sex has become a taboo subject within Indian culture. It is talked about in "hushed tones" within the family, and ignorance is often thought of as being a good thing because it protects young people.

It is not surprising, then, that in Indian schools, health and sex education have long been matters of fierce debate. Questions relating to whether to introduce such issues as part of the curriculum, when to start teaching sex education in schools, how much knowledge to impart, and how to deliver this knowledge always raise many vociferously voiced concerns.

The debate relating to these questions has been fierce within all sections of society, and opinions diverge markedly. Many feel that sex education should be made mandatory because it "is a lifelong learning process of acquiring information, developing skills and forming attitudes and beliefs about sex, sexuality, relationships and feelings" (Patel-Kanwal & Lenderyou, 1998, p. 17). Others argue it should be an optional subject. And others again—a good many—consider it should not be taught at all.

The issue is thus an emotive one that pits modernists against conservatives. The conservative generation, faced with a new generation of young people raised on a diet of Western soap operas, cable television, and increasingly globalized values, battles fiercely to resist change. Progressive educators see the need to develop sex and health education programs in order to combat such endemic health concerns as HIV/AIDS, sexual abuse, and teenage pregnancy.

The increasing incidence of these concerns in the country has brought a new sense of urgency to addressing them. However, attempts by state governments to introduce sex education as a compulsory part of the curriculum have generally received harsh criticism from opposition political parties who claim, for example, that sex education is contrary to Indian culture and would actively mislead

N. Taylor, F. Quinn, M. Littledyke and R.K. Coll (Eds.), Health Education in Context, 183–190.
© 2012 Sense Publishers. All rights reserved.

children. Parents, as well as teachers, raise opposition on both academic and ethical grounds, claiming, for example, that young minds may misinterpret such information.

One thread of the debate relates to efforts made to bring sex-related issues into the open. But this approach, too, has divided educators between those who say that sex education will reduce, for example, HIV/AIDS rates, and their critics who fear it will "corrupt" young minds. In India, textbooks on sex education are attacked as obscene, and are even considered a threat to Indian values.

SEX EDUCATION: THE COLLAPSE OF A POLICY

Alldred and David (2007) rightly call sex education a contentious political topic that, on the one hand, is described as a basic human right and, on the other, as a factor corrupting children's innocence. These two extreme opinions have created considerable turmoil in India.

On 16 November 2005, the Supreme Court of India ruled against the proposal that sex education in schools be brought under the ambit of young people's fundamental rights by making it a part of their "right to education." This judgment was made in response to a public interest litigation filed by a non-government organization (NGO) that suggested sex education should be compulsory in schools. In this instance, the NGO argued that sex education in the school curriculum could do much to check, amongst other concerns, the rise in the number of rape cases in the country (Sharma, 2005).

The debate raged at both national and regional levels. In 2007, the efforts of the Central Board of Secondary Education (CBSE), the country's largest education board, to introduce sex education for all classes in schools under the Adolescence Education Programme (AEP) failed in the state of Maharashtra. At the national level, the Ministry of Human Resource Development and the National AIDS Control Organisation had collaborated with others, including especially the National Council of Educational Research and Training (NCERT), to develop this school-based program, which drew on UNICEF materials. At the regional level, the Maharashtra state government banned CBSE's sex education books, and announced that, henceforth, there would be no plan to introduce the subject in the state's school curriculum.

The AEP, with its primary aim of combating population growth and HIV infection, was set to address issues related to reproductive and sexual health as well as HIV/AIDS. When the Minister of State for School Education announced the program in India's House of Representatives, noisy scenes broke out, with members of the Opposition (some of whom believed that sex education corrupted young minds) shouting slogans and otherwise expressing their anger against the introduction of sex education as a subject in school syllabus. They also tore up the CBSE books ("Maharashtra Government Bans CBSE Sex Education Books," 2007). At this point, the government succumbed to demands from both opposition and ruling party members.

The Maharashtra state government's decision to ban sex education provoked considerable criticism among various people and agencies. The decision was termed regressive: experts denigrated the state government for not consulting stakeholders on this sensitive issue, and demanded that the decision not to allow sex education in schools be immediately retracted. They argued that the matter had to be discussed by everyone involved, and who were likely to be involved, and not determined by political leaders alone ("Decision to Ban Sex Education," 2007).

Following in the footsteps of the Maharashtra state government, as many as 11 of India's 29 other state governments then either suspended or were in the process of dropping sex education altogether from school programs in all state-run schools. The state of Madhya Pradesh, for example, banned sex education in schools on the grounds that the instruction manual for teachers contained obscene illustrations. And according to the chief minister of Madhya Pradesh at that time, Shivraj Singh Chauhan, Indian culture and tradition, not sex education, should be taught to students (Gupta, 2007).

While these local bans were a setback to central government efforts, the implementation of the project remained stalled only during 2007 because the Ministry of Human Resource Development ordered that sex education be implemented in all states from 2008 onwards. The education departments in Maharashtra and the other states consequently had to take steps to formulate a syllabus. On 22 April 2008, the Maharashtra state government unveiled its plan to bring in legislation on "rights to education" that would enable it to introduce sex education in the state on its own terms ("Maharashtra to Bring in Legislation," 2008).

The many divisions were not just at state level, or between local and central government, but also within central government, where various of its members and agencies proposed but then rejected Western-style sex education programs. They argued that these would not help solve the problem of teenage pregnancy but rather exacerbate it by promoting sexual promiscuity. An example of this happenstance is a government report relating to the aforementioned ARP that was issued in March 2009 in response to a citizen-launched petition. Issued by a parliamentary committee of the Rajya Sabha, the upper house of the Indian Parliament, the report rebutted the decision by the Union Ministry of Human Resource Development to implement the AEP. The report's authors stated that the program had "shocked the conscience" of the country, a claim that aligned with comment in some media where, for example, the program was described as "frightening" ("Indian Government: Sex Education," 2009). If implemented, the report's authors said, the program would "promote promiscuity of the worst kind." They rejected the AEP on the grounds that India's "social and cultural ethos was such that sex education had absolutely no place in it" (Sengupta, 2009). The authors also argued that the introduction of sex education in India's schools should at least be delayed until the issue had been fully debated in public.

Religious conservatives rejected outright the initial draft of the AEP's instruction manual, and objected strongly to the idea of sex being discussed openly in classrooms. According to Ram Madhav, a member of the Hindu nationalist Rashtriya Swayamsevak Sangh Organisation, "Sex education is un-Indian" (quoted in McDowall & Dhillon, 2008). Madhav blamed sex education for all serious current issues, such as divorce, adultery, and teenage pregnancy. Malviya (2007) likewise argued that India is a land of culture and values, and that one of the dominant Indian values is to educate children to "hold out against sex." This comment chimes with the view of Dr. Balaji, advisor to NCERT, that "many people think that neither sex education nor AIDS education is compatible with their notion of Indian culture" (Sharma, 2005).

THE NEED

Young people account for almost one quarter of the population in India, and our contention is that their reproductive health needs are generally poorly understood and ill-served. There is lack of attention to almost every dimension of their sexual health, including sexuality, reproductive morbidity, abortion-seeking, and reproductive choice (Jejeebhoy, 1998). The Indian government's coyness about sex education for young people, who are becoming increasingly promiscuous, is fuelling the spread of AIDS ("India's Shyness," 2002). Teenage girls continue to marry and become pregnant. According to the National Family Health Survey 3 (International Institute for Population Sciences, 2005/2006), nearly half of all women in India marry before age 18.

Research continues to reveal how badly India needs sex education. A study conducted by the Ministry of Women and Child Development in 2007 argued that more than 50% of children admitted to having faced one or more forms of sexual abuse. Such children lack the knowledge and the means to protest and are unable to handle these issues adequately.

A four-year study of 500 students by Mamta, a health institute for mothers and children (Mamta Health Institute, 2004), showed that sex education can improve the health of young girls and also control the birth rate. Four schools in the state of Haryana, two urban and two rural, participated in this study, which was conducted in 2004. Before the classes, only about 5% of the rural schoolgirls and 10% of the urban ones had any awareness of condoms. After receiving the sex education classes, as many as 78% of the rural girls and 33% of the urban girls said that they would "decline sex without a condom" (Mamta Health Institute, 2004). Results from this study can be used as evidence in support of implementation of the AEP in school settings.

The aims of sex education are commonly defined in terms of reducing unplanned pregnancies and reducing the spread of sexually transmitted diseases (Thomson, cited in Alldred & David, 2007). Proponents of comprehensive sex education believe that a common approach to sex education is necessary to reduce risky behavior, such as unprotected sex, and to cquip individuals to make informed decisions about their personal sexual activity.

This argument is supported by a survey of 35 sex education projects conducted by the World Health Organization (WHO) in 1993. On the basis of the findings of this study, the researchers involved argued that sex education in schools did not encourage young people to have sex at an earlier age or more frequently (WHO, 1993). Importantly, the survey showed that early sex and relationships education, coordinated with sexual health services, can work: the approach actually delays the start of sexual activity, reduces sexual activity among young people, and encourages those already sexually active to have safer sex.

Researchers have found no support for the contention that sex education encourages sexual experimentation or increased activity (see, for example, WHO, 1993; NHS Centre for Reviews and Dissemination, 1997). Harris (1974, p. 19) convincingly argued that "the more educated a person is, the better he [or she] is able to make a responsible and informed choice between possible courses of behavior."

These and other similar studies support the contention that adolescents should be provided with appropriate information at an appropriate time so they can be educated to take sensible and responsible decisions. Education about sex does not mean leading adolescents on to a forbidden path. Rather, the right knowledge, provided effectively, is highly likely to encourage a healthy approach to sex and relationships.

ARGUMENTS GOING FORWARD

Sengupta (2009) rightly argues that implementation of comprehensive sex education in India continues to be an elusive goal. In such a context, the Maharashtra state government's decision to reject the AEP on the grounds that sex before marriage is "immoral, unethical and unhealthy" and that sex outside marriage is against the social ethos of the country can be easily refuted given the current climate of sexual openness in the mass media in the country (Sengupta, 2009). Such vague concepts of morality and decency seem inadequate in the face of the concrete reality of HIV/AIDS, sexual abuse, and the high incidence of teenage pregnancy. The culture and ethos of any country needs to change with changing times and adapt to shifting realities.

While the traditional rigid mindset that has been a barrier in the way of sex education will take time to change, some NGOs are undertaking exemplary work to both change attitudes and develop sex education programs and resources. They take heart from comments from prominent people such as Renuka Chowdhary, the former Minister of State for Women and Child Development, who has pointed out to the people of India that "sex education does not mean you are encouraging sex, which is how it's interpreted … sex education is insurance for your child: it will protect your child" (Mukherjee, 2007).

Mindful of the vehement opposition to sex education from many politicians and parents, the central Ministry of Human Resource Development has worked toward a compromise by deleting graphic references and explicit phrases from the sex education booklets, including the instruction manual for teachers. These revised versions are, in the words of the health minister, mellowed-down ones. According to Sujatha Rao, who helped draft the revised version of the instruction manual, the message in it remains the same but has been expressed more sensitively and appropriately. For example, all references to homosexuality, which is still a criminal offence in India, have been dropped from the manual. Rao admits that, instead of simply imitating the West when developing sex education resources, those involved in preparing them have to bear in mind India's moral and cultural norms. There is, she says, a huge difference between Western and Eastern ideals.

These sorts of compromise represent a positive step forward. As long as those developing programs and resources keep all the arguments for and against sex education in mind, it should be possible to present sex education as much more than just imparting knowledge about sex and sex-related issues. This area of education also provides a means of helping young people understand and respect their bodies, learn to distinguish between right and wrong, and learn to be responsible human beings. Innovations such as the mobile educational units that visit towns and villages along with comic books used to spread health awareness (Sengupta, 2009) are welcome ones. These relatively small developments are also steps in the right direction.

While schools and colleges in India should become the main hubs for creating awareness of sexual health issues through sex education, parents must be heavily involved in educating their children in these sensitive matters. Unfortunately, experience and research suggests that the majority of parents are not aware of their role in imparting knowledge about sex to their children. According to Alldred and David (2007), adults need to "get real" about teenagers and sex.

CONCLUSION

The situation surrounding the development of and attempts to deliver the AEP is just one instance of the tensions that arise when India's traditions and orthodoxy are faced with serious issues such as high rates of HIV/AIDS, sexual abuse, and teenage pregnancy. We might expect that the social advances surrounding India's booming economy and the strides the country has made in the fields of information and technology would make people more aware of and receptive to the need to actively address these matters through a comprehensive, nationwide program of sex education. As renowned psychiatrist Rajendra Barve states, "Sex education should be about carrying out the duties of an adult, not just sexuality" (Bamzai, 2007). We concur: let the adolescents be equipped with adequate knowledge, and let them decide what is right and wrong for them.

REFERENCES

Alldred, P., & David, M. (2007). *Get real about sex: The politics and practice of sex education.* London, UK: Open University Press.
Bamzai, K. (2007, June 18). The wrong touch. *India Today.* Retrieved from http://www.india-today.com/itoday/20070618/education.html.

Decision to ban sex education comes under fire. (2007, April 15). *Daily News and Analysis*. Retrieved from http://www.dnaindia.com/mumbai/report_decision-to-ban-sex-education-comes-under-fire_1089058.

Gupta, S. (2007, March 20). Chauhan bars sex-education classes in MP. *The Times of India.* Retrieved from http://articles.timesofindia.indiatimes.com/2007-03-20/india/27881394_1_education-classes-aids-awareness-arjun-singh.

Harris, A. (1974). What does "sex education" mean? In R. Rogers (Ed.), *Sex education: Rationale and reaction* (pp. 18–23). London, UK: Cambridge University Press.

Indian government: Sex education "has absolutely no place" in our schools. It "promotes promiscuity." (2009, June 12). *LifeSiteNews.com.* Retrieved from http://www.lifesitenews.com/news/archive/ldn/2009/jun/09061202.

India's shyness towards sexual education fuelling AIDS. (2002, November 1). *The HIV Update International*, *37*(2). Retrieved from http://www.childrensaidsfund.org/resources/upi023.htm#12.

International Institute for Population Sciences. (2005/2006). *National Family Health Survey, India.* Mumbai, India: Author. Retrieved from http://www.nfhsindia.org/factsheet.html.

Jejeebhoy, S. (1998). Adolescent sexual and reproductive behavior: A review of the evidence from India. *Social Science & Medicine*, *46*(10), 1275–1290.

Maharashtra government bans CBSE sex education books. (2007, April 2). *The Hindu.* Retrieved from http://www.hinduonnet.com/2007/04/02/stories/2007040202541100.htm.

Maharashtra to bring in legislation on right to education. (2008). *Indiaserver.com* [website]. Retrieved from http://www.india-server.com/news/maharashtra-to-bring-in-legislation-on-494.html.

Malviya, C. (2007, August 20). Sex education among children in India. *Articlesbase* [website]. Retrieved from http://www.articlesbase.com/home-and-family-articles/sex-education-among-children-in-india-200963.html.

Mamta, Health Institute for Mother and Child [website]. (2004). Retrieved from http://www. mamta-himc.org/.

McDowall, A., & Dhillon, A. (2008, April 6). India censors school sex education booklet. *The Telegraph.* Retrieved from http://www.telegraph.co.uk/news/worldnews/asia/india/1584136/India-censors-school-sex-education-booklet.html.

Mukherjee, K. (2007, July 14). Sex education creates storm in AIDS-stricken India. *The Washington Post.* Retrieved from http://www.washingtonpost.com/wp-dyn/content/article/2007/07/14/AR2007071401390.html.

NHS Centre for Reviews and Dissemination. (1997). *Preventing and reducing the adverse effects of unintended teenage pregnancies.* London, UK: Her Majesty's Stationery Office.

Patel-Kanwal, H., & Lenderyou, G. (1998). *Let's talk about sex and relationships.* London, UK: National Children's Bureau Enterprises.

Sengupta, A. (2009, August 16). India in denial over sex education. *The Guardian.* Retrieved from http://www.guardian.co.uk/commentisfree/2009/aug/16/sex-education-india.

Sharma, P. (2005). Sex education still off the charts. *India Together.* Retrieved from http://www.indiatogether.org/2005/dec/edu-notaboo.htm.

Went, D. (1985). *Sex education: Some guidelines for teachers.* London, UK: Bell & Hyman.

World Health Organization (WHO). (1993). *Effects of sex education on young people's sexual behavior.* Retrieved from http://www.who.int/.

Mala Sharda and Mike Watts
Brunel University
London
United Kingdom
email: Mike.Watts@brunel.ac.uk

21. MALAYSIAN TRADITIONAL KNOWLEDGE AND HERBAL GARDENS

Informal Education on Plant Resources for Health

INTRODUCTION TO HEALTH ISSUES IN MALAYSIA

Malaysia is a country of 329,750 square kilometers. The country's two main regions are separated by the South China Sea, with Peninsular Malaysia at the southern tip of South East Asia, and East Malaysia, comprising the states of Sabah and Sarawak, on the island of Borneo. With a total population of 28 million, Malaysia is a well-known melting pot that includes Malay, Indian, Chinese, Kadazan, Iban, and many other ethnic groups (Department of Statistics Malaysia, 2010). The Malays and the indigenous ethnic groups of Malaysia make up 65% of the population, the Chinese make up 26%, and Indians, 8%. The rest of the population is comprised of other ethnic groups (Department of Statistics Malaysia, 2010).

Once Malaysia gained independence from the British in 1957, the country progressed throughout the following decades. In 1991, the then prime minister announced the target of "Vision 2020," by which time Malaysia aspires to be a self-sufficient industrial, united nation with a confident society that embraces moral values and exhibits desirable behavior. More recently, the current prime minister tabled a remit calling for the Malaysian parliament to focus on three core strategies, one of which is for the country to become a high-income economy. The other two themes are sustainable development and people's welfare. As preparation for the 10th Malaysia Plan (covering the years 2011 to 2015), the 2010 budget provided the context for the new economic model. Under this model, issues of health have certainly become more important, especially with respect to the third core strategy—addressing people's welfare.

The Ministry of Health Malaysia is committed to the Ottawa Charter (Canadian Public Health Association, Health and Welfare Canada, & WHO, 1986), which maintains that health promotion is the process of enabling people to exert control over the determinants of health so that they can improve their own health. The key strategies of health promotion advocated in the charter are building a healthy public policy, creating a supportive environment, developing personal skills, strengthening community action, and re-orienting health services to meet future needs.

The Malaysian government has done reasonably well in addressing health issues and managing emergency health cases. Hospitals and health clinics are

N. Taylor, F. Quinn, M. Littledyke and R.K. Coll (eds.), Health Education in Context, 191–198.
© 2012 Sense Publishers. All rights reserved.

easily accessible even in remote areas where indigenous people live. Several other agencies besides the Ministry of Health provide public healthcare facilities. They include the Ministry of Education, the Ministry of Defense, and other agencies such as the Department of Aboriginal Affairs. Malaysia has more than 200 private hospitals and over 5,000 general practitioners. These numbers include hospitals run and practitioners employed by non-governmental agencies (NGOs) (Li, 2010).

However, like other countries experiencing industrialization, urbanization, and exposure to globalization of fast food products, there is concern in Malaysia about the escalation in the number of overweight and obese adults and children, especially given these problems are associated with many other health problems (WHO, 2002). The number of Malaysians with diabetes has increased by 250% over the past 20 years (Kadir, 2009). Heart, blood pressure, and cancer problems are also becoming significant health issues. Chronic diseases now account for about 70% of all deaths. Obesity is linked with changes in lifestyles and dietary intake. Pre-prepared and fast foods have changed the meal menus in Malaysia. Both parents working and spending less time at home has also contributed to the convenience lifestyle of modern Malaysian families. Traditional local cuisine that is heavy with carbohydrate and fat might have worked well in the past but is no longer suitable for the more sedentary lifestyle of today. Most Malaysians are now free from engaging in physical labor in the tropical heat and are employed in air-conditioned offices with mechanized transport; a very different lifestyle from that of agricultural workers of 40 years ago.

Malaysia has therefore undergone a transition from under-nutrition to relative over-nutrition within a period of 30 years—the fastest rate of decline in underweight prevalence in the East Asia and Pacific regions (UNICEF, 2007). Among the different ethnic groups, overweight levels are highest among Indians, followed by Malays, Chinese, and the Aboriginals (Khambalia & Seen, 2010).

From the early 1990s to 2000, the reported proportion of underweight Malaysian children fell dramatically from 55% to 14.4% while the proportion of overweight children rose from 4% to 9.8%,, mostly in Kuala Lumpur (Kamarzamen, Bruce, & Tan, 2009). In 1996, the National Health and Morbidity Survey reported a 16.6% and 4.4% prevalence of overweight and obesity, respectively. Results show a small rise in overweight adults in the years 1996, 2003, and 2006 (20.7%, 26.7%, 29.1%, respectively) and a much more dramatic increase in obesity in 1996, 2003, 2004, and 2006 (5.5%, 12.2%, 12.3%, 14.0%) (Khambalia & Seen, 2010). It is projected that the prevalence of overweight females 30 years of age and over will rise to 56% by 2015 while figures for males will remain constant at 29% (WHO, 2002).

ENHANCING HEALTH THROUGH PARTNERSHIPS

The mission statement of the Ministry of Health is to build partnerships for health that will facilitate and support people to fully attain their health potential and that will motivate them to appreciate health as a valuable asset and take positive action to sustain it. The contribution of NGOs to this mission is very much recognized.

In Malaysia, various NGOs work on health promotions within society; these tend to be specific to certain health issues. Most partnerships between the Ministry of Health and NGOs have been developed through forums and dialogue; increasing numbers of NGOs are attending the ministry's annual dialogue sessions. The ministry and NGOs often jointly organize public awareness campaigns, which usually take the form of talks, public forums, exhibitions, walks, and runs. The NGOs also support the ministry's health campaigns and programs, such as the Healthy Lifestyle Program and Reduce Sugar Consumption Campaign. NGO support is also required in the health camps and medical camps that the ministry sets up on a community basis. The NGOs furthermore contribute to public health by disseminating health education materials and conducting training directed at capacity building.

Both the government and the informal health sectors promote many programs designed to foster healthy lifestyles and so prevent obesity problems. As part of measures to address obesity problems, the Malaysian Council on Obesity Prevention was formed in January 2008. Given the association between obesity and other health ailments, 13 professional associations and NGOs serve as members of this council. They include the National Diabetes Institute, Malaysian Association for the Study of Obesity, Malaysian Dietitians Association, Malaysian Pediatric Association, National Kidney Foundation of Malaysia, Malaysian Diabetes Association, Federation of Malaysian Consumers Associations, Malaysian Medical Association, Malaysian Endocrine & Metabolic Society, Nutrition Society of Malaysia, National Heart Foundation, and National Heart Association of Malaysia.

The Malaysian Council on Obesity Prevention and its affiliates have identified four priority areas that they, along with other organizations and industry, need to address:

- Research on the prevention of overweight and obesity;
- Incorporating measures designed to combat overweight and obesity into policies and legislations;
- Childhood overweight and obesity prevention;
- Increasing awareness of overweight and obesity (Malaysian Council for Obesity Prevention, 2010).

The council's educational activities include an interactive website, which is freely accessible to members, as well as health events, forums, and discussions.

TRADITIONAL HEALTH REMEDIES FOR OBESITY PREVENTION AND ASSOCIATED DISEASES

Many government agencies are now promoting traditional health remedies as alternatives for holistic health. The relatively low percentage of overweight individuals among the group of Aboriginal or indigenous people is thought to be indicative of their healthier and more natural lifestyles. Many indigenous people still depend on the natural products from the forest and local farms for their medicinal sources as well as for food.

Although medicinal knowledge is often passed on through practices and word of mouth from one generation to the next, there has been an increase in published information—newspapers, magazines, and books—in this area. Promotions by pharmaceutical companies have also intensified as people become more aware that maintaining an ideal weight helps keep the body healthy. Because of their greater exposure, the traditional preventive measures and medicinal plant remedies are increasingly being viewed as a cheaper and a natural way to keep Malaysians healthy. There is heightened interest in traditional health medication and practices for general health and wellbeing and for the treatment of specific ailments.

Because 50% of Malaysia is still forested, medicinal plants from the forest are easily obtainable. Malaysians, down through the generations, have cultivated useful plants in their gardens and backyards for family and community use. Traditional medicine men and women known as *bomoh* are locally available in the villages and are still referred to for many types of physical and spiritual ailments. Medicinal plants are often the usual recommendations in these traditional healing processes.

Medicinal plants are popular because they are relatively easily obtained in forests, backyards, and gardens, are comparatively cheap and effective, and are believed to be natural and without side-effects. In addition, they do not need to be formally prescribed. With the development, 40 years ago, of hospital and clinic facilities, the use of traditional medication lessened but then, 20 years on, began to increase. This was when the medicinal properties of natural products started being researched and documented by research institutes such as the Forest Research Institute of Malaysia, the Malaysian Agriculture Research and Development Institute, the Institute of Medical Research, and the universities. These organizations disseminate their findings to the public and work with companies to commercialize the researched medicinal products.

As a result of the scientific findings of these institutes, several plants have been recently popularized in the form of herbal tea sachets and beverages. These are mainly used for preventing obesity, hypertension, and diabetes. Plants used specifically as anti-hypertensives, for cholesterol reduction, and because of their slimming properties include *Androgaphis paniculata*, *Centella asiatica*, *Cymbopogon citratus*, *Orthosiphon stamineous*, and *Garcinia atroviridis*. Details of their medicinal properties and methods of intake are described by Burkill (1966), Mastura, Izanudin, and Mirfat (2008), and Mastura and Khozirah (2001).

It is timely that government agencies are backing the promotion of medicinal plants, with agencies such as the Forest Research Institute of Malaysia, the Malaysian Agriculture Research and Development Institute, and the Institute of Medical Research, as well as the universities in Malaysia, actively doing research to ensure the safety and the relevance of medicinal plants in the marketplace. The Ministry of Health has an endorsement program for products. The public is informed via newspapers and the internet of products that do not comply. This approach has encouraged many private companies to work with research organizations to ensure that their products are endorsed and thus marketable.

EDUCATION AND TRAINING

With the growth in popularity of medicinal plants comes the need for adequate education and training. Education is beneficial in terms of ensuring continuation of traditional knowledge and keeping culture and traditions alive. It is also essential with respect to ensuring safety and standards. More creative ways of delivering advice and information about natural preventive and alternative methods need to be explored. Dissemination via non-formal and informal education methods offers one important approach, but those involved in this work need to ensure that they remain mindful of scientific findings pertaining to traditional health-care methods and products. Although government agencies are now promoting traditional health remedies in non-formal and informal ways, they have yet to provide well-organized training on traditional medicinal use among villagers and members of the rural population. One reason for this situation may be the notion that local communities know more about this field, not only because it is their normal practice to use such remedies but also because they have passed this knowledge on from generation to generation. That said, there are many traditional knowledge projects in Malaysia associated with the management of natural resources. They focus on learning the old ways and on how to disseminate the information to urban people as well as the international community. The Forest Research Institute of Malaysia has organized various such workshops for communities and relevant stakeholders.

As part of an exercise designed to promote herbs as natural cures and prompt health-care awareness among Malaysians, the Forest Research Institute of Malaysia organized the Herbal Asia conference in 2007 and 2008. Similar conferences were jointly organized with the *Journal of Tropical Medicinal Plants* in 2005 and in 2009. One was specifically dedicated to women's health and Asian traditional medicine (WHAT). The WHAT conference was also supported by the Malaysian Ministry of Science, Technology, and Innovation, the Malaysian Ministry of Women, Family, and Community Development, the Malaysian Ministry of Art, Culture, and Heritage, Malaysia Tourism, and an international team of scientists and traditional medicine practitioners from Oxford University Medical School, and Columbia University, USA. Malaysian scientists from the Forest Research Institute and universities also attended. Under the theme "Promoting Complete Healthcare for Women," the conference focused on Asian healthcare traditions used by generations of women to care for their families and their own health needs (WHAT Medicine, 2009).

Apart from conferences on medicinal plants, many seminars have been held to address issues of health care. These events aim to encourage the use of more herbal plants as alternatives for treatment of ailments such as diabetes and related diseases. Companies such as Nona Roguy and Jamu Mak Dara give talks and lectures, especially to women. Health and beauty care using traditional herbs and natural resources is usually the focus of these seminars and workshops.

Training herbal entrepreneurs and individuals is also necessary to maximize the benefits and safety of traditional medicines. The Forest Research Institute's technical training for herbal entrepreneurs and individuals has provided awareness about extraction techniques and product development practice. Herbal products are now being produced in a safe and cleaner manner. The Herbal Product Quality Improvement Program, a joint effort by the Forest Research Institute and the Ministry of Entrepreneur and Corporative Development, is another example of a quality enhancement program. Ten selected bio-herbal entrepreneurs were trained for 12 months and exposed to various methodologies related to the safety and efficacy of their products. This training is helping these individuals determine that, in accordance with the standards set by the National Bureau of Pharmaceutical Control, their traditional products are safe and of high quality, are effective, and are therefore suitable for sale to the public.

Education through Herbal Gardens

Awareness about the usefulness of plants also needs to be accompanied with education about proper identification of the right plants and awareness of their sources, as well as ensuring the availability of resources. The best way to do this is to introduce "self-developed" herbal gardens. Medicinal gardens are becoming popular, as they can be a source of food and a resource for outdoor education within parks or schools, and they have the added benefit of not requiring as much space as that required by forest trees.

As an institute interested in sustainable use of natural resources, particularly tropical plants, the Forest Research Institute of Malaysia has embarked on many projects related to herbal garden establishments, advising on the choice of species, as well as landscaping techniques for herbal garden establishment, to schools and private holdings. For example, through the Demonstrator Application Grant Scheme's eco-garden projects for schools in the Klang Valley of Malaysia, many schools chose herbal gardens to suit their small compounds. In a project on biodiversity gardens funded by the United Nations Development Programme, the Forest Research Institute advised an NGO, Treat Every Environment Special (TReeS), on creating sustainable gardens. The advice offered encompassed medicinal plants, rainwater harvesting, and composting.

Some schools harvest their garden products for sale. It is very important in this type of project that proper identification and interpretation of the value of natural resources is imparted to teachers and students.

In 2000, an ethno-botanical garden was established within the Forest Research Institute campus, a venture which has added to the forested grounds and provided another attraction for the public. Visitors can learn about medicinal plants, scientifically labeled and interpreted, and backed with research conducted by institute scientists. Kitchen gardens arc also available at the institute. Here, casual visitors can learn about healthy resources, notably spices and herbs. These gardens provide insight into the traditional values of plants and into their use as a healthy alternative to processed food.

Establishing self-made medicinal gardens promotes a healthy, natural, and sustainable life. The physical aspect of gardening can itself be a form of exercise, especially for those in urban areas with a sedentary lifestyle. It will be a good exercise for members of the family and for education in nature as well.

CONCLUSION

The many races with rich backgrounds in traditional knowledge in Malaysia mean that the country's citizens have the option of practicing traditional exercises and alternative medication. Many consider these to be more natural and usually much less costly than Western-developed pharmaceutical products and gymnasium facilities.

We cannot over-emphasize that people and organizations need to work together to promote health issues in Malaysia. Events co-organized by government agencies and NGOs are good examples of how traditional health methods can be promoted and made safe. Conferences, workshops, and other forms of training organized by commercial, technical, and practical organizations are also very useful. The work being conducted at the Forest Research Institute of Malaysia provides evidence of the increasing demand for training in traditional health. This demand, of itself, is indicative of earlier, successful dissemination of information about Malaysia's traditional health care and medicines.

Although health education in Malaysia has yet to be proven effective in reducing cases of chronic disease associated with unhealthy lifestyles and obesity, both formal and informal education need to be continued. Such ongoing education will help to ensure that Malaysian health promotion is successful in building a healthy public policy, creating a supportive environment, developing personal skills, strengthening community action, and re-orienting health services to meet future needs.

REFERENCES

Burkill, I. (1966). *A dictionary of the economic products of the Malay Peninsula* (2nd ed.). Kuala Lumpur, Malaysia: Ministry of Agriculture and Co-Operatives.

Canadian Public Health Association, Health and Welfare Canada, & WHO. (1986). *Ottawa Charter for Health Promotion.* Presented at the First International Conference on Health Promotion, Ottawa, Canada, November 21, 1986. Retrieved from http://www.who.int/hpr/NPH/docs/ottawa_charter_hp.pdf.

Department of Statistics Malaysia. (2010). *Official website of the Department of Statistics, Malaysia.* Retrieved from http://www.statistics.gov.my/portal/index.php?option=com_content&view=category&id = 35&Itemid=53&lang=en.

Kadir, K. (2009, July 8). Malaysians facing diabetes "catastrophe". *Monash University Newsletter* (online). Retrieved from http://www. monash. edu.au/news/monashmemo/stories/20090708/uni-news1.html.

Kamarzamen, S., Bruce, N., & Tan, G. (2009). *Childhood Obesity in Malaysia study.* Perth, Western Australia: Centre for Integrated Human Studies, University of Western Australia. Retrieved from http://www.ihs.uwa.edu.au/research/obesity-malaysia.

Khambalia, A. Z., & Seen, L. S. (2010). Trends in overweight and obese adults in Malaysia (1996–2009): A systematic review. *International Association for the Study of Obesity, 11*(6), 403–412.

Li, J. (2010, January 7). Building a healthy Malaysia. *Asia-Pacific FutureGOV* (online newsletter). Retrieved from http://www.futuregov.asia/articles/2010/jan/07/building-healthy-malaysia/.

Malaysian Council for Obesity Prevention. (2010). *Malaysian Council for Obesity Prevention official website*. Retrieved from http://www.preventobesity.my/article.php?aid=14.

Mastura, M., Izanudin, Z., & Mirfat, A. H. S. (2008). *Khazanah Alam Untuk Kesihatan dan Kecantikan* [Khazanah Alam for health and beauty]. Kepong, Selangor, Malaysia: Forest Research Institute Malaysia.

Mastura, M., & Khozirah, S. (2001). Cures from the forest. In J. L. P. Wong (Ed.), *Forestry and forest products R&D in FRIM* (pp. 88–98). Kepong, Selangor, Malaysia: Forest Research Institute Malaysia.

National Cancer Council. (2010). *National Cancer Council of Malaysia official website*. Retrieved from http://www.makna.org.my/services.asp.

United Nations Children's Fund (UNICEF). (2007). *Health education in Malaysia*. Retrieved from http://www.unicef.org/ malaysia/health_education_7258.html.

WHAT Medicine. (2009). *Natural remedies for health and wellness, 19–21 June 2009*. Retrieved from http://www.whatmedicine.org/.

World Health Organization (WHO). (2002). *The impact of chronic disease in Malaysia*. Retrieved from http://www.who.int/chp/chronic_disease_report/media/impact/malaysia.pdf.

Noor Azlin Yahya and Nor Azah Mohd. Ali
Forest Research Institute Malaysia (FRIM)
Kepong
Selangor
Malaysia
email: azlin@frim.gov.my

22. SUPPORTING HEALTH EDUCATION IN THAI CONTEXTS

Conceptualizing and Evaluating the Change

BACKGROUND

Thailand, located in the center of Southeast Asia, covers an area of 513,115 square kilometers. Thailand is a constitutional monarchy and the King is highly respected by all Thais. Thailand's population is relatively homogeneous. Of the 64 million citizens, an estimated 10 million live in Bangkok, the capital city. Thai is the national and official language; over 85% of the population speaks a dialect of Thai, while English is widely spoken and understood in major cities, particularly in business circles and tourist areas. The primary religion in Thailand is Buddhism, which has a large influence on the culture and attitudes of Thai people. Thailand experienced rapid economic growth between 1985 and 1995, and is a newly industrialized country that greatly benefits from tourism.

According to the mores of Thai culture, people respect one another as sisters and brothers, and social relationships are very important. Members of extended families and local society have traditionally had a strong influence on people's behaviors (Pinyuchon & Gray, 1997). However, that influence is waning as families in Thailand have become smaller, with extended families increasingly being replaced by nuclear families. Family size began to decrease markedly between 1999 and 2002. Today, only about 30% of families can be classified as extended.

The decrease in the number of extended families has meant that parents have had to assume more responsibility for day-to-day care of their children, but typically do not have sufficient time to do this. Society has also become more individualized and people more independent of one another. Children and youth now spend more time within the school setting than any other context. Commentators agree that schools have thus become the most important influence in children's and young people's lives. As such, schools today play a critical role in the healthy development—including physical, behavioral, and moral—of Thailand's youngsters.

HEALTH EDUCATION IN THE THAI CURRICULUM

In 1960, the Ministry of Education of Thailand specified its National Health Recommendation (NHR). This not only established good health as an important principle guiding health education within primary schools but also provided 10

N. Taylor, F. Quinn, M. Littledyke and R.K. Coll (eds.), Health Education in Context, 199–210.

guidelines on healthy behaviors and practices. In 1978, health education, science, and social science were integrated into the education curriculum as "life experience subjects," and the NHR was defined according to a new term—"health behavior."

In 1992, the Ministry of Public Health of Thailand began to reform the NHR in response to a rapid increase in various health problems. The key emphasis this time was on children's and young people's health-related behaviors, and it was given impetus through six goals pertaining to personal health, food and nutrition, exercise, mental health, accidents, and environmental health.

On 28 May 1996, the government approved the new NHR, which again included 10 guidelines on healthy behaviors and practices.

1. Keep your body and belongings clean.
2. Take care of your teeth by brushing them correctly after meals.
3. Wash your hands before eating and after using the toilet.
4. Eat cooked food and avoid food containing artificial coloring, additives, or preservatives.
5. Avoid indulging in cigarette smoking, alcohol, drugs, gambling, and many sexual affairs.
6. Cultivate a warm relationship in the family.
7. Prevent accidents by being careful.
8. Engage in regular exercise and have a health examination once a year.
9. Keep your mind clean and healthy at all times.
10. Maintain a strong civic sense with regard to both public and community property (see also Health Education Division, Ministry of Public Health, 1990, 1999; Sukabanyad, 2010).

The education reforms of 1999 were followed in 2001 by development of Thailand's Basic Education Curriculum, with health education addressed in the subject areas of health and physical education. Health education thus became one subject taught across all grade levels (i.e., 1 to 12) of basic education (Department of Curriculum and Instruction Development, Ministry of Education, 2002). One of the goals set out under the five standards of the new curriculum established physical exercise as a means of securing good physical and mental health. Success indicators with respect to health education for all grade levels aligned with the following practices and situations:

- Eating foods that are healthy and meet daily nutrition requirements;
- Engaging in regular exercise;
- Preventing behaviors detrimental to good health—illness, accidents, addictive substances, "vices";
- Performing actively and rigorously;
- Experiencing warm, secure human relationships and (as a corollary) emotional wellbeing;
- Meeting normative standards of physical and mental growth and development.

The most recent reform of the national curriculum for basic education—the 2008 Basic Education Core Curriculum for Grades 1 to 12—again positioned health within the learning areas of health and physical education (Department of Curriculum and Instruction Development, Ministry of Education, 2008). This time, key aims concerned strengthening and maintaining good health and bringing about a good quality of life for individuals, families, and communities. The new curriculum makes specific the need for learners to *concurrently* develop attitudes and behaviors that allow them to secure knowledge, acquire a sound system of values, act morally, and adopt healthy practices.

The subject area of health and physical education within the 2008 curriculum includes five strands, each of which covers a number of standards, as outlined by the Bureau of Academic Affairs and Education Standards, Office of Basic Education Commission, Ministry of Education (2009).

1. *Human Growth and Development*
    Standard H1.1—Understanding the nature of human growth and development
2. *Life and Family*
    Standard H2.1—Understanding and appreciating family: the focus is on sex education, life skills
3. *Movement, Physical Exercise, Games, Thai and International Sports*
    Standard H3.1—Understanding and possessing kinesthetic skills: the focus is on movement, physical exercise, games, and sports
    Standard H3.2—Developing a preference for and engaging in physical exercise: the focus is on regularly playing games and sports, observing rights, rules, and regulations, exhibiting both a sporting and a competitive spirit, and appreciating the aesthetics of sports
4. *Robust Health, Sickness Prevention, Health Capacity*
    Standard H4.1—Appreciating the need to strengthen and maintain one's health: the focus is on the skills and practices that lead to and maintain good health, including practices that prevent sickness and increase capacity for maintaining good health
5. *Safety throughout Life*
    Standard H5.1—Preventing and avoiding risk factors: the focus is on behaviors detrimental to health, such as accidents, drugs and addictive substances, and violence.

HEALTH EDUCATION ISSUES IN THAILAND

Although Thailand's health curriculum has kept pace with societal changes, health problems such as obesity and HIV have become major concerns. Rapid urbanization and modernization have adversely affected the lifestyles of many children, who now tend to consume more fast food and do less exercise than their predecessors. They also spend a considerable portion of their time on computers and the internet and can more easily than children of the past access sexual material and violent games and movies. Today, children are at greater risk of obesity, developing aggressive behaviors, and engaging in unsafe sexual practices. These developments could be seen as evidence that health education is not achieving its goals. The validity of this perception can be gauged from the following discussion of the issues just mentioned.

HIV/AIDs and Sex Education

In 1997, the World Bank concluded from relevant data that combining public education with targeted interventions (such as condom distribution) in Thailand was an effective means of lowering the incidence of HIV/AIDS in Thailand. However, a report recently published by the National AIDS Prevention and Alleviation Committee (2010) revealed that the main risk group for HIV in Thailand has become young people. Premarital sex has become more common among young Thais, and their first sexual encounter typically occurs when they are between 14 and 18 years of age. This statistic also shows that Thailand's young people are beginning sexual activity earlier than past generations of Thais (Institute for Population and Social Research, Mahidol University, 2006; Isarabhakdi, 2000). Also, it seems that only 20% to 30% are consistently using condoms, although the available data on this matter are not recent (Reproductive Health Division, Ministry of Public Health, 2003).

Nevertheless, it is clear that unsafe sex among young people has made them increasingly vulnerable to sexually transmitted diseases and HIV infection. Between 1984 and 2003, the rate of HIV infection in people aged 10 to 24 years reached just over 11% of the total HIV/AIDS population. There is conjecture that around 85% of Thai youth are not concerned about HIV. Gasonbou's (2005) study of the incidence of AIDS and unwanted pregnancies through unsafe sex in a group of Grades 8 through 11 Thai students revealed that these young people were the ones most likely in the Thai population to engage in high-risk behavior in relation to AIDS. The findings also showed that females younger than 19 had the highest pregnancy rate of any group of women in the reproductive age bracket.

In 2008, about 77,000 female adolescents gave birth. Young women who become pregnant have to leave school, which means they miss out on completing their education (Iamyaem, 2005). However, at the time of writing, the Ministry of Public Health was endeavoring to push a Reproductive Health and Privacy Protection Bill through government, the provisions of which would allow pregnant students to continue their studies (Information and Public Relations Office, Ministry of Public Health, 2010). Whatever the outcome of this initiative is, teenage pregnancy is an issue within Thai culture that needs to be seriously discussed.

The need for children and adolescents to receive sex education of a kind that will help address the above problems should have been made more explicit in health policy. That it has not is probably because of cultural sensitivity about sexual matters (Pinyuchon & Gray, 1997; Thato, Jenkins, & Dusitsin, 2008). Sex education in schools is academic in nature, focusing upon the biology of sexual reproduction but not on sexual *practice* in a social context. In Thai culture, sexual activity is typically framed as something that should occur between a husband and wife, and sex between unmarried young people is unacceptable. Open discussions between parents and young people or in classrooms about sex are generally taboo (Noppakunthong, 2007). Thus, sexual intercourse among teenagers remains clandestine.

One attempt to address this issue involved a television campaign (launched in 2007) promoting condom use. The campaign was not well received, with some arguing that it was antithetical to Thai culture and encouraged sexual activity among teenagers. These attitudes undermined the influence of the campaign. So, too, did school textbooks, which were not up to date with the changing mores of Thailand's young people and the risks they were taking with respect to pregnancy and contracting sexually transmitted diseases, including HIV. Helping young people understand not only the mechanics but also the emotions associated with sex—desire, pleasure, and love—tends to be a part of health and sex education overlooked by teachers; the same can be said of adolescents' sexual rights, such as knowing how to engage in safe sex. This situation again reflects the mainstream perspective of Thai society that sex is a distasteful and obscene matter and so is not an appropriate classroom subject.

However, the government has not been entirely remiss in recent years. Various agencies have been developing more comprehensive sex-education resources and working to educate parents on sexuality, in the hope of equipping them with the skills to discuss sex and sexuality with their children. These developments are commensurate with the government's recent long-term plan (2002 to 2011) with respect to children and youth development.

In 2003, the first sex education guidebooks for Thai teachers, *Grades 6–11 Comprehensive Sexuality Education*, were developed by PATH (HIV Policy.org— an online database of HIV/AIDS policies for the Pacific region). PATH received support for this work from the Global Fund to Fight AIDS, Tuberculosis, and Malaria and from the Ministry of Public Health. The guidebooks were piloted in 118 primary and secondary schools during 2003 to 2006 and were then sent out, after being launched by the Ministry of Education, to schools nationwide in 2007. The guidebooks provide teachers with stories, learning activities, and tips, and cover six areas—sexual development, interpersonal relationships, prevention of sexual harassment, sexual behavior, sex-related health issues, and sex within societal and cultural contexts (PATH, 2007). Teachers also had opportunity at this time to attend teacher training/orientation programs on AIDS and sex education. Organized by government and non-governmental agencies at national, regional, and provincial levels, the programs trained a large number of school teachers in how to teach these areas more effectively.

These formal school-based efforts have been accompanied by informal community-based education initiatives. In recent years, the United Nations Population Fund, World Health Organization, and the Thai government have given the Department of Health's Family Planning Population Division as well as non-governmental organizations (NGOs) in Thailand money to produce documents, leaflets, cassette tapes, articles, and handbooks relating to reproductive health. The money has also been used to mount nationwide radio campaign programs. The many healthcare services around the country, such as the Integration of

Reproductive Health Services, Health Promotion Hospital, and the Model of Adolescent Reproduction Health Service (Reproductive Health Division, Ministry of Public Health, 2003) have also been working to educate people about reproductive health.

Obesity

Obesity has become a major health problem in many countries, both developed and developing (Kantachuvessiri, 2005), and Thailand has not been immune. A report documenting a Thailand food nutrition survey shows a considerable increase in the prevalence of obesity among school-children. From 1995 to 2003, the proportion of primary school children classified as obese rose from 10% to 15%; the corresponding increase among secondary school students was 10% to 17% (Health Education Division, Ministry of Public Health, 2009). In 2007, Aree et al. (2007) explored the nutrition status of 5,773 adolescents (Grades 5–9) in two schools in northern Thailand. They found that 14.7% of the students surveyed were overweight, and 7.5% were obese. The Thailand Global School-Based Students' Health Survey in 2008 found that 4.4% of students in Grades 7 to 10 (ages 13–15) were overweight (Kramomtong, Pujchakarn, & Junpong, 2010).

The critical factors associated with the increases in weight and obesity are unhealthy food choices and lack of physical activity. According to recent evidence (e.g., Health Education Division, Ministry of Public Health, 2010), just over 40% of Thai students consume unhealthy snacks and soft drinks five or more days a week. Kramomtong et al. (2010) reported that only 15.3% of the students they surveyed had engaged in active physical exercise for at least 60 minutes per day during the previous seven days. In addition, 37.6% of the survey respondents reported sitting in front of the television or computer for more than three hours a day over the past week.

A report put out by the National Statistical Office Thailand (2010) confirmed that children and youth are the biggest group of computer users in the Thai population. Just over 60% of children 6 to 14 years of age and 55% of young people 15 to 24 years of age said they used computers. The study, conducted during 2007 and 2008, also reported that 13.3% of Thai children and youth between 9 to 15 years of age had become addicted to computer games, and that the games that they preferred involved fighting, sex, and special (armed) forces. This information adds to concerns about the adverse effects of this involvement on Thai children and youth, such as health problems, misconceptions about sex, and aggressive behavior.

In the curriculum for basic education, food and nutrition are part of science and health education. Students learn about healthy food, unhealthy food, and the type and amount of nutrition that are appropriate at each age level. Students in all grades also undertake physical education at least one hour a week. However, this information and level of activity are not enough to encourage children and young people to adopt good health behaviors.

One way that schools can make what provision is available more effective is to forge collaborations with families and communities. Korwanich, Sheiham, Srisuphan, and Sisilapanan (2008) found that parents, school staff, and community members, working together, have a strong influence on reducing children's consumption of unhealthy food. This type of activity is supported by campaigns launched by government agencies. Examples include the Ministry of Public Health's *Suitable Eating for Thai Happiness*, the Ministry of Public Health and the Department of Health's *KhonThai Raipoong* ("No Tummy") and *Global Strategy on Diet, Physical Activity, and Health*, and the Thai Health Promotion Foundation's *To Move Equals to Exercise*, *After School Exercise*, and *There Are Always Opportunities to Exercise*.

Aggressive Behavior

Thailand is witnessing an increase in the number of children and young people involved in such activities as fighting, gang violence, crime, and motorbike racing. Over the five years prior to 2009, the number of young people charged with property-based offences increased, on average, 13.2% per year. Illegal drug use rose by an average of 14.9% per year, and physical violence 12.1% per year (Kanchanachitra et al., 2009). These increases are reflected in the number of juvenile vocational training centers in Thailand. In 1952, there was only one center. By 2006, there were 76 (Meepien, Iamsupasit, & Suttiwan, 2010).

Another issue of increasing and major concern in Thailand, especially over the last five or so years, is that of students from different schools fighting one another in public. This behavior is mostly seen among males, but incidents involving females have also been recorded. These incidents are often captured in video clips and then sent to other young people via mobile phones or are posted on websites. In addition, more Thai female students than ever before are engaging in at-risk behaviors that have generally been associated with males, notably drinking, frequenting entertainment venues, and having more than one sexual partner at the same time (Kanchanachitra et al., 2009).

The increasing severity and complexity of the types of violence now being perpetrated by children and young people reflect the weaknesses of formal and informal education, particularly in terms of Thai society not facing up to and addressing these challenges. As mentioned earlier, families of today tend to be smaller, which means parents have to assume responsibility for child care and moral development formerly undertaken by older members of the family (grandparents, aunts, and uncles). Work commitments mean that parents have less time to spend with their children. Young people are becoming increasingly materialistic and spoiled. Family, community, and religious institutions are becoming weaker, while the mass media, particularly television and internet, are becoming more accessible and difficult to control.

The findings of a study conducted by Mathews, Kronenberger, Wang, Lurito, Lowe, and Dunn (2005) revealed that adolescents who play violent videogames for as little as 30 minutes can experience strong and violent emotions. According to

Meepien et al. (2010), if no effort is made to curtail aggressive behavior in children and adolescents, this behavior will continue to increase with serious consequences for both the young people involved and society. Again, one of the best means of addressing concerns relating to aggression and violence amongst youngsters is likely to be through school-based initiatives and collaborative work with parents and communities.

HEALTH EDUCATION PROJECTS

Over time, Thailand has implemented highly successful government-sponsored health care projects. These include family planning, childhood immunizations, and control of infectious diseases, such as the influenza viruses H5N1 and H1N1. Most of these health care projects draw on the idea of collaboration between health institutes, family, and communities. By 2007, Thailand had over 800,000 health volunteers nationwide engaged in this work, with the Society and Health Institute playing a support role (Chuengsatiansup & Suksuth, 2007). Thailand also benefits from several cooperative projects that are supported by organizations such as the Ministry of Public Health, WHO, and NGOs. The following account provides brief descriptions of health care projects and organizations that have particular relevance for health education within Thailand's schools and wider community.

- *Health Promoting Schools (HPS) Program:* evident in many primary and secondary schools throughout Thailand, this program is overseen by the Ministry of Public Health and WHO. The program provides a good example of how collaboration facilitates the provision of health education for children and youth in both formal and informal educational contexts. By 2003, 84% of public primary and secondary schools were participating in the HPS program. Of these schools, 21% had achieved all of the standards criteria set down by the program (Reproductive Health Division, Ministry of Public Health, 2003).
- *PATH:* this database, mentioned earlier in this chapter, has received official recognition from Thailand's International Development Cooperation Agency (TICA), which has operated under the auspices of Thailand's Ministry of Foreign Affairs since 1980. It also has projects that target students and sex educators in secondary schools. One project, which encourages students to talk openly about sexual issues and sexual rights, has been linked to a drop in unwanted pregnancies among participating students (PATH, 2007). PATH also utilizes contemporary media, including website and interactive information and communications technology, to promote (e.g., through role plays) sexual health.
- *The Thai Health Promotion Foundation (ThaiHealth):* established in 2001 under the Health Promotion Foundation Act 2001, the foundation is one of the most important health promotion organizations in Thailand. ThaiHealth acts as a catalyst for projects that work to change values, lifestyles, and social environments under the banner of "Sustaining the Wellbeing of Thai People." Its health-promotion efforts reach out to Thai people of all ages in accordance with various aspects of the country's national health policies: reducing the

consumption of alcoholic beverages and tobacco; building the capacity of communities to address health issues; carrying out research to determine the elements of effective health promotion; and developing information campaigns directed at building health-related awareness and, from there, changing attitudes and behaviors.

Most of the foundation's campaigns use various means to communicate health promotion to the public. These include social marketing and sponsorship of sports, the arts, and popular culture (ThaiHealth, 2008). A particular example is the Science Projects for Better Health initiative, which is a collaboration between the foundation and Thailand's National Science and Technology Development Agency. The main aim of this project is to encourage young people to develop life skills through the medium of science projects. Between the middle of 2007, when the project began, and 2010, Thailand's young people had developed over 700 health science projects (Science and Health, 2010).

CONCLUSION

It is readily understood that the health problems that Thailand's children and young people of today are experiencing arise not only out of lack of understanding and knowledge but also out of rapid changes within Thai society. Social change inevitably affects children's and young people's lifestyles, which can become characterized by health and social problems, such as HIV, engaging in risky sexual behaviors, obesity, and aggression. Despite health education being a clear component of Thailand's core curriculum for Grades 1 to 12, these health problems have continued to escalate. This escalation indicates that health education in both formal and informal contexts is not being sufficiently effective. Addressing this situation requires modifying the curriculum—in terms of both content and implementation—to meet the demands of social change.

Because the health issues discussed in this chapter are matters that need to be addressed by parents, teachers, and society, collaboration between and across schools and homes is likely to be one of the best remedial actions. Certainly, this approach has proved effective with respect to other health care initiatives in Thailand, such as immunization. Implementation of this model, along with the fact that health education in Thailand receives strong support from many organizations, both governmental and non-governmental (and national and international) should provide a platform from which Thailand can continue its efforts to facilitate attitudes and behaviors conducive to good health amongst its youngest citizens.

REFERENCES

Aree, P., Wangsrikhun, S., Kantawang, S., Boonyasopun, U., Kumwong, P., Buranapin, S., Sennone, P., Tananoon, P., Wongchettha, S., Danosuwon, R., & Sennone, S. (2007). Nutritional status, food consumption, and physical activity in adolescents: A pilot study. *Nursing Journal, 34*(2), 98–104.
Bureau of Academic Affairs and Education Standards, Office of Basic Education Commission, Ministry of Education. (2009). *Benchmarks and core standards for health and physical education learning*

area following core education curriculum B.E. 2551 (2008). Nontaburi, Thailand: The Agricultural Co-operative Federation of Thailand Publisher.

Chuengsatiansup, K., & Suksuth, P. (2007). Health volunteers: Potentials and development strategies in the context of changes. *Mohanamai, 17*(3), 7–20.

Department of Curriculum and Instruction Development, Ministry of Education. (2002). *Basic education curriculum B.E. 2544 (A.D. 2001).* Bangkok, Thailand: The Express Transportation Organization of Thailand Publisher.

Department of Curriculum and Instruction Development, Ministry of Education. (2008). *Basic Education Curriculum B.E. 2551 (A.D. 2008).* Bangkok, Thailand: The Express Transportation Organization of Thailand Publisher.

Gasonbou, C. (2005). *The effects of a participatory learning sexual health education program on self-efficacy of sexual health behaviors among 6th grade students.* Unpublished Master's thesis, Mahidol University, Bangkok, Thailand. Retrieved from http://mulinet10.li.mahidol.ac.th/e-thesis/4336844.pdf.

Health Education Division, Ministry of Public Health. (1990). *Guidelines for extra-curriculum activities following national health recommendations in secondary school.* Nontaburi, Thailand: The Agricultural Co-operative Federation of Thailand Publisher.

Health Education Division, Ministry of Public Health. (1999). *National health recommendations.* Nontaburi, Thailand: Author.

Health Education Division, Ministry of Public Health. (2009). *Health Education Division highlights projects in 2009* [PowerPoint presentation]. Nontaburi, Thailand: Author.

Health Education Division, Ministry of Public Health. (2010). *Thai children's health standards* (draft). Bangkok, Thailand: Author.

Iamyaem, W. (2005). *One-night stands among adolescents in Bangkok metropolis.* Unpublished Master's thesis, Chulalongkorn University, Bangkok, Thailand.

Information and Public Relations Office, Ministry of Public Health (2010, July 12). *Jurin [Public Health Minister] pushes draft of Reproductive Health and Privacy Protection Act to all health care center services for consultation on ensuring reproductive health for all ages* (press release). Retrieved from http://www.moph.go.th/show_hotnew.php?idHot_new=32799,%2012%20Aug%202010.

Institute for Population and Social Research, Mahidol University. (2006). *Thai health 2006.* Nakhorn Pathom, Thailand: Institute of Population and Social Research.

Isarabhakdi, P. (2000). *Sexual attitudes and experience of rural Thai youth.* Nakhorn Pathom, Thailand: Institute for Population and Social Research, Mahidol University.

Kanchanachitra, C., Podhista, C., Archavanitkul, K., Pattaravanich, U., Siriratmongkhon, K., Tipsuk, P., & Jarassit, S. (2009). *Thai health 2009: Stop violence for well-being of mankind.* Nakhon Pathom, Thailand: Institute for Population and Social Research, Mahidol University.

Kantachuvessiri, A. (2005). Obesity in Thailand. *Journal of the Medical Association of Thailand, 88*(4), 554–562.

Korwanich, K., Sheiham, A., Srisuphan, W., & Sisilapanan, P. (2008). Promoting healthy eating in nursery school children: A quasi-experimental intervention study. *Health Education Journal, 67*(1), 16–30.

Kramomtong, P., Pujchakarn, S., & Junpong, P. (2010). Thailand Global School-Based Student Health survey 2008. *Thailand Journal of Health Promotion and Environmental Health,* April–June, 53–72.

Mathews, V. P., Kronenberger, W. G., Wang, Y., Lurito, J. T., Lowe, M. J., & Dunn, D. W. (2005). Media violence exposure and frontal lobe activation measured by functional magnetic resonance imaging in aggressive and nonaggressive adolescents. *Journal of Computer Assisted Tomography, 29*(3), 287–292.

Meepien, D., Iamsupasit S., & Suttiwan, P. (2010). Effects of self-control training to reduce aggressive behaviors of female adolescent offenders in Ban Pranee Juvenile Vocational Training Center. *Journal of Health Research, 24*(1), 35–38.

National AIDS Prevention and Alleviation Committee. (2010). *UNGASS country progress report Thailand.* Retrieved from http://data.unaids.org/pub/Report/2010/thailand_2010_country_progress_report_en.pdf.

National Statistical Office Thailand. (2010). *ICT household 2009.* Bangkok, Thailand: Statistical Forecasting Bureau, National Statistical Office.

Noppakunthong, V. (2007, September 4). Talking about sex in the classroom. *Bangkok Post.* Retrieved from http://www.bangkokpost.com/education/site2007/cvse0407.htm.

PATH. (2007). *Comprehensive sexuality education for Grades 6–11 students.* Bangkok, Thailand: Author.

Pinyuchon, M., & Gray, L. A. (1997). Understanding Thai families: A cultural context for therapists using a structured approach. *Contemporary Family Therapy, 19*(2), 209–228.

Reproductive Health Division, Ministry of Public Health. (2003). *Thailand reproductive health profile.* Retrieved from Regional Office for South-East Asia, WHO website: http://www.searo.who.int/LinkFiles/Reproductive_Health_Profile_completebook.pdf.

Science and Health. (2010, August). *Pueng Sangsuk Newsletter, 5,* 2–3.

Sukabanyad. (2010). *History of Sukabanyad.* Retrieved from http://www.sukabanyad.com/history/history_1.php.

ThaiHealth (Thai Health Promotion Foundation). (2008). *Annual report 2008.* Retrieved from http://documents.scribd.com.s3.amazonaws.com/docs/7jhfu9v534m552v.pdf?t=1279714522.

Thato, R., Jenkins, R. A., & Dusitsin, N. (2008). Effects of the culturally-sensitive comprehensive sex education programme among Thai secondary school students. *Journal of Advanced Nursing, 62*(4), 457–469.

World Bank. (1997). *Confronting AIDS: Public priorities in a global epidemic.* New York: Oxford University Press.

Tussatrin Kruatong
Kasetsart University
Nakhon Pathom
Thailand

Chanyah Dahsah
Srinakharinwirot Unviersity
Bangkok
Thailand
email: chan_yah@yahoo.com

EMMY MAN YEE WONG AND MAY MAY HUNG CHENG

23. PRIORITIES FOR HEALTH EDUCATION IN HONG KONG IN RELATION TO NON-COMMUNICABLE DISEASES

BACKGROUND

Chronic non-communicable diseases (NCDs) are increasing rapidly worldwide and therefore have considerable implications for health education. Like other advanced countries, Hong Kong, which is a special administrative region of Mainland China, has experienced an epidemiological transition wherein chronic NCDs have overtaken communicable diseases as the major cause of mortality and morbidity. Registered deaths due to infectious and parasitic diseases decreased from 10.1% in 1964 to 2.8% in 2004, while the mortality rate due to neoplasms and diseases of the circulatory system increased twofold, from 30.9% to 59.5% in the same period of time (Department of Health, 2008a).

This epidemiological transition relates largely to rapid changes in the economic, social, and demographic conditions brought about by Mainland China's introduction of economic reforms and its open policy in the 1970s (Wong & Shen, 2002). The effective economic management of Mainland China accelerated industrialization, urbanization, globalization, and regional integration between Hong Kong and Zhujiang Delta, affecting the prosperity of the region. Mainland China's subsequent development improved the standards of educational attainment, employment, work environment, housing, and living conditions of people living in Hong Kong. Today, the causes of death in Hong Kong are largely comparable to those in other developed countries (Mathers et al., 2003). In 2006, the top five leading causes of death in Hong Kong were NCD related. They included cancers (32.3%), heart diseases (15.0%), pneumonia (11.2%), cerebrovascular diseases (8.8%), and external causes of morbidity and mortality (5.2%) (Lam, 2007).

In general, Hong Kong people enjoy a good quality of life health-wise. One survey indicated that nearly 60% of Hong Kong people self-rated their general health status as being from good to excellent (Department of Health & Department of Community Medicine, 2005). However, some behaviors are having a negative impact on people's health. Hong Kong people have increased their consumption of tobacco, and they now experience obesity, an unhealthy diet, physical inactivity, and other unhealthy lifestyles (Department of Health, 2008b). These unhealthy behaviors are important determinants of NCDs, which result in the long-term disease processes that account for nearly 60% of global deaths and 46% of the global burden of disease (World Health Organization [WHO], 2001, 2002a).

In order to facilitate health policy planning and to support health promotion and disease prevention programs, the Hong Kong government several years ago

N. Taylor, F. Quinn, M. Littledyke and R.K. Coll (eds.), Health Education in Context, 211–222.

conducted a heart health survey to determine the prevalence and risk factors of cardiovascular disease (Ho, Woo, Tao, & Sham, 2006). The results from a behavioral risk factor survey enhanced understanding of the health-related behaviors of the Hong Kong adult population (Department of Health, 2008b). Six priority areas were identified for further action: prevention of communicable diseases, nutrition, physical activity, injury prevention, mental health, and tobacco control (Lam, 2007).

A child health survey (CHS) conducted by Lau, Low, Cheung, Lee, Wong, and Lam (2009) provided information on the physical and psychosocial health, behaviors, and lifestyle practices of children 15 years and under. The CHS was the first population-based health survey of children in this age group. Findings indicated that Hong Kong children have a high risk of visual problems, pay little attention to healthy eating, have a sedentary lifestyle, experience early initiation into smoking and drinking alcohol, and do not adopt safe practices, such as wearing a helmet when riding a bicycle. The study also found that some children are left alone at home. The study's findings furthermore confirmed the importance of developing healthy habits in the earlier stages of life, such as school age.

Childhood obesity and drug abuse are two examples that illustrate the severity of the public health impacts of NCDs. The prevalence of obesity among primary students increased from 11.3% to 20.6% for boys and 8.9% to 14.2% for girls respectively between 1993 and 2004. Sum and Hui (2007) found a 70% increase over 11 years in the prevalence of childhood obesity in Hong Kong. Lam (2007), drawing on 2007 data, noted that one out of every five primary school children is obese in Hong Kong. This trend of childhood obesity implies a strong likelihood of multiple risk factors for chronic cardiovascular, metabolic, and psychological problems beginning to affect these children in 10 years' time. In other words, a variety of co-morbidities before or during early adulthood is occurring (Chan, 2008).

Obesity is becoming a rapidly growing economic burden on the health care system. Hospitalization expenses for obesity prevention, medical investigation, and treatment of related health problems amounted to HK\$B2.29 (US\$B0.29) in 1998 and HK\$B3.36 (US\$B0.43 billion) in 2002, totals that account for 8.2% to 9.8% of total public expenditure on health (Ko, 2008). Other soft costs such as proprietary medicine and commercial health products cost HK\$54.00 (US\$6.90) per family per month in 2000 (Census and Statistics Department, 2006).

The trend of increased drug abuse among Hong Kong youth is also alarming. The number of reported drug abusers under 21 years of age increased from 2,278 in 2005 to 3,430 in 2008, an increase of 51% in three years, while the total number of reported drug abusers increased by 0.4% over the same period of time. More worrying is the rising trend of young drug abusers, especially those in the age group 12 to 17 (Central Registry of Drug Abuse, 2010). A recent survey investigated drug use among 158,089 primary, secondary, and university students (Li, Tam, & Tam, 2010). The results indicated that drugs are circulating in more than 90% of primary and secondary schools, where one out of 27 students admits to having tried some form of drug. The government has earmarked three billion

Hong Kong dollars for anti-drug initiatives, detoxification treatments, and rehabilitation (Tang, 2010).

These priority areas are largely related to unhealthy behavior, such as poor eating habits and insufficient physical activity in the case of obesity. Early school health education is considered an important starter measure for improving the health of school children and then of the community. The Education Bureau (2007) noted that health education needs to be strengthened in the mainstream education curriculum. The government has also urged schools to develop healthy school policies directed at building up positive values and attitudes among students from an early age (Legislative Council Secretariat, 2010).

HEALTH EDUCATION IN HONG KONG

In order to keep pace with social and economic development in Hong Kong, Hong Kong's education system has undergone huge reform. Opportunities for health education were few in the packed school curriculum of the past. At the primary level (ages 6 to 12), the components of health education are today included under the subject of general studies. General studies is an integration of personal, social, and humanities education, science education, and technology education. In 2007, a new senior secondary school (NSS) curriculum (for 16- to 18-year-olds) was promulgated with the introduction of a core subject, liberal studies. One sixth of this subject's content is health related. Liberal studies, as one of four compulsory subjects under the new system, includes the teaching elements of science, the humanities, and technology.

Another elective subject within the NSS is health management and social care (HMSC). Compared to liberal studies, this subject has a higher proportion of its content focused on health promotion and social care services. Elective subjects in the NSS allow students to select a range of subjects within the choices offered by their schools, so that they can develop their interests and abilities and open up their pathways into further studies and career goals. Although the NSS HMSC is a new subject and although only a few students take this elective, the Education Bureau has nevertheless organized professional development sessions on it for teachers. Teachers are encouraged to study a wide range of reference books, related policy documents, research findings, information leaflets, newspapers, and websites before they teach HMSC in order to keep up with the ever-changing content of this subject. Teachers also have access to HMSC resource kits and a web-based HMSC resources database (Curriculum Development Council, 2009). The rationale behind the HMSC curriculum is that of advancing students' understanding of the determinants of health and enabling them to participate in building a healthy and supportive society. HMSC not only benefits students' own wellbeing but also lets students master a macroscopic view of public health issues in both local and global contexts (Curriculum Development Council & the Hong Kong Examinations and Assessment Authority, 2007). HMSC represents a big step forward in the promotion and implementation of school-based health education.

Despite these advances, local health education still suffers from a lack of emphasis in the comprehensive-school-based curriculum. This curriculum is a diverse one in terms of its structure and content, but it does not encompass a coherent health education curriculum or position health education as a key learning area on its own. At present, health education is subsumed under the key learning area of personal, social, and health education. Some provisions of teacher training, curriculum materials, and supports for schools and teachers for health education are available to ensure progression in learning across the primary and secondary levels of the education system. While efforts are being made to implement quality skills-based health education to increase students' capacity for making healthy choices (Clarke, Bundy, Lee, Maier, McKee, & Becker, 2003), health education continues to be project-based and heavily reliant on university support, a situation that is limiting schools' ability to autonomously develop this area of the curriculum.

THE EVOLUTION OF HEALTH PROMOTING SCHOOLS

School is an important place in which to build up a healthy lifestyle for teachers, students, and parents. In 1998, the Centre for Health Education and Health Promotion of the Chinese University of Hong Kong launched a health promoting schools (HPS) program for primary schools and secondary schools (Lee, Cheng, & St Leger, 2005). The HPS program follows the World Health Organization's global school health initiatives (WHO, 2010), and its development was based on concepts inherent in the Ottawa Charter of Health Promotion (WHO, 1986) and the Bangkok Charter for Health (Smith, 1992). The program provides a structured framework within which schools can promote, through various supports, the healthy development of school children. These supports include and/or relate to health policies, health services, personal health skills, community relationships, the social environment, and the physical environment. The program's aims are focused on improving not only the health of students but also the health of school personnel, families, and other community members.

The health promotion strategy also gives impetus to school health programs by providing guidelines for further improvement, building up the networks that help schools become health promoting schools, and strengthening connections between health and education institutes by having them develop strategies and programs that schools can use to promote their students' health. Schools have thus become a model of a healthy setting for living, learning, and working.

The success of HPS is evaluated by measuring its outcomes against six areas noted in the healthy school award (HSW) scheme:

- Strategic partnerships for health and education;
- Strategic partnerships for health promotion and good governance;
- Leadership of and mentoring in health promotion;
- Health promotion infrastructure and financing;
- Communication; and

- Effectiveness with respect to health promotion and alleviating the worldwide diseases burden (WHO, 1996, 2002b).

Although, as noted earlier, the school-based HPS projects focus on different health-promotion programs in schools because of their collaboration with different institutions, the latter institutions rather than the schools or teachers direct the strategies. Since the initiation of the scheme, however, over 200 kindergartens, primary schools, secondary schools, and special schools have become HPSs and involved in various health campaigns. One such is the healthy eating campaign named EatSmart@school.hk. Launched in 2007, the program's aims are to combat childhood obesity and reduce the incidence of NCDs (Lam, 2007). The Centre for Health Education and Health Promotion provides school teachers and health-related personnel with training not only on the concepts that inform the scheme but also on its implementation. The center has additionally developed practical guidelines that participating schools can use when planning and implementing school-based health initiatives. It furthermore provides teachers with professional development support and continual guidance, as well as health-related teaching tools and resources (Lee, 2004). These projects have significantly improved school children's health behaviors (Lee, Cheng, Fung, & St Leger, 2006; Lee, Ho, & Keung, 2010; Lee, Lee, Tsang, & To, 2003). The recently launched two-year Health Promoting Schools Built-on Project, which is based on the successes of previous projects, also aims to sustain the good practices of HPS (Centre for Health Education and Health Promotion, 2009).

But again, despite these gains and despite many schools having facilitated environmental protection measures, established safety guidelines, and implemented strategies for managing students with emotional problems, a number of researchers have revealed the ongoing lack of health policies throughout Hong Kong schools (see, for example, Lee, St Leger, Cheng, & Hong Kong Healthy Schools Team, 2007; Wong, Lee, Sun, Stewart, Cheng, & Kan, 2009). Other issues include insufficient staff trained in health promotion and education, and students and staff finding it difficult to access health services in their schools. It seems that many schools and school teachers are not yet ready to take a leadership role in health education.

IMPROVING THE IMPLEMENTATION OF SCHOOL HEALTH EDUCATION

Driven by the School Sector

The success of HPS depends largely on teachers' efforts to promote the health and social development of children. Teachers play an important role in fostering the building blocks of health-promotion skills and experiences. However, regardless of the focus on partnerships and leadership roles for schools in the HPS program, health education is still driven primarily by the medical profession instead of being a joint effort of both the health and education sectors in Hong Kong. Schools and teachers are still seen as a receptacle for health messages, materials, and prevention programs. The findings of a local study that explored school teachers' needs with respect to addressing infectious disease outbreaks showed that the teachers relied on Department of Health-provided information on preventive measures and contingency plans (Wong, Cheng, & Lo, 2010). According to the researchers, teachers said that they wanted to receive even more such support from health professionals.

Schools appear to acknowledge the rhetoric about community partnership, but see the meaning of partnership in terms of resource acquisition, such as having visiting speakers and information kits. Accordingly, the existing school health projects rely mainly on health-driven models rather than on collaborative activities. The latter would mean that schools are treated as partners on an equal footing with health professionals. In this connection, school health education requires a new mindset. Schools need to expand their leadership roles so that they lead health education in a way that produces stronger health-based organizations and communities. The work of teams, organizations, and networks can be better positioned to accomplish systemic and social change. The power of this collective action should also enhance the productivity of teams. In short, schools should have a more prominent leadership role in the HPS initiative.

Developing School Health Policies

A school health education program is effective if school health policies are clearly defined and development directions and strategies clearly set out. Resource allocation needs to be based on the directions set by schools according to the priorities they each give to health issues (Lee et al., 2005). Schools also should decide whether to take a curriculum-focused or a comprehensive approach to addressing multiple health issues as well as the confusion created by multiple agencies at multiple levels. Schools furthermore should take a holistic view of health and wellbeing, and they should have the option of having in place either a program directed at preventing just one health issue (a priority issue) or a program able to address several health problems simultaneously.

Teachers' Understandings of Health Education

The success of the HPS program depends largely on school teachers' understandings of health education and on teachers' capacity to implement related programs. This is because teachers are the ones who can most easily identify the needs of their respective students and communities. Although teachers understand the notion of local school community within the context of health education in terms of teaching needs and the resources available, they do not seem to see local community members and agencies as partners in planning, implementing, and reviewing school health programs and school health policies (Lee et al., 2003).

The reason for this perception may relate to the fact that school teachers plan their curriculum for their own class, and that they usually tackle health matters on an issue-related or ad hoc basis. For example, teachers responded to the outbreak of H1N1 influenza in terms of concern about the spread of the infection. They strongly supported closing all primary schools, kindergartens, child care centers, and special schools immediately after the discovery of the first case of H1N1. Their responses were reactive rather than proactive. It was not until an infection such as H1N1 emerged that schools and teachers wanted to put in place health education related to infectious diseases. They looked closely at the H1N1 information that the government, including the Department of Health and the Education Bureau, sent out to them, and they invited health care professionals to give talks about the prevention and treatment of infectious diseases (Wong et al., 2010).

What is apparent from this example is that schools and teachers will address health issues when they become widespread and are the source of considerable community concern. The challenge in the personal health skills area and with respect to NCDs is for the education and health sectors to work together to promote and implement health education as on ongoing area of educational provision rather than as a piecemeal or reactive one. If this aim is to be realized, teachers will need to receive from government and adjunct health agencies consistent messages about health education. They will also need support in delivering it. More importantly, teachers will need to receive professional development that will help them become competent developers of school-based health policies.

Hong Kong lacks teachers with the competence to professionally develop and implement a school health policy. Health education for Hong Kong teachers is based on basic training of science subjects, including biology, integrated science, liberal science, and general science. A recent study (Wong et al., 2010) found no difference between what science teaching and what non-science teaching teachers perceived they needed when faced with an emerging infectious disease crisis. However, today's era of globalization and rapid social, technological, and economic change means that teachers continually have to deal with controversy about health and are bombarded with new information in the health field. They cannot afford to remain complacent about or uninterested in this area of education.

FUTURE DEVELOPMENTS

A holistic school approach is needed with respect to HPS. This approach includes the development of a better health education curriculum (Parsons, Stears, & Thomas, 1996). Teacher training needs to be strengthened so that teachers can better support the initiation and development of a school-based health policy. Because health education is a lifelong process, school-based health policies need to evolve over time if they are to properly address contemporary health issues. Adequate health education training is needed for teachers to prepare the new generation for an unpredictable future and to contribute to the human capacity development needed to meet new challenges. Moreover, health education should be taught by qualified, trained teachers (Marx, Wooley, & Northrop, 1998). There is also a commensurate and urgent need to provide more health education resources for teacher educators (Keung, Lee, Cheng, Yuen, & Ho, 2003).

This understanding recognizes the need to build capacity in the education systems, agencies, and professions that deliver school health education. There should be greater recognition that schools are not simply convenient recipients of health messages and materials. The high need for communities to receive quality health education makes it essential that more resources are directed toward designing a health education curriculum for teachers. Without this support, teachers will not be able to take on the important role of helping educate the community about health issues.

Professional development programs focused on health education are also essential for pre-service and in-service teachers, especially given that in-service school teacher training provisions typically comprise one-off activities related to a specific health issue. If teachers are to be encouraged to participate in health-related professional development, they need to be assured that the program they experience balances their need for health knowledge with their need to acquire the skills required to develop school-based health policy and sustain HPS (Wong et al., 2010). That said, schools and teachers need to change their attitudes toward the provision of health education. They need to acknowledge the relevance and importance of collaborating with school and health professionals, and to see all involved as equal partners. They need to move away from their over-reliance on materials and services from external health-related organizations or institutes. And they need to reshape their current working relationships by engaging in those that embrace integrative and collaborative action.

The success of health education requires the support of a well-planned curriculum and school policy developed jointly by school teachers and management personnel. Hong Kong can build on the success of HPS that has been demonstrated both locally and internationally by establishing more resilience-enhancing activities. Support from health and from educational authorities is essential in order to accomplish these objectives (Wong et al., 2010). Those formulating a coordinated response to NCDs need to remain mindful that an effective health strategy is one that reiterates the importance of inter-sectorial action and the leadership role that schools and their teachers can play. As a starting point, a review of current health education approaches should provide the basis of a comprehensive and integrated approach to further strengthening strategies for preventing NCDs.

CONCLUSION

Healthy children are children who lead a healthy lifestyle and adopt behaviors that prevent or reduce their risk of physical and mental harm. By involving parents and other community partners, schools can do much to improve the health and limit the risk-related behaviors of children and young people. One way of addressing the promotion of positive health is through the school health initiative. Hong Kong has made moves in this direction by adopting the health promoting schools program. It is important, however, that schools develop their own plans and create an infrastructure that reflects their needs and the needs of their communities. Schools also need to promote partnerships that include teachers, education system administrators, and health education policymakers. Schools, though, are unlikely to implement these measures unless their teachers receive support from targeted and ongoing professional development.

REFERENCES

Chan, C. (2008). Childhood obesity and adverse health effects in Hong Kong. *Obesity Reviews, 1*, 87–90.

Census and Statistics Department. (2006). *The 2004/05 Household Expenditure Survey and the rebasing of the consumer price indices*. Hong Kong: Census and Statistics Department.

Central Registry of Drug Abuse (CRDS). (2010). *Central Registry of Drug Abuse fifty-eighth report: 1999–2008*. Hong Kong: Narcotics Division, Security Bureau.

Centre for Health Education and Health Promotion. (2009). *Health Promoting Schools Built-on Project*. Retrieved from http://www.cuhk.edu.hk/med/hep/HPS/Built_on/e_index.html.

Clarke, D., Bundy, D., Lee, S., Maier, C., McKee, N., & Becker, A. (2003). *Skills for health: Skills-based health education including life skills—an important component of a child-friendly/health-promoting school*. Geneva, Switzerland: World Health Organization.

Curriculum Development Council. (2009). *The future is now: From vision to realisation (Secondary 4–6), Booklet 6. Quality learning and teaching resources: Facilitating effective learning (senior secondary curriculum guide)*. Hong Kong: Author.

Curriculum Development Council & the Hong Kong Examinations and Assessment Authority. (2007). *Health management and social care curriculum and assessment guide (Primary 4–6)*. Hong Kong: Education and Manpower Bureau.

Department of Health. (2008a). *Hong Kong population health profile series 2005/06. Non-communicable diseases*. Hong Kong: Author.

Department of Health. (2008b). *Behavioural risk factor survey*. Hong Kong: Surveillance and Epidemiology Branch, Centre for Health Protection, and Department of Health.

Department of Health, & Department of Community Medicine. (2005). *Report on population health survey 2003/2004*. Hong Kong: Departments of Health and Community Medicine, the University of Hong Kong.

Education Bureau. (2007). *Healthy schools*. Retrieved from http://www.edb.gov.hk/index.aspx?nodeID=5024&langno=1.

Ho, S. C., Woo, J. L. F., Tao, V., & Sham, A. (2006). *Heart health survey 2004/2005*. Hong Kong: Department of Community and Family Medicine, the Chinese University of Hong Kong.

Keung, M. W., Lee, A., Cheng, F. F. K., Yuen, S. K., & Ho, M. (2003). *School health education and promotion in Hong Kong: The current status in schools*. Hong Kong: The Chinese University of Hong Kong.

Ko, G. T. (2008). The cost of obesity in Hong Kong. *Obesity Reviews, 1*, 74–77.

Lam, P. Y. (2007). *Department of Health annual report 2006/2007*. Hong Kong: Department of Health.

Lau, Y. L., Low, L., Cheung, Y. F., Lee, S. L., Wong, W., & Lam, T. H. (2009). *Child health survey 2005–2006*. Hong Kong: Surveillance and Epidemiology Branch, Centre for Health Protection, Department of Health.

Lee, A. (2004). The concept of health promoting schools to enhance positive youth development. *Asia Pacific Journal of Public Health, S16*, S3–6.

Lee, A., Cheng, F., Fung, Y., & St Leger, L. (2006). Can the concept of health promoting schools help to improve students' health knowledge and practices to combat the challenge of communicable diseases? Case study in Hong Kong. *Journal of Epidemiology and Community Health, 60*, 530–536.

Lee, A., Cheng, F. F. K., & St Leger, L. (2005). Evaluating health promoting schools in Hong Kong: The development of a framework. *Health Promotion International, 20*(2), 177–186.

Lee, A., Ho, M., & Keung, V. (2010). Healthy school as an ecological model for prevention of childhood obesity. *Research in Sports Medicine, 18*(1), 49–61.

Lee, A., Lee, S. H., Tsang, K. K., & To, C. Y. (2003). A comprehensive "healthy schools program" to promote school health: The Hong Kong experience in joining the efforts of health and education sectors. *Journal of Epidemiology and Community Health, 57*, 174–177.

Lee, A., St Leger, L., Cheng, F. K., & Hong Kong Healthy Schools Team. (2007). The status of health-promoting schools in Hong Kong and implications for further development. *Health Promotion International, 22*(4), 316–326.

Legislative Council Secretariat. (2010). *The youth drug abuse problem in Hong Kong.* Hong Kong: Research and Library Services Division, Legislative Council Secretariat.

Li, R., Tam, M., & Tam, N. (2010). *The 2008/09 survey of drug use among students.* Hong Kong: Narcotics Division, Security Bureau.

Marx, E., Wooley, S. F., & Northrop, D. (1998). *Health is academic: A guide to coordinated school health programs.* New York: Teachers College Press.

Mathers, C. D., Bernard, C., Iburg, K. M., Inoue, M., Ma Fat, D., Shibuya, K., Stein, C., Tomijima, N., & Xu, H. (2003). *Global burden of disease in 2002: Data sources, methods, and results* (Global Program on Evidence for Health Policy Discussion Paper No. 54). Geneva, Switzerland: World Health Organization.

Parsons, C., Stears, D., & Thomas, C. (1996). The health promoting school in Europe: Conceptualising and evaluating the change. *Health Education Journal, 55*, 311–321.

Smith, C. (1992). The health promoting school: Progress and future challenges in Welsh secondary schools. *Health Promotion International, 7*, 151–152.

Sum, R., & Hui, S. (2007, May 25). *CUHK Sports Science and Physical Education Department releases survey results on childhood obesity in Hong Kong* (press release). Retrieved from http://www.cuhk.edu.hk/cpr/pressrelease/070525e.htm.

Tang, H. (2010, June 26). *"Fight drugs together" activities launch* (press release). Retrieved from http://www.info.gov.hk/gia/general/201006/26/P201006260219.htm.

Wong, E. M. Y., Cheng, M. M. H., & Lo, S. K. (2010). Teachers' risk perception and needs in addressing infectious disease outbreak. *Journal of School Nursing, 26*(5), 398–406.

Wong, K. Y., & Shen, J. (2002). *Resource management, urbanization and governance in Hong Kong and the Zhujiang Delta.* Hong Kong: Chinese University Press.

Wong, M. C. S., Lee, A., Sun, J., Stewart, D., Cheng, F. F. K., & Kan, W. (2009). A comparative study on resilience levels between WHO health promoting schools and other schools among a Chinese population. *Health Promotion International, 24*(2), 149–155.

World Health Organization (WHO). (1986). *Ottawa Charter for Health Promotion* (presented at the First International Conference on Health Promotion, Ottawa, Canada, November 21, 1986, WHO/HPR/HEP/95.1).

World Health Organization (WHO). (1996). *Regional guidelines for the development of health-promoting schools: A framework for action.* Manila, the Philippines: Regional Office for the Western Pacific, World Health Organization.

World Health Organization (WHO). (2001). *The world health report 2001: Mental health—new understanding, new hope.* Geneva, Switzerland: Author.

World Health Organization (WHO). (2002a). *Non-communicable diseases in the South-East Asia region: A profile.* New Delhi, India: Regional Office for South-East Asia, World Health Organization.

World Health Organization. (WHO). (2002b). *Workshop on capacity-building for health promotion.* Manila, the Philippines: Regional Office for the Western Pacific, World Health Organization.

World Health Organization. (2010). *School and youth health*: Global school health initiative. Geneva, Switzerland: Retrieved from http://www.who.int/school_youth_health/gshi/en.

Emmy Man Yee Wong
The Hong Kong Institute of Education
Hong Kong
China
email: emmywong@ied.edu.hk

May May Hung Cheng
University of Oxford
Oxford
United Kingdom

IRENE POH-AI CHEONG

24. WORKING TOWARDS A HEALTHIER BRUNEI

BACKGROUND

Brunei Darussalam is a small equatorial country of 5,765 square kilometers that lies on the north-west coast of the island of Borneo. An affluent nation, its economy is based mostly on oil and gas. Brunei's GDP per capita of US$50,117 places the country fifth highest on this index internationally (International Monetary Fund, 2010). The population of Brunei is about 398,000, with Malays, who are Muslims, forming the majority (just under 67% of the country's people) (Prime Minister's Office, 2008). The annual population growth rate is just over 2.0%; life expectancy is 75 years (Central Intelligence Agency, 2010). Brunei meets all 10 global health indicators of the World Health Organization (WHO) as well as the UN Millennium Development Goals (WHO, 2004). The Human Development Index (HDI) level of 0.919 ranks Brunei 30 out of 177 countries (United Nations Development Program [UNDP], 2009).

Brunei's health services are ranked amongst the best in Asia (WHO, 2009a). The ratio of general practitioners to people is 1:992 (Mohamad, 2008). Health and education expenditure per capita constitutes 5.1% and 9.1% of total government expenditure, respectively (UNDP, 2009). Brunei's citizens receive free public healthcare and have access to overseas specialized medical treatment if their needs cannot be met in Brunei.

Brunei's long-term vision is to diversify its activities to overcome dependency on oil and gas, as well as to achieve a well-educated, highly skilled population who enjoy a high quality of life and live within a sustainable economy (Brunei Economic Development Board, 2008).

HEALTH ISSUES IN BRUNEI DARUSSALAM

Brunei has an enviable record in being almost free of major communicable diseases. WHO declared the country malaria-free in 1987, poliomyelitis-free in 2000 (WHO, 2009b), and free of seasonal infectious diseases such as SARS (severe acute respiratory syndrome) and H1N1 (subtype of the influenza A virus). However, non-communicable illnesses, such as cancer, heart diseases, diabetes mellitus, cerebrovascular diseases, hypertensive diseases, and respiratory diseases (bronchitis, chronic and unspecified emphysema, asthma, influenza, and pneumonia) are the leading causes of death (Ministry of Health, 2008). The modifiable behavioral risk factors of these diseases are unhealthy diet, obesity, lack of physical activity, and smoking (WHO, 2009b).

Brunei has a diabetes prevalence rate of about 25%, and its younger population, with a high incidence of obesity, risks developing Type 2 diabetes (Dash 1999;

N. Taylor, F. Quinn, M. Littledyke and R.K. Coll (eds.), Health Education in Context, 223–234.

"Diabetes: A Brunei Affliction," 2009; Van Eekelen, Stokvis-Brantsma, Frolich, Smelt, & Stokvis, 2000). Obesity is alarmingly on the rise among children in Brunei; 33% were classified as overweight or obese in 2008 (Ishak, 2008) compared to 9.1% in 1999 (Ministry of Health, 1999, cited in Tee, 2002). Weight disorders are also common, particularly among Malays, people of middle age, and females (Chong & Abdullah, 2008).

The common occurrence of abandoned newborns as a result of teenage pregnancies is also an issue. At least 18 cases were reported between 1995 and 2002 ("Increase in Abandoned Babies," 2003), and five cases in 2009 ("Abandoned Baby Needs Mother's Milk," 2010). The Ministry of Health asked parents and the public to partner with them to deal with this problem ("Need Public–Parents Partnership," 2010). Calls for introducing sex education as a separate subject into the education system ("Teach Sex Education in School," 2010) have been made in order to address "the number of babies born out of wedlock to teenagers aged less than 19 years" (Rasidah, 2010). Brunei also recognizes the need to achieve the WHO standard in dental health (Ottoman, 2006).

Because intoxicants such as alcohol and drugs are *haram* (forbidden) to Muslims, their sale and public consumption is banned. However, compared to other ASEAN (Association of South East Asian Nations) countries, the rate of drug use in Brunei is relatively high. Brunei thus needs to focus on psychological and sociocultural settings to prevent drug abuse among its youth (United Nations Office on Drugs and Crime, 2009). Islamic-based organizations play a key role in helping youth say "no to drugs" through motivational talks and workshops. The ban on smoking in public places, which came into effect on June 1, 2008, is enforced through the Tobacco Act of 2005 and its 2007 regulations (Razak & Ong, 2007). However, smoking is still prevalent, and is the major cause of cancer in Brunei.

HEALTH EDUCATION IN BRUNEI DARUSSALAM

Community Health Education

To promote good health, education materials, posters, and pamphlets on health topics are made available to all (Ministry of Health, 2010). A major initiative has been the National Health Care Plan 2000–2010, which aimed to increase public awareness of non-communicable diseases. Strategies focused on supporting people to embrace a healthier lifestyle through community participation and inter-sectorial collaboration directed at seven priority areas: nutrition, food safety, tobacco control, mental health, physical activity, health environments/settings, and women's health. These priorities were promoted through special events, publicity about major health issues, and appropriate measures for modifying lifestyles (WHO, 2008).

An example of these health promotion initiatives is a program that teaches healthy lifestyles to selected people with a body mass index of over 30. The three-month program consists of group sessions for physical activities, such as walking, hiking, trekking, and obstacle games. The program offers presentations and discussions on healthy diet, motivation, stress management, time management, and a range of physical exercises. It also involves fostering a commitment to physical activities, advice on how to prevent relapses, and ways of overcoming barriers to participation in physical activities. It furthermore includes shopping trips directed at identifying and buying healthy food. Individual consultations with a psychologist, dietician, and physiotherapist are followed up every six months. However, success rates, as defined by a weight loss of five percent, have been   low—at between 11.9% and 17.3% (2008/2009 data).

World Diabetes Days (Ishak, 2008) are observed through charity walkathons, healthy *mukim* (village) programs, free health examinations, exhibitions, and distribution of posters to schools. A national diabetes plan, involving parents, teachers, and other community leaders as well as healthcare providers, is currently in the planning stage. Its aim is to educate people about how to prevent diabetes and its complications ("Diabetes: A Brunei Affliction," 2009).

Drug, alcohol, and smoking education is conducted via public talks, open dialogues, exhibitions, information in pamphlets, sports activities, mass urine screening, and anti-drug campaigns. Interventions such as the "Demand Reduction Strategy," Anti- Drug Badge project, trade fairs, and counseling sessions are also in place. Efforts to counteract smoking include education programs on the hazards of smoking that encompass road shows, health talks, exhibitions, and smoking cessation clinics (Wilson, 2010).

Formal Health Education in Brunei Darussalam

Between 2006 and 2008, much attention was given to providing sports facilities in schools and increasing human resources for physical education. About 40.5% of total expenditure for the Ministry of Education Building Improvement of School and Infrastructure program was allocated to providing and upgrading sports facilities in government schools (UNDP, 2009).

The school curriculum is implemented in a didactic manner and is taught according to prescribed syllabi; students rely on drill and memorization to pass examinations that enable them to move to the next grade level. Much health education in the school system and in the community focuses on knowledge dissemination instead of changing behavior. Although the school curriculum has been revamped in recent years (Ministry of Education, 2010), much of the content in terms of health education remains the same as it was 10 years ago. Positive change, however, has included integrating within the curriculum core values and attitudes relevant to health education, such as self-confidence, self-esteem, self-reliance, and independence, along with caring, concern, and sensitivity. Health and physical education has been allocated as a separate area of study, and emphasis on school-based assessment may allow for greater innovation in health education. Descriptions of two relatively recent innovative programs initiated in Brunei with direct or indirect implications for health education follow.

The first program, an interdisciplinary one called English and Physical Education for Health Education, was trialed in a secondary school. Strategies focused on integrating healthy concepts into English-language learning and providing students with opportunities to increase their physical activity. Students' health concerns, such as nutrition, sexuality, and physical activities, were investigated. On Healthy Food days, students contributed money so that teachers could provide healthy food. Discussions were held as to why the teachers chose certain foods and how students could establish healthy eating habits. Students also examined their school lunch-boxes to identify the categories of food they contained. Students' correspondence with pen-friends in Australia contributed to building up their self-esteem in general. Extracurricular activities promoted physical activities, with students contributing to the running of these activities (Williams, 2003).

The second initiative saw university students engaged in community problem-solving projects, some of which involved local health-related concerns. Three of these serve as examples. Concerns related to disposal of cooking oil led students to discover that restaurants were disposing of some of their waste cooking oil by giving it free to food vendors. Their actions were creating health problems for the community (Ibrahim, Hassim, Lamit, & Rangga, 2008). The students produced pamphlets for the public that addressed how to cook without oil, the harmful effects of cooking with waste cooking oil, and proper ways of disposing of waste cooking oil, which included recycling it for diesel-engine fuel or soap-making.

During the second project, students endeavored to make the community aware that the common use of polystyrene food containers meant that styrene was leaching into hot and oily food (Abdul Rahman, Eu, Muhammad Kincho, & Muhamad, 2008). The students let vendors know why they needed to change containers, and they suggested alternatives, such as reusable steel containers.

The third project focused on the use of cars as the main means of transporting children to and from school (Zakaria, Wahab, Ismail, & Abdullah Bayoh, 2010). The university students proposed to schools that they needed to encourage parents to let students use healthier transport options, such as walking, taking the school or public bus, and cycling.

CHALLENGES FOR HEALTH EDUCATION IN BRUNEI DARUSSALAM

Health education programs designed to overcome preventable diseases and solve present and future health problems need to be implemented in such a way that they can bring about positive changes not only in attitudes and beliefs but also in behavior. The National Center for Chronic Disease Prevention and Health Promotion (Division of Adolescent and School Health, 2008) considers curricula that overemphasize teaching scientific facts about health matters in order to increase student knowledge of them are relatively ineffective. Health education curricula should accordingly be based on sound research evidence and emphasize the teaching of essential health-related concepts. Personal values that support healthy behaviors also need to be emphasized, as does shaping group norms that value healthy lifestyles and helping students develop the skills necessary to adopt, practice, and maintain health-enhancing behaviors.

The essential challenge for Brunei is to bring into play a full commitment to a health education policy that enables education institutions and health-promotion agencies to develop and implement new and innovative ways of markedly improving the health of Bruneians. Although some efforts commensurate with this aim have been taken, they are neither widespread nor publicized. Innovative health education programs must be underpinned with modes of assessment that allow practitioners and educators to determine the extent to which people have the skills and ability to identify and work toward alleviating their health problems. Assessment and development of affective factors that are important drivers of healthy lifestyles, such as caring for others and valuing oneself, is an important accompanying aspect of such programs. The next sections of this chapter focus on four types of program that contain these components and so should help secure a healthier Brunei.

Life Skills Programs

In order to tackle its obesity problems, Brueni could implement long-term life skills programs, such as the Kitchen Garden Program (Brock & Johnson, 2009) and the School Lunch Initiative (Rauzon, Wang, Studer, & Crawford, 2010). These types of program also promote the eating of vegetables and fruits. Life skills programs furthermore involve campaigns directed at preventing teenage pregnancies. Youth are taught skills such as assertiveness and negotiation and are encouraged to engage in open discussion and communication with one another, teachers, and health professionals about specific sexual practices (Smith, Kippax, Aggleton, & Tyrer, 2003). An example of a successful such program is Abstinence Only. Its content includes information and discussion on parenthood, dating, sexual refusal skills, and remaining true to oneself (McGuire, Walsh, & LeCroy, 2005). Another useful program, described by Henderson (2010), uses inquiry-based approaches that enable students to develop links between values and decisionmaking skills and from there make informed choices about their health, wellbeing, and general resilience.

Action-Oriented Projects

Health literacy is not just about transmitting information, distributing pamphlets, putting up posters, and making appointments to see health professionals (Nutbeam, 2000). It is also, and more importantly, about taking action on the social, political, and economic determinants of health. In practice, this means teaching students the critical components of health literacy, such that they understand the determinants of health and have the skills to take remedial action when necessary. However, little, if any recognition, has been given to this type of teaching in Brunei's schools, and this lack appears to be one of the main impediments to bringing about the type of curriculum change necessary to accomplish a critical level of health literacy. Also, as Gould, Mogford, and DeVoght (2010) remind us, health educationalists and professionals themselves need to be educated.

A particularly needed emphasis within the health curriculum is that of action learning. This type of learning helps empower young people to live healthily and to promote healthy living conditions (National Institute of Child Health Greece, 1997). The three examples of community problem-solving projects by Brunei university students described above provide just one possible action-competence approach that Brunei could adopt in this regard. Experience in Denmark (Jensen, 2004) shows the success of such initiatives.

Religious and Cultural Practices

Brunei has adopted, as its guiding national philosophy, Melayu Islam Beraja, or MIB (Malay Islamic Monarchy). Education strategies are guided by the culture and traditions inherent in this philosophy (Charleston, 1998). Much of Brunei's educational provision emphasizes cognitive outcomes rather than affective and competency-based ones. For example, a study funded by the Joint United Nations Programme on HIV/AIDS found that education systems in some countries, including Brunei, employ HIV/AIDS-related education that is largely information-bound. Sex education is conducted in a mechanistic way, focusing mainly on human reproduction and anatomy (Smith et al., 2003). The study also found that when education programs cater to the cultural sensitivities of the majority of the population, the effectiveness of those programs can be compromised because they do not address certain health issues, often because of inherent gender bias. From her study of Bruneian health textbooks, Elgar (2004) found that the gender bias evident in them meant concealment of issues affecting women's health.

Hinyard and Kreuter (2006) suggest that because oral story-telling plays a significant role in Malay culture, it could be used to promote positive health behavior. Cheong and Thong (2004) have done just this with respect to promoting pro-environmental attitudes in Brunei. Also, because Muslims in Brunei adhere strictly to the teachings of the *Quran*, passages from it could be used to promote healthy lifestyles, such as this one:

> O Children of Adam! Wear your beautiful apparel
> At every time and place
> Of prayer: eat and drink:
> But waste not by excess,
> For Allah loveth not the wasters. (al-A'rāf:31) ('Alī, 1989)

Reference could also be made to passages in *Hadith*, which records the traditions or sayings of the Prophet Muhammad. An example is this excerpt, which refers to eating and drinking in moderation.

> The Prophet (peace and blessings be upon him) said:
> No human ever filled a container more evil than his belly. The few
> morsels needed to support his being shall suffice the son of Adam.
> But if there is no recourse then one third for his food, one third for

his drink and one third for his breath. (Narrated by Turmudzi, Ibnu Majah, dan Muslim) ("Eating and Drinking," 2010)

Reference could also be made to religious edicts published for use in education. Those relating to use of medicines (Kasule, 2008) and models for eating set out in the Quran (Muhammad as-Sayyid, 2006) are just two examples.

Using ICT for Positive Health Behavior

Although giving out leaflets on health matters is thought to be effective in some countries (see, for example, Murphy & Smith, 1993), research conducted by Paul, Redman, and Sanson-Fisher (2003) suggests that even pamphlets that are well designed and include adequate content may not be an effective means of relaying information and changing behavior. Better ways of communicating information are needed. Information and communication technologies (ICT) have the potential to deliver, at low cost, programs aimed at changing people's health-related behaviors. They are particularly likely to appeal to students from the "digital generation." Ferney and Marshall (2006) identify the utility of websites that include simple interactive features, such as online community noticeboards, personalized progress charts, email access to expert advice, and access to information on specific local physical activity facilities and services. The online social networks that have become particularly popular amongst young people in recent years could provide an especially valuable means of imparting health education.

CONCLUSION

If Brunei is to achieve its aspiration of bringing about a high quality of life for all of its people, much greater effort than that currently being exercised is needed, especially with respect to people's health. Better health education within both schools and the wider community is a key to realizing this aim. There is a need to change behaviors and convert problems to solutions instead of just focusing on improving knowledge and attitudes. There is also a need to implement in health education programs attitudes and practices learned from research, especially those that take a holistic approach to health and health education. Adopting an interdisciplinary approach to education and health and empowering the young to act in ways that exemplify healthy living are essential.

Psychosocial determinants of health behavior also need to be incorporated in schools' health curriculums and assessment practices. These determinants, which are grounded in the belief that each of us can exercise the control needed to change and improve our health-related habits for the better, encompass motivation, the perseverance needed to succeed, ability to recover from setbacks and relapses, and ability to maintain changed habits (Armitage & Conner, 2000).

Health changes can only be effective if supported by social systems (Bandura, 2004), which include infrastructural, personnel, and policy aspects. For example, involving health education personnel in making health reports has proved effective in promoting healthy lifestyle practices (Kwong & Seruji, 2007). Providing safe facilities for walking and cycling and encouraging use of public transport are also part of this process (Brownson et al., 2000; Pucher & Dijkstra, 2003; Saelens, Sallis, Black, & Chen, 2003). Brunei takes pride in the many jungle walking trails available to its residents. However, many of these trails need to be better mapped and made more accessible if the public is to continue using them safely. In essence, a healthier Brunei is reliant on inter-sectorial partnerships within and across government as well as non-government agencies—partnerships that are committed to the same goals and the same means of achieving them.

REFERENCES

Abandoned baby needs mother's milk to survive. (2010, May 28). *The Brunei Times*. Retrieved from http://174.142.62.49/index.php/2010052722054/Fourth-Stories/abandoned-baby-needs-mothers-milk-to-survive.html.

Abdul Rahman, S. N. F., Eu, C. N. L., Muhammad Kincho, K., & Muhamad, N. A. (2008). *Waste cooking oil in Brunei*. Retrieved from http://foodpackaginginbrunei.blogspot.com/.

'Ali, 'A. Y. (1989). *The Holy Qur'ān: Text, translation, and commentary*. Washington: Amana Corp.

Armitage, C. J., & Conner, M. (2000). Social cognition models and health behavior: A structured review. *Psychology and Health, 15*, 173–189.

Bandura, A. (2004). Health promotion by social cognitive means. *Health Education Behavior, 31*, 143.

Brunei Economic Development Board. (2008). *Brunei's national vision*. Retrieved from http://www.bedb.com.bn/why_nationalvision.htm.

Brock, K., & Johnson, B. (2009). *Final report to the Stephanie Alexander Kitchen Garden Foundation*. Retrieved from http://www.kitchengardenfoundation.org.au/uploads//02%20ABOUT%20THE%20PROGRAM/pdf/kgevaluation_key_findings.pdf.

Brownson, R. C., Housemann, R. A., Brown, D. R., Jackson-Thompson, J., King, A. C., Malone, B. R., & Sallis, J. F. (2000). Promoting physical activity in rural communities: Walking trail access, use, and effects. *American Journal of Preventive Medicine, 18*(3), 235–241.

Central Intelligence Agency (CIA). (2010). *The world factbook: Life expectancy at birth*. Retrieved from https://www.cia.gov/library/publications/the-world-factbook/fields/2102.html.

Charleston, R. (1998). *Implementing a developmental perspective of learning in the first year of school: Brunei Darussalam*. Paper presented to the Australian Association for Research in Education Conference, Research in Education, Adelaide, November 29–December 3. Retrieved from http://www.aare.edu.au/98pap/cha98080.htm.

Cheong, I. P. A., & Thong, L. K. (2004). *Story-telling in science teaching*. Retrieved from http://202.160.7.83/cgi-bin/infoviewer/igp_infoviewer_cpe/load_framework?catalog_item_id =300b08e7&sid=2ef0142eedb18ade944bb7aa37cdc8bc&language=en.

Chong, V.-H. & Abdullah, M.-A. (2008). Health of our patients based on body mass index. *Brunei Journal of Health, 3*, 45–51.

Dash, R. J. (1999). A glimpse of diabetes mellitus in Brunei Darussalam. *Brunei International Medical Journal, 1*, 241–247.

Diabetes: A Brunei affliction. (2009, November 14). *The Brunei Times*. Retrieved from http://news.brunei.fm/2009/11/14/diabetes-a-brunei-affliction/.

Division of Adolescent and School Health. (2008). *Characteristics of an effective health education curriculum*. Retrieved from http://www.cdc.gov/healthyyouth/SHER/characteristics/index.htm.

Eating and drinking in moderation. (2010, February 2). Retrieved from http://www.islamonline.net/servlet/Satellite?c=Article_C&cid=1264249983529&pagename=Zone-English-Living_Shariah/LSELayout.

Elgar, A. G. (2004). Science textbooks for lower secondary schools in Brunei: Issues of gender equity. *International Journal of Science Education, 26(7)*, 875–894.

Ferney, S. L., & Marshall, A. L. (2006). Website physical activity interventions: Preferences of potential users. *Health Education Research*, *21*(4), 560–566.

Gould, L., Mogford, E., & DeVoght, A. (2010). Successes and challenges of teaching the social determinants of health in secondary schools: Case examples in Seattle, Washington. *Health Promotion Practice*, *11*(22S). Retrieved from http://hpp.sagepub.com/content/11/3_suppl/26S. full.pdf.

Henderson, D. (2010). Values, wellness and the social sciences curriculum. *International Research Handbook on Values Education and Student Wellbeing*, *1*, 273–289.

Hinyard, L. J., & Kreuter, M. W. (2006). Using narrative communication as a tool for health behavior change: A conceptual, theoretical, and empirical overview. *Health Education Behavior*, *34*, 777.

Ibrahim, R., Hassim, H., Lamit, S., & Rangga, J. M. Q. (2008). *Waste cooking oil in Brunei*. Retrieved from http://wastecookingoil.blogspot.com/.

Increase in abandoned babies. (2003, January 25). *Brunei Direct*. Retrieved from http://acr.hrschool.org/LatestNews/latestnewsdecarticles.htm.

International Monetary Fund (IMF). (2010). *World economic outlook database—April 2010*. Retrieved from http://www.imf.org/external/pubs/ft/weo/2010/01/weodata/index.aspx.

Ishak, A. P. D. H. (2008, November 16). Obese youth in Brunei at risk. *Borneo Bulletin*. Retrieved from http://old.brudirect.com/public_html/DailyInfo/News/Archive/Nov08/161108/nite03.htm.

Jensen, B. B. (2004). Environmental and health education reviewed from an action oriented perspective: A case from Denmark. *Journal of Curriculum Studies*, *36*(4), 405–425.

Kasule, O. H. K. (2008). Patterns and trends of religious edicts (Fatwa Mufti Kerajaan & Irsyad Hukum) on medical matters in Brunei Darussalam 1962–2005. *Brunei Journal of Health*, *2*, 13–15.

Kwong, J. T. L., & Seruji, L. H. (2007). A report on the healthy lifestyle initiative at Brunei Shell Petroleum Company Sdn Bhd, Negara Brunei Darussalam. *Public Administration and Development*, *11*(1), 67–78. Retrieved from http://www.onepetro.org/mslib/servlet/onepetropreview?id=SPE-108639-MS&soc=SPE.

McGuire, J. K., Walsh, M., & LeCroy, C. W. (2005). Content analyses of little V abstinence-only education programs: Links between program topics and participant responses. *Sexuality Research and Social Policy*, *2*(4), 18–31.

Ministry of Education. (2010). *What is SPN21?* Retrieved from http://www.moe.edu.bn/web/spn21/kurikulum?p_p_id=86&p_p_action=1&p_p_state=normal&p_p_mode=view&p_p_col_i d=&p_p_col_pos=0&p_p_col_count=0&.

Ministry of Health. (2008). *Health information booklet 2008*. Retrieved from http://www. moh.gov.bn/satisticshealthguidelines/download/HIB_2008.pdf.

Ministry of Health. (2010). Health promotions: Health topics. Retrieved from http:// www.moh.gov.bn/healthpromotions/healthtopics.htm.

Mohamad, L. (2008, November 3). Brunei may have a new hospital. *Borneo Bulletin*. Retrieved from http://www.brudirect.com/DailyInfo/News/Archive/Nov08/031108/nite01.htm.

Muhammad as-Sayyid, A.B. (2006). *Pola Makan Rasulullah: Makanan sehat berkualitas menurut al-Quran dan as-Sunnah* [Rules of the Prophet on food: Quality healthy food according to the Quran and as-Sunnah]. Jakarta, Indonesia: Almahira.

Murphy, S., & Smith, C. (1993). Crutches, confetti or useful tools? Professionals' views on and use of health education leaflets. *Health Education Research*, *8*(2), 205–215. Available online at http://her.oxfordjournals.org/cgi/content/abstract/8/2/205.

National Institute of Child Health Greece. (1997). *The health promoting school: An investment in education, health and democracy*. Retrieved from http://www.schoolsforhealth.eu/upload/pubs/TheHPSaninvestmentineducationhealthanddemocracy.pdf.

Need public–parents partnership, Minister. (2010, July 1). *The Brunei Times*. Retrieved from http://www.brudirect.com/index.php/2010063024183/Local-News/need-public-parents-partnership-minister.html.

Nutbeam, D. (2000). Health literacy as a public health goal: A challenge for contemporary health education and communication strategies into the 21st century. *Health Promotion International, 15*(3), 259–267. Retrieved from http://www.rotarydexter.org/program/material/Nutbeam_article.pdf.

Ottoman, A. (2006, November 28). Dental health not up to standard. *Borneo Bulletin*. Retrieved from http://www.moh.gov.bn/news/20061128a.htm.

Paul, C. L., Redman, S., & Sanson-Fisher, R. W. (2003). Print material content and design: Is it relevant to effectiveness? *Health Education Research, 18*(2), 181–190.

Prime Minister's Office. (2008). *Brunei Darussalam key indicators 2008*. Bandar Seri Begawan: Department of Economic Planning and Development, Prime Minister's Office, Brunei Darussalam.

Pucher, J., & Dijkstra, L. (2003). Promoting safe walking and cycling to improve public health: Lessons from the Netherlands and Germany. *American Journal of Public Health, 93*(9), 1509–1516.

Rasidah, H. A. B. (2010, May 17). Concern over teen abortions in Sultanate. *Brunei Times*. Retrieved from http://www.brudirect.com/index.php/2010051721443/Local-News/concern-over-teen-abortions-in-sultanate.html.

Rauzon, S., Wang, M., Studer, M., & Crawford, P. (2010). *Students' knowledge, attitudes, and behavior in relation to food: An evaluation of the School Lunch Initiative*. Berkeley, CA: Dr Robert C. and Veronica Atkins Center for Weight and Health, University of California at Berkeley. Available online at http://www.schoollunchinitiative.org/downloads/sli_eval_full_report_2010.pdf.

Razak, A., & Ong, J. (2007, July 1.). Brunei joins fight against smoking. *Brunei Times*. Retrieved from http://www.bt.com.bn/news/2007/07/01/brunei_joins_fight_against_smoking.

Saelens, B. E., Sallis, J. F., Black, J. B., & Chen, D. (2003).Neighborhood-based differences in physical activity: An environment scale evaluation. *American Journal of Public Health, 93*(9), 1552–1558.

Smith, G., Kippax, A., Aggleton, P., & Tyrer, P. (2003). HIV/AIDS school-based education in selected Asia-Pacific countries. *Sex Education, 3*(1), 3–21.

Teach sex education in school. (2010, June 2). *Brunei Times*. Retrieved from http://www. brudirect.com/index.php/2010060122372/Local-News/teach-sex-education-inschools.html.

Tee, E.-S. (2002). Obesity in Asia: Prevalence and issues in assessment methodologies. *Asia Pacific Journal of Clinical Nutrition, 11*(3), 694–701.

United Nations Development Program (UNDP). (2009). *Human development report 2009*. Retrieved from http://hdr.undp.org/en/media/HDR_2009_EN_Complete.pdf.

United Nations Office on Drugs and Crime. (2009). *Commonwealth Youth Program, Government of Brunei and UNODC collaborate to fight drug abuse in Brunei*. Retrieved from http://www.unodc.org/india/en/brunei-cyp-workshop.html.

Van Eekelen, A., Stokvis-Brantsma, H., Frolich, M., Smelt, A. H. M., & Stokvis, H. (2000). Prevalence of glucose intolerance among Malays in Brunei. *Diabetes Care, 23*(9), 1435–1436.

Williams, R. (2003). *Three soccer balls, two netballs and no health education: Can healthy outcomes be achieved? A case study of one teacher's efforts to promote healthy lifestyles in a SE Asian high school*. Unpublished paper, School of Education, Murdoch University, Murdoch, Western Australia. Retrieved from http://fulltext.ausport.gov.au/fulltext/2002/achper/Williams.pdf.

Wilson, C. (2010, April 8). Smoking top cause of cancer deaths in Brunei. *Brunei fm!* Retrieved from http://news.brunei.fm/2010/04/08/smoking-top-cause-of-cancer-death-in-brunei/.

World Health Organization (WHO). (2004). *Brunei Darussalam environmental health country profile*. Retrieved from http://www.wpro.who.int/NR/rdonlyres/CC03E151-7FCA-47A1-A587-6443C 7F05 1E7/0/brunei_ehcp_19Nov2004.pdf.

World Health Organization (WHO). (2008). *Ministry of Health's mission, vision and objectives*. Retrieved from http://www.wpro.who.int/countries/2008/bru/national_health_ priorities.htm.

World Health Organization (WHO). (2009a). World Health Organization Regional Office for the Western Pacific 2005–2010. Retrieved from http://www.wpro.who.int/countries/2007/bru/national_health_priorities.htm.

World Health Organization (WHO). (2009b). *Health situation and trends: Communicable and noncommunicable diseases, health risk factors and transition*. Retrieved from http://www. wpro.who.int/countries/bru/2010/health_situation.htm.

Zakaria, M., Wahab, M., Ismail, K., & Abdullah Bayoh, M. R. F. (2010). *Transport 2010*. Retrieved from http://www.transport2010.blogspot.com/.

ACKNOWLEDGEMENT

The author wishes to thank the following for assisting with the preparation of this chapter: Peck-Yoke Oh for her assistance in proof reading this chapter, officers from the Health Promotion Centre of the Ministry of Health and the Health Education Unit of the Ministry of Education for sharing information, views and experience on health education in Brunei, and Dr Hj Gamal Abd Nasir Hj Zakaria and Dr Hjh Salwa D. Hj Mahalle for their advice on references to the *Quran* and *Hadith*.

Irene Poh-Ai Cheong
University Brunei Darussalam
Brunei Darussalam
email: irenecpa2007@yahoo.com

25. INTEGRATION OF HEALTH EDUCATION FOR SUSTAINABLE DEVELOPMENT

Sabah's Initiatives

INTRODUCTION

Sabah, located north of Borneo, is bordered by Sarawak on its south-west and by East Kalimantan of Indonesia to the south. The area that Sabah encompasses— 73,711 square kilometers—makes the state the second largest in Malaysia. Sabah is popularly known as "the land below the wind."

About 60% of Sabah's population is distributed in the rural areas while the remaining 40% are concentrated in the major towns. Sabah's interior is mountainous and hilly and is traversed by several rivers with vast stretches of forest. Sabah has one of the highest population growth rates in Malaysia. In 2000, the population was estimated to be just over three and a half million. With an average increase of six percent per year, the population by 2010 is expected to reach almost five and a half million (Siang Chin & Johan Ipe, 2000). Sabah has 38 ethnic groups, of which the largest indigenous ethnic group is Kadazandusun, followed by Bajau and Murut; the largest non-indigenous group is Chinese (eMas Sabah, 2010).

Sabah is the poorest state in Malaysia; the per capita income of 16% of its households is below the poverty line (Mohd Yusof, 2009). Sabah has the second and fourth largest number of primary and secondary schools in Malaysia, respectively, with about 88% (1,131) of schools located in rural areas (Nuri, 2010). However, in 2005, Sabah recorded only a 55% school enrolment compared to the national average of a little more than 77%. Among the reasons identified for poor enrolment are lack of awareness of the importance of education, lack of access to schools, location of schools, poverty, and mountainous terrain (Dullah, Kassim, Mori, Christina, & Nai'mah, 2010).

Some remote or rural areas are still inaccessible by road, so communication is either by river or helicopter and dependent on weather conditions and seasons. The poverty, difficult accessibility, and lack of infrastructure and public facilities associated with many rural areas affect the health of primary and secondary school students. For example, about 60% of students in the islands and coastal areas have stunted growth because they and their parents live in poverty and have poor knowledge of good nutrition (Dullah et al., 2010). The Third National Health and Morbidity Health Survey 2006 (NHMS III) (Ministry of Health, Institute for Public Health, 2008) found that just under 30%

of students (under 18 years old) were underweight and nearly 53% had stunted growth.

Poverty and accessibility are also the main factors, particularly in rural areas in Sabah, contributing to lack of awareness about health education (Osman, 2010). Lack of infrastructural and basic facilities, quality teachers, parental involvement in education, and motivation and encouragement also contribute to the low level of education in general in rural areas (Nuri, 2010). Inadequate electricity and piped water may provide other reasons for the poor performance of Sabah secondary schools in rural areas (Dullah et al., 2010). For example, studies in the rural schools (Center for Rural Education and Development, 2007) show that 42% of the schools do not have clean water and around 92% have no electricity supply.

Urban areas also show health issues, with an unhealthy diet common among urban primary and secondary school students due to their parents' lifestyles. According to Asma', Nawalyah, Rokiah, and Mohd Nasir (2010), eating food away from home (bought from a mobile stall or canteen) is fast and convenient. Even students who lead healthy lifestyles (e.g., good eating habits, sufficient physical activity) are at risk of contracting food and waterborne diseases such as cholera, in part because of lack of awareness of good hygiene and food-handling techniques among workers in the school canteen. Also, some students in urban areas come from unhealthy settlements where lack of sanitation is often associated with diseases such as malaria.

HEALTH, EDUCATION, AND SUSTAINABLE DEVELOPMENT

The United Nations Division for Sustainable Development lists 44 themes under sustainable development. According to UNESCO (2009), all themes involve social, environmental, economic, or cultural aspects of development, and relate to both time and space. These four aspects of sustainable development take into account the needs of future generations, and equally the needs of the present generation. The concepts of sustainability can be seen as conserving natural resources, the complexity of relationships between material and social living conditions, generational equity, and justice in the distribution and development of resources, affluence, and quality of life (German Commission for UNESCO, 2010). Health is clearly related to all four of these aspects, particularly sustainable social development (UNESCO, 2009). The integration of sustainability concepts into health and education needs to draw out the interconnections between social, environmental, cultural, and economic problems and achievements.

UNESCO has identified four major thrusts of education for sustainable development (ESD):

- Improving basic education (access to quality education);
- Reorienting existing education systems to address sustainable development;
- Developing public understanding and awareness; and
- Providing training programs for all sectors of society, including business, industry, and government (UNESCO, 2007).

UNESCO (2009) defines ESD as a learning process or approach to teaching. It implies transformation brought about by bringing sustainable development into all facets of school life at both primary and secondary levels. Integration of health education for sustainable development can be seen not only as health equity but also as justice in terms of equitable distribution and development of infrastructural and basic facilities, teachers' skills and personal attributes, parental involvement, and motivation and encouragement in Sabah rural primary and secondary schools.

Another initiative is the Millennium Development Goals (MDG), which focus specifically on elevating health status and alleviating disease. The initiative consists of eight goals:

1. Eradication of extreme poverty and hunger;
2. Universal primary education;
3. Gender equality;
4. Reduction in child mortality;
5. Improved maternal health;
6. Combating HIV/AIDS, malaria, and other infectious diseases;
7. Environmental sustainability; and
8. Global partnerships for development (WHO, 2010).

Because ESD and MDG are almost directly linked, they support each other and so make it easier to enhance the health-related and other attitudes, behaviors, and awareness of rural and urban primary and secondary school students.

In order to create sustainable school development with respect to health education, relevant agencies carry out planned learning activities, both formal and informal. Sustainable school development promotes integration of health and education, which leads to sustainable student development in terms of knowledge, skills, and good values. This concept of sustainable school development is based on an integrated approach that involves the school community as a whole, the students' families (through parent–teacher associations), local communities (e.g., village committees), the government (the Ministries of Health and Education), and the private sector, as well as non-governmental organizations.

Ideally, the benefits of sustainable school development and sustainable student development provide parents and students with more educational opportunities. These, in turn, raise students' learning motivation and increase their ability to master knowledge and skills. There is also opportunity to shape the competency and personality of students by:

• Acculturating courtesy and good manners;
• Strengthening the 3K Programme (cleanliness, health, and safety); and
• Enhancing student discipline (Zainal Abidin, Omar, & Hamoon, 2009).

Incorporation of health issues into the ESD framework thus makes health education more relevant and interesting to students, and enhances the outcome and quality of education overall.

Health Education for Sustainable Development

The World Health Organization (WHO, 2010) defines health not only as an absence of disease or infirmity but also as a state of complete physical, mental, social, and spiritual wellbeing. This definition implies that health affects and is affected by education generally and by sustainable development specifically (UNESCO, 2009). The presence of poverty and inequality, as highlighted by the MDG agenda (WHO, 2010), makes integration of health and education a crucial means of achieving sustainable development.

The Bonn Call for Action on Promoting Sustainable Global Health (2007, p. 4) emphasizes that:

... good health is good wealth—health is the bedrock of economic prosperity, and fosters improved human productivity and, consequently, better investment opportunities; good health is good governance. A healthy workforce, safe living and working conditions, social health protection, and access to water and sanitation foster stable cities, rural areas, and societies; and good health is good for security and peace building. Providing sufficient health services to all is not only an expression of social solidarity, but the foundation of social stability and sustainable development, and an indispensable pillar of human security.

The Dakar Framework for Action, in its expanded commentary (Education World Forum, 2000, p. 11), similarly suggests that good health relates to the achievement of education for all (EFA) "as an input and condition necessary for learning; as an outcome of effective quality education; and as a sector that must collaborate with education to achieve the goal of EFA."

SABAH'S INITIATIVES

Over the first decade of the 21st century, Sabah's federal and state governments, along with the state's Ministries of Education and Health, sought to develop health education that would enhance health-related attitudes, behaviors, and awareness. However, despite these agencies' efforts, little has been achieved in terms of realizing these aims. Although Malaysian health education at primary and secondary school levels covers psychomotor, affective, and cognitive wellbeing, it seems that the determinant of poor performance in rural primary and secondary schools is a lack of sustainable development. For example, eating disorders amongst primary and secondary school students arising out of poverty adversely affect students' learning. There is thus, in the case of Sabah, an urgent need to provide every individual primary and secondary school student (and particularly students in remote or rural areas) with ways of practicing good health care (Marzuki, 2009; Osman, 2010). This need has implications for the school environment, classroom teaching practices, and teacher education (Luepker, Murray, Jacobs, Mittelmark, Bracht, & Carlaw, 1994).

Although Malaysia was not included in the UNESCO report titled *A Situational Analysis of Education for Sustainable Development in the Asia Pacific*, it tried to address matters in the report by proposing changes to the Ministry of Education Malaysia's efforts to promote sustainable development education in the primary and secondary education system (Zainal Abidin et al., 2009). One of the authors of this chapter has been involved in teaching the course ESD to primary school leaders at the University of Malaysia Sabah (UMS). Because of experience gained while conducting this course, he went on to conduct another initiative—the Sustainable Community Development Project. This took place from October 2010 to November 2011 and received funding from UMS and Sabah's parliament.

The project promoted health education by targeting primary school children at the individual level. The children were encouraged to practice a healthy lifestyle in terms of personal hygiene, such as hand-washing, dental and oral health care, and taking regular baths. The project also endeavored to heighten community awareness about the importance of cleanliness, good nutrition, and the eating of traditional foods as well as the importance of efforts focused on combating pollution and climate change.

The medical faculty at the UMS recently introduced an initiative called the UMS–Community Partnership in Wellness Program. The partnership focuses on promoting family health and sending health-care professionals to work amongst the indigenous people of Sabah's rural areas (Osman, 2010). This initiative is seen as the most powerful source of influence on an individual student's development. Through this program, the community is taught the correct way of taking medicine and is empowered to take care of their health by knowing how to avoid communicable diseases such as dengue fever, tuberculosis, HIV infection, malaria, hepatitis B, and cholera.

Sabah school students' engagement in health education is also influenced by their levels of reading and writing literacy, which naturally have an impact on all aspects of their education, including health. Literacy among primary and secondary school students in Sabah varies because of the difficulties associated with accommodating the language and cultural needs of Sabah's 38 ethnic groups, which differ in their speech, attire, music, dance, and craft (Sabihah, Paul, Asmady, Mohammad Tahir, & Aliaakbar, 2010). As a collective, the groups speak nearly 100 dialects.

Among the more recent initiatives for raising the standard not only of education but also of health among Sabah primary and secondary school students are tuition voucher schemes and the Poor Children Trust Fund. The Ministry of Education encourages healthy and responsible lifestyles through programs such as Family Health Education (FHE), as well as co-curricular activities in schools. In primary schools, specified aspects of FHE are taught through the curriculum subject physical and health education. In secondary schools, health and sex education is also taught through physical and health education, as well as through science, biology, and moral and Islamic education. Islamic education is a compulsory school subject, and the teaching of sexual and reproductive health under its auspices means that Islamic values and good conduct are made a part of that teaching. However, some current social problems and youth misconduct suggest limitations to the success of sex education in schools. In addition, many teachers avoid teaching this component or are not skilled or trained to deal with these sensitive issues.

Nonetheless, health education in Sabah has improved over recent decades, with various health programs initiated in cooperation with the State Education Department and the Ministry of Health. These programs extend to a range of settings other than schools, including communities, worksites, health-care settings, homes, and the consumer marketplace, thus enhancing the targeting and communication of health messages and healthy practices to people in Sabah, including those in remote areas (Mullen et al., 1995). Today, there is a greater emphasis than previously on health education within health service delivery places such as primary-care settings, physicians' offices, health maintenance organizations, public health clinics, and hospitals (King, Rimer, Balshem, & Engstrom, 1993; Walsh & McPhee, 1992).

CONCLUSION

Given changing attitudes, behaviors, and awareness within the context of health education, there is a need to take a closer look at how the people of Sabah interact with their environment. There is also a need to pay greater heed to community health, school health practices, and the establishment of supportive environments. It is important that the government be more proactive in creating the incentives, regulations, and benefits that allow the establishment and continuance of an integrated system of health education between it and the schools. Achievement of this aim requires more communication between government and schools. New conceptualizations about the changing nature of health education need critical consideration in terms of the attitudinal, behavioral, and awareness components of health education programs.

The increasing age of the population with the associated issues of elder care, childcare, and working mothers, as well as issues relating to rural and remote areas and the increasing cultural diversity of workers (i.e., issues relating to language and low income) call for new strategies focused on sustainable development. Strategies, preferably within long-term projects, designed to combine health goals with wellness goals in the most efficient ways possible must be initiated to meet the needs and expectations of a healthy population. Communicating health-promoting information within schools and among practitioners, researchers, and teachers relies on engaging this diverse representation in information dissemination, planning, and decisionmaking. This approach should also have the benefit of creating better dialogue and partnering amongst researchers and practitioners, especially with respect to implementing understandings drawn from current research in health education.

Sabah's initiatives with respect to health education for sustainable development rely on strategies that combine the goals for health and the environment. As such, there is considerable need for research within the sphere of health education that focuses on environmental health. In order to promote and develop this need, there must be collaboration amongst health providers, such as government agencies, non-governmental organizations, and schools. That collaboration must take into account the realities of the ever-changing attitudes, behaviors, and awareness of both rural and urban communities, and it must be presented in environmental health terms—not health promotion terms—through non-formal initiatives in Sabah schools. Finally, it must have an ecological perspective.

REFERENCES

Asma', A., Nawalyah, A. G., Rokiah, M. Y., & Mohd Nasir, M. T. (2010, July). *Food at home (FAH) and food away from home (FAFH) among married couples in an urban community in Selangor, Malaysia.* Paper presented at the International Conference on Sustainable Development, Universiti Putera Malaysia, Selangor.

Bonn Call for Action on Promoting Sustainable Global Health. (2007). Retrieved from http://www.ilo.org/public/german/region/eurpro/bonn/download/bonndeclaration_ef.pdf.

Center for Rural Education and Development. (2007). *Rural school index.* Kota Kinabalu, Sabah: Universiti Malaysia Sabah.

Dullah, M., Kassim, M., Mori, K., Christina, P. L., & Nai'mah, Y. (2010). Quality of living: Poverty, infrastructure, health and education. In D. Ramzah, A. Marja, & O. Sabihah (Eds.), *Sabah priority issues: Setting the course for change* (pp. 13–33). Kota Kinabalu, Sabah: Universiti Malaysia Sabah.

Education World Forum. (2000). *The Dakar Framework for Action. Education for all: Meeting our collective commitments.* Retrieved from http://www.unesco.org/education/efa/ed_for_all/framework.shtml.

eMas Sabah. (2010). *Sabah population.* Retrieved from http://www.sabah.org.my/archive/penduduk_1.htm.

German Commission for UNESCO. (2010). *Universities for sustainable development: Declaration by the German Rectors' Conference and the German Commission for UNESCO on higher education for sustainable development.* Bonn, Germany: Hochschulrektorenkonferenz.

King, E., Rimer, B., Balshem, J. S. A., & Engstrom, P. (1993). Promoting mammography use through progressive interventions. *American Journal of Public Health, 84*(1), 1644–1656.

Luepker. R. V., Murray, D. M., Jacobs, D. R., Mittelmark, M. B., Bracht, N., & Carlaw, R. (1994). Community education for cardiovascular disease prevention: Risk factor changes in the Minnesota Heart Health Program. *American Journal of Public Health, 84*, 1383–1393.

Marzuki M. I. (2009). Primary health care setting in Sabah: Issues and challenges. In *Proceedings of Second International Conference on Rural Medicine.* Kota Kinabalu, Sabah.

Ministry of Health, Institute for Public Health. (2008). *The Third National Health and Morbidity Survey 2006 (NHMS III).* Kuala Lumpur, Malaysia: Ministry of Health.

Mohd Yusof, I. (2009). Issues of rural health in Sabah. In *Proceedings of workshop on future direction of rural medicine.* Kota Kinabalu, Sabah.

Mullen, P. D., Evans, D., Forster, J., Gottlieb, N., Kreuter, M., Moon, R., & Strecher, V. (1995). Settings as an important dimension in health education/promotion policy, programs, and research. *Health Education Quarterly, 22*, 329–345.

Nuri, U. (2010, July 6–8). *Science and mathematics in rural and remote areas of Sabah: Challenges of teaching and learning from perspectives of Sabah Education Department.* Paper presented at the Science and Mathematics Education Workshop for Stakeholders 2010, Kota Kinabalu, Sabah.

Osman, A. (2010, October). *Rural health: The way forward.* Paper presented at the University of Malaysia Sabah professorial inaugural lecture. Kota Kinabalu, Sabah: Universiti Malaysia Sabah.

Sabihah, O., Paul, P. Asmady, I., Mohammad Tahir, M., & Aliaakbar, G. (2010). Sabah chapter: Revisiting the layout. In D. Ramzah, A. Marja, & O. Sabihah (Eds.), *Sabah priority issues: Setting the course for change* (pp. 1–4). Kota Kinabalu, Sabah: Universiti Malaysia Sabah.

Siang Chin, T., & Johan Ipe, J. (2000, June 10–13). *Information systems for the integration of Sabah Health Services.* Paper presented at the Health Vision 2010, Sabah Health Department, Kota Kinabalu, Sabah.

UNESCO. (2007). *United Nations Decade of Education for Sustainable Development (DESD 2005–2014): The first two years.* Paris: Author. Retrieved from http://unesdoc.unesco.org/images/0015/001540/154093e.pdf.

UNESCO. (2009). *Review of contexts and structures for education for sustainable development: United Nations Decade of Education for Sustainable Development (DESD, 2005–2014).* Paris, France: Author.

Walsh, J., & McPhee, S. (1992). A systems model of clinical preventive care: An analysis of factors influencing patient and physician. *Health Education Quarterly, 19,* 157–176.

World Health Organization (WHO). (2010). *Millennium Development Goals (MDGs).* Retrieved from http://www.who.int.

Zainal Abidin, S., Omar, O., & Hamoon, K. D. (2009). *The situational analysis of the Malaysian primary education systems towards sustainable development.* Penang, Malaysia: Regional Centre of Expertise on Education for Sustainable Development.

Mohd. Zaki Ishak and Hamzah Md. Omar
University of Malaysia Sabah
Sabah
Malaysia
email: mokish@tm.net.my

HOANG-MINH DANG AND BAHR WEISS

26. MENTAL HEALTH EDUCATION AND TRAINING IN VIETNAM

The Role of Clinical Psychology

BACKGROUND

In 1975, at the end of a long and destructive war, Vietnam faced severe economic and social problems. Eleven years on, in response to the economic challenges, Vietnam began to move from its previously highly centrally controlled economy to a more mixed, market-based economy. After two decades of this reform, known as Doi Moi ("renovation"), Vietnam reached a point where it was evident that the country had achieved significant economic progress. GDP growth stabilized at around 8% per year, a rate of growth which makes Vietnam the second most rapidly developing economy in the world, although the recent global economic downturn has seen the rate drop to around 5.5% per year (World Bank, 2010).

Although the policies of Doi Moi are generally deemed successful in economic terms, concerns have been raised over the lack of a commensurate growth in social policy, particularly with regard to health. Gabriele (2006), for example, points to the social costs and ills brought about by rapid economic growth, noting in particular the increasing stress that these are having for families in general and children in particular.

We begin this chapter with a review of the mental health challenges facing Vietnamese children subsequent to the changes brought about by the Doi Moi policy shift. We then discuss different approaches to addressing these challenges, one of which is the provision of mental health education to both students and teachers, with content designed not only to correct misconceptions about mental health but also to provide the adaptive skills needed to improve mental health. We also focus on the training of counselors and mental health clinicians, practitioners who need to intervene when mental health education is not sufficient. Finally, we review our initiative to develop a graduate program in clinical psychology at Vietnam National University. This program is the first such program in Vietnam.

MENTAL HEALTH CHALLENGES IN VIETNAM

Challenges Facing Vietnamese Children

The rapid, uncontrolled economic change arising out of the Doi Moi reforms has had the unfortunate side effect of limiting families' traditional ability to

N. Taylor, F. Quinn, M. Littledyke and R.K. Coll (eds.), Health Education in Context, 243–252.

successfully protect their children and socialize them into healthy, adaptive adults (Korinek, 2004). For example, in response to increased economic opportunity, parents often work long hours, with many leaving their young children alone for long periods of time without adult supervision (Ruiz-Casares & Heymann, 2009).

This situation is one particularly faced by rural parents and children who move away from their home village, the members of which have known one another for generations. Families typically move to urban areas where they lack the generations-old social support and child-rearing networks available in their rural homeland. These changes place Vietnamese children at increased risk of developing mental health problems (United Nations Vietnam Youth Theme Group, 2010).

Status of Vietnamese Children's Mental Health

Several studies have investigated Vietnamese children's mental health. Overall, the studies suggest that many Vietnamese children face significant stress in their lives, and experience a high incidence of mental health problems. In their study of northern Vietnamese secondary school children in Hanoi, Hoang-Minh and Tu (2009) found that about 25% of the children met diagnostic criteria for a psychiatric disorder. In southern Vietnam, Anh, Anh, Quyen, and Hang (2007) conducted an assessment of social and behavioral problems among high school students in Ho Chi Minh City. Sixteen percent of the students were experiencing significant affective problems, 19% had social relationship problems, and 24% were judged as having behavior problems. Several years earlier, Tran et al. (2003) found similar results when conducting their Young Lives Project. This epidemiological survey of the developmental and health outcomes of children across Vietnam (as well as in several other countries) found Vietnamese children facing a wide range of stressors, with 20% having experienced or experiencing significant mental illness.

Mental Health Resources in Vietnam

At the beginning of Doi Moi, the Vietnamese government decided to focus its limited financial resources on direct economic development, a response that is typical of most developing countries. The social services, among them education and health (including mental health), were accorded low priority (Stern, 1998), which meant a limited availability of resources for treating mental health conditions (Gabriele, 2006; Schirmer, Cartwright, Montegut, Dreher, & Stovall, 2004). According to a World Health Organization (WHO) report on the mental health system in Vietnam (WHO, 2006), the total number of personnel working in this field per head of population in Vietnam is low, as reported in Table 1. This lack of resourcing is especially evident with respect to children. For example, Vietnam currently has only about 15 child psychiatrists.

When we first began working in children's mental health in Vietnam, we and our colleagues conducted a needs assessment (Weiss, Tu, Ngo, & Sang, 2002), which saw us meeting with 23 educational and mental-health-related agencies in six cities across Vietnam. Twenty-two of these agencies stated that children's mental health represented a very serious problem in Vietnam and that there was an almost complete lack of research and clinical training available in this area of health provision. We drew the following conclusions from our survey of the state of child mental health in Vietnam:

- Both professionals and laypeople see children's mental health problems as a serious problem facing the country;
- Clinical infrastructure to effectively treat these mental health problems is lacking;
- The research infrastructure needed to inform the development of effective mental health treatments is lacking; and
- There is no training infrastructure whatsoever dedicated to improving teachers' and other related professionals' knowledge of mental health, and there has been no development of clinical and research infrastructures.

Table 1: Mental health personnel in Vietnam

Personnel	Total number	Per 100,000 population
1. Psychiatrists	286	0.35
2. Non-psychiatric physicians	730	0.90
3. Nurses	1,700	2.10
4. Psychologists	50	0.06
5. Social workers	125	0.15
6. Occupational therapists	4	0.01
7. Other health/mental health workers (non-physician primary health care workers, health assistants, medical assistants, etc.)	650	0.80

MENTAL HEALTH EDUCATION AND TRAINING PROGRAMS AT VIETNAM NATIONAL UNIVERSITY

Several approaches can be used to reduce the effects of the problems just cited. We consider that one of the most efficient ways is the provision of mental health education in primary and secondary schools. Mental health education (MHE) has been defined as education and training that enables individuals and groups of people to behave in a manner conducive to the promotion, maintenance, and restoration of mental health. It comprises intentionally constructed learning opportunities designed to improve mental health knowledge and attitudes and to develop skills beneficial to individual and community mental health (WHO, 1998).

Two points should be highlighted in this definition. First, MHE involves development of attitudes and knowledge, as well as development of skills. Second, mental health education enhances not only the mental health of the individuals involved in this form of education but also the members of their community. MHE has, we believe, particular relevance to the situation in Vietnam because it provides the type of socialization and training that families challenged by the rapid social change have found difficult to provide. MHE also addresses the newer health challenges that many families now face, such as drug abuse.

The most sustainable way to provide MHE in the schools is through teacher training because this approach targets both teachers' general classroom management skills as well as the acquisition of specific MHE programs for students (Han & Weiss, 2005). The most efficient and sustainable way to educate teachers about MHE is to include it in pre-service teacher training curricula and in professional development courses for in-service teachers, as indicated in Table 2.

Table 2: Outline of teacher-focused school-based MHE programs

---

Trainees
- Integrated into the teacher training curriculum of teacher education colleges
- Training of teachers already in the field

Program content
- Knowledge about and identification of attitudes toward students' emotional and behavioral/mental health problems
- Skills
  - General classroom management skills
  - Specific MHE programs (e.g., life skills training)

At the Vietnam National University (VNU) School of Education, all student teachers are now taught MHE. Teachers first learn knowledge designed to modify their attitudes toward and understanding of students' emotional and behavioral problems. In Vietnam, teachers often view these problems as willful and intentional, and this attitude is associated with harsh punishment that is counter-productive. For instance, teachers perceive children who are disruptive in class as willfully disrespectful of the teacher, yet often the child is simply reflecting what he or she has learned (or failed to learn) at home (Anh et al., 2007). Mental health education helps teachers understand that, regardless of how they feel about their students' behavior, these young people are simply responding in ways that align with what they experience and learn during their everyday lives at home and school. Accordingly, if a teacher wants a student to behave differently, the teacher needs to change the environment.

For this reason, student teachers at VNU also learn skills that will allow them to modify classroom environments to maximally support their students' mental health. They furthermore learn about the importance of reinforcing students' positive behaviors, and the most effective ways of doing this. A study conducted in the United States found that teachers provide approximately one-tenth of the optimal level of positive reinforcement for their students (Sutherland, Wehby, & Copeland, 2000). The study also made clear that if students exhibiting challenging behaviors did not receive this support, they had difficulty replacing these behaviors with positive ones.

Life Skills Training for Enhanced Mental Health Functioning

In addition to providing teachers with training in general classroom skills, the VNU School of Education provides both pre-service and in-service teachers with a *life skills* MHE program. (The program is mandatory for the student teachers.) Life skills are a set of skills that allow individuals to deal effectively with the challenges that they encounter in everyday life. They represent a broad concept, but are considered to include decisionmaking skills, critical thinking skills, skills for managing emotions (in particular, anger, grief, and anxiety), skills for coping with stress, and adaptive interpersonal skills, including conflict management skills and assertiveness skills (Clark & Crosland, 2009). Ordinarily, these skills are acquired directly through life experience, but when this is not sufficient, they can be taught through intentional training (Grand, 2000). This need for intentional training often occurs in settings experiencing rapid transition or change (WHO, 1999).

The MHE life skills program is offered to in-service teachers throughout the country. The first such program took place in 2010, in Haiphong (northern Vietnam) and in Dalat (southern Vietnam). Participants were civics education teachers, and educators from provincial departments of education. Each province in Vietnam sent five representatives to the two training events, which meant an overall attendance of 325. The program was positioned as a "train the trainer" model in which the participants, having learned about the skills, were expected to train additional people in their own provinces. The training itself focused on both values education (content included the theoretical framework of values education and drew in values pertaining to caring and cooperative behavior), and the life skills education program, which focused on self-awareness, conflict resolution, anger management, and problem-solving. The training also included didactic presentation as well as extensive role-playing with feedback.

MENTAL HEALTH INTERVENTION IN VIETNAM

Sometimes, MHE is insufficient, and direct intervention becomes necessary. As we noted above, at the time we began our work at VNU, the limited availability of resources was stymying opportunity to train child mental health researchers and practitioners. A review of literature provided us with three possible ways of increasing mental health research and treatment capacity: (1) short-term in-country seminars conducted by "foreign experts," (2) overseas training, and (3) mentored-research and program-implementation projects. Thus, our next goal was to evaluate each of these approaches for their effectiveness and sustainability with regard to increasing mental health research and clinical capacity.

Over a period of several years, we conducted a series of two-week mental health research and practice training seminars, led by people with the relevant expertise from the United States, Canada, and Australia. Seminar participants included people from across Vietnam. We concluded from this experience that the short-term in-country seminars could be useful for providing focused training for mid- to advanced-level professionals. However, because the seminar did not offer extensive basic training, they did not address the fundamental need for developing new professionals. We also found that the seminars were of little or no value without extensive follow-up supervision or collaboration.

We also evaluated the utility of young professionals receiving training in foreign institutions. These individuals were supported by the Vietnamese, United States, and French governments. We found this provision to be very effective for the individuals involved, but also so expensive that it could not be sustained. The approach also carried the very real risk that the young professionals studying abroad would find life in the United States or some other affluent Western country so attractive that they would not return to their home country. One young professional who participated in this program gave up a university faculty position in Cambodia to remain illegally in the US making donuts.

The third method that we considered led to us providing mid- to upper-level professionals with one-on-one mentoring. Our rationale for this approach was that often the best way to learn something is through direct experience guided by someone more senior than oneself (Allen & Eby, 2007). We planned, conducted, and evaluated seven medium-term, mentored research projects focusing on such topics as mental health epidemiological surveys in schools, assessments of the mental health functioning of street children and individuals addicted to drugs, and development of a model for school-based mental health intervention. The results of these projects are reported in Dang and Weiss (2007).

Our conclusion at the end of this process was that long-distance mentoring is feasible and very useful for training mid- to advanced-level professionals and is probably more useful than short-term seminars. The projects also helped us identify factors that supported the long-distance mentoring. These included:

- The mentored researchers' strong commitment to improving their abilities;
- An entrepreneurial spirit that allowed the researchers to resolve implementation problems; and
- The researchers working together as a close-knit network.

We also identified factors that impeded successful long-distance mentoring, notably:

- Different supervision styles (e.g., our Vietnamese colleagues view it as impolite to remind a teacher/mentor to do something whereas United States and Australian trainees rarely hesitate to act in this way); and

- A lack of research infrastructure, such as a basic pool of valid mental health-assessment instruments.

However, in line with our overall conclusion regarding the short-term seminars, we decided that this mentoring still did not provide us with a best way of developing new professionals.

VNU School of Education Doctoral Program in Clinical Psychology

Having completed our evaluation of these three approaches to increasing mental health capacity and having concluded that none of them was sufficiently effective, efficient, and sustainable, we decided on another approach. We considered that the most sustainable, albeit highly challenging, approach would be to support development of a child-focused, research-oriented, clinical-psychology doctoral program at VNU School of Education. The research focus was deemed essential because we could not assume that mental health programs developed and found effective in the West would be suitable for Vietnam. In all likelihood, such programs would need to be adapted.

We obtained funding from the United States' National Institutes of Health Fogarty International Center to support this project, which began in 2006. The key activities informing program development have been:

- Providing two Vietnamese psychologists, who will eventually become key faculty members of the VNU program, with PhD-level training in the United States;
- Providing post-doctoral training to two Vietnamese clinical psychologists, who will also become key faculty members;
- Securing technical assistance to develop the program's curriculum; and
- Gaining support from people able to offer instructional assistance and course supervision for the first few years of the program.

Program development has been underpinned by three important principles:

1. The program must be culturally appropriate;
2. It must be sustainable in a low-resource environment; and
3. It must follow scientifically rigorous research methods.

An early stage of program development involved reviewing the curricula of United States, Canadian, and Australian clinical psychology programs, followed by discussion with Vietnamese education and mental health professionals. During the first phase of development, we began offering, in 2009, a two-year Master's in Clinical Psychology. Sixteen graduate students made up the first cohort of Master's students.

The Master's program consists of nine specialty clinical-psychology courses and six non-specialty courses. Courses are jointly taught by a Western and a Vietnamese instructor, with the same instructors teaching the same course across years. Sustainability comes from the expectation that Vietnamese instructors will take responsibility for the course after three years of co-teaching and is also enhanced by a tight focus on the curriculum—that is, not teaching outside its parameters. In the United States, clinical psychology programs approved by the American Psychological Association must include "breadth" requirements. This means that graduate students are required to take courses in cognitive psychology, physiological psychology, and so forth. Although these courses are an important part of training for clinical psychologists in the affluent West, they are a luxury in Vietnam and so are not included in the curriculum.

We have also had to address cultural issues pertaining to instruction. For instance, although the Western instructors are all highly experienced classroom teachers, and for the most part Vietnamese by birth (e.g., Vietnamese-American), it has been difficult for us to gauge students' reactions to our material. Unlike Western students, Vietnamese students express their reactions more subtly. Western students' facial expressions give a clear expression of confusion when they do not understand material!

CONCLUSION

Addressing children's mental health needs in developing countries such as Vietnam requires a range of approaches, from the provision of basic MHE in the schools to comprehensive MHE programs at tertiary education level, with the latter probably the most difficult to develop. Although this approach requires a relatively large initial investment, we believe that development of self-sustaining programs such as our Master's in Clinical Psychology program represents the best long-term sustainable solution to addressing mental health needs and education in an environment such as that found in Vietnam. This type of program allows for Vietnamese professionals to develop a high level of competency, for cultural adaptation of mental health programs, and for the development of long-term international collaborations.

REFERENCES

Allen, T. D., & Eby, L. T. (2007). *The Blackwell handbook of mentoring: A multiple perspectives approach.* Malden, MA: Blackwell.

Anh, L.V., Anh, P. T. N., Quyen, N. T., & Hang, N. M. (2007). A proposed model for school counseling in general education schools. In B. L. Dang & B. Weiss (Eds.), *Research findings from the Vietnam children's mental health research training program* (pp. 455–484). Hanoi, Vietnam: National University Publishing House.

Clark, B., & Crosland, K. A. (2009). Social and life skills development: Preparing and facilitating youth for transition into young adults. In B. Kerman, M. Freundlich, & A. N. Maluccio (Eds.), *Achieving permanence for older children and youth in foster care* (pp. 313–336). New York: Columbia University Press.

Dang, L. B., & Weiss, B. (2007). *Research findings from the Vietnam Children's Mental Health Research Training Program.* Hanoi, Vietnam: Educational Publishing House.

Gabriele, A. (2006). Social services policies in a developing market economy oriented towards socialism: The case of health system reforms in Vietnam. *Review of International Political Economy, 13,* 258–289.

Grand, I. C. (2000). *The life skills presentation guide.* Hoboken, NJ: John Wiley & Sons.

Han, S. S., & Weiss, B. (2005). Sustainability of teacher implementation of school-based mental health programs. *Journal of Abnormal Child Psychology, 33,* 665–679.

Hoang-Minh, D., & Tu, H. C. (2009). The mental health of secondary students in Hanoi and the need for school counseling. *Vietnamese Journal of Social Sciences and Humanities*, *25*, 11–16.

Korinek, K. (2004). Maternal employment during Northern Vietnam's era of market reform. *Social Forces*, *83*, 791–822.

Ruiz-Casares, M., & Heymann, J. (2009). *Children home alone unsupervised: Modeling parental decisions and associated factors in Botswana, Mexico, and Vietnam.* Montreal, Québec, Canada: Institute for Health and Social Policy, McGill University.

Schirmer, J. M., Cartwright, C. M, Montegut, A. J., Dreher, G. K., & Stovall, J. A. (2004). A collaborative needs assessment and work plan in behavioral medicine curriculum development in Vietnam. *Families, Systems, and Health*, *22*, 410–418.

Stern, L. M. (1998). *The Vietnamese Communist Party's agenda for reform: A study of the Eighth National Party Congress.* Jefferson, NC: McFarlane.

Sutherland, K. S., Wehby, J. H., & Copeland, S. R. (2000). Effect of varying rates of behavior-specific praise on the on-task behavior of students with EBD. *Journal of Emotional and Behavioral Disorders*, *8*, 2–8.

Tran, T., Pham, T. L, Harpham, T., Nguyen, T. H., Tran, D. T., Tod, B., & Nguyen, T. V. H. (2003). *Young Lives preliminary country report: Vietnam.* London, UK: Southbank University.

United Nations Vietnam Youth Theme Group. (2010). *United Nations position paper on young people in Viet Nam 2008–2010.* New York: United Nations.

Weiss, B., Tu, H. C., Ngo, V. K., & Sang, D. (2002). *2002 NIH D43-TW05805NIH progress report.* Nashville, TN: Vanderbilt University.

World Bank. (2010). *Gross national income per capita 2009.* Washington, DC: Author.

World Health Organization (WHO). (1998). *Health promotion glossary.* Geneva, Switzerland: Author.

World Health Organization (WHO). (1999). *Partners in life skills education.* Geneva, Switzerland: Author.

World Health Organization (WHO). (2006). *WHO-AIMS report on mental health system in Vietnam.* Hanoi, Vietnam: Author.

ACKNOWLEDGEMENT

We gratefully acknowledge the support of the US National Institutes of Health Fogarty International Center in the preparation of this chapter and for the research and training described in this chapter, in particular grants D43-TW007769, R21-TW008435, R03-TW007923, and D43-TW007769.

Hoang-Minh Dang
Vietnam National University
Hanoi
Vietnam
email: minhdh@vnu.edu.vn

Bahr Weiss
Vanderbilt University
Nashville
Tennessee
USA
email: bahr.weiss@vanderbilt.edu

YIMIN WANG

27. HEALTH EDUCATION IN CHINA (1978–2010)

Challenges and Reforms

BACKGROUND

Since 1978, China has undergone rapid socioeconomic development and several waves of school and curriculum reform at the national level. These developments have included significant efforts to improve health education and management in both primary and secondary schools. However, several reforms have not been implemented as successfully as their creators had hoped, partly because China has large rural–urban and cross-provincial disparities, especially in terms of the economy, which have had a significant impact on the development of health education.

Standards for and outcomes of health education also vary in different regions and under different circumstances. Glaring gaps exist in both the education and health-care arenas—gaps that are again associated with the stratified economic development status of each area. For example, the needs and the agenda for health education in the more remote and impoverished areas of China tend to focus on teaching students knowledge of and practices for a healthy, hygienic lifestyle. However, in relatively well-off metropolitan areas, youth diabetes is a major health problem and a trend typical in wealthy areas. In these areas, health education is perceived as the province of teachers who usually teach physical education, as well as of homeroom teachers.[1] Matters relating to mental and psychosocial health education are slowly being incorporated into the topics and concerns of health education in China, especially in some élite urban schools, but the extent of inclusion nationwide is still far from what is needed.

ISSUES

In this section, I discuss two types of issues relating to health education provision in China. The first concerns health education topics taught in the formal K–12 schooling system. The second encompasses health education efforts in the arena of informal educational settings. These efforts include information campaigns, extracurricular activities and events, and practices such as distributing health-education posters and pamphlets on school campuses and to members of the general public.

N. Taylor, F. Quinn, M. Littledyke and R.K. Coll (eds.), Health Education in Context, 253–260.

Before considering these matters, however, I consider it is important to examine how health education is envisioned at the policy level. On 6 August 1951, the Council of Government Affairs issued a report titled *Decision on Improving Students' Health in Educational Institutions at all Levels*. This publication was the first government document to address health education. It pointed out that "improvement of students' health bears great significance to guaranteeing students' success in learning and fostering a modern generation of youths with a robust body" (China Education and Research Network, n. d., ¶ 1). In 1990, the State Council of China issued a report titled *Operational Rules on Health Work in Educational Institutions*. It stated that:

> The major elements of health work in educational institutions are to monitor students' health, to offer healthcare courses for students and help them cultivate better habits of sanitation, to improve the school sanitation environment and improve sanitation conditions for teaching [in order] to strengthen prevention and treatment of contagious and common disease among students. (China Education and Research Network, n. d., ¶ 1)

These two policy documents laid the foundation for health education in China, although neither specifically addressed issues related to curriculum or pedagogy. In terms of actual curriculum and pedagogy, health education for students has been a key part of China's recent reform of the country's standard K–12 curriculum, and it tends to be a focal point of national campaigns signaled in the Chinese government's annual resolution briefs (Liu & Zhang, 2008). However, numerous challenges and many systematic problems exist at the implementation level. In 1986, the Ministry of Education in China initiated a policy mandating all public primary and secondary schools in China to include a component of health education in their curriculum, but they gave schools autonomy to formulate their own definitions of health education.

Today, the majority of inconsistencies in the curriculum standards exist in underdeveloped areas of China, where teachers and administrators lack the necessary awareness and knowledge of health education to describe it, much less to teach it effectively. Therefore, various other forms of physical education unlikely to achieve the desired goal often supplant the mandated component of health education. Also, because health education is not a mandated part of teacher training curricula, teachers as a body have no shared, unified understanding of what health education encompasses, and little, if any, understanding of how to teach it. Health education is also challenged by financial constraints, including those that limit needed teacher training.

Three other aspects of China's formal education system hinder the promotion and implementation of health education-related topics and materials. First, Chinese education, especially at the primary and secondary school levels, is generally perceived as an examination-oriented system. Although this constraint is slowly lessening, the examination culture still dominates what is taught and how it is taught in most Chinese schools. Because health education is predominantly concerned with the wellbeing of individuals and the community, it is difficult to measure learning outcomes in the short term. Also, other than a few facts-based questions, content related to health education cannot be included in the competitive, high-stakes college entrance examination. This situation makes it difficult for schools to give attention to health education beyond ensuring that students are aware of the basics of good hygiene.

The second challenge lies in the perceived relationship between families and schools, as well as in the school's perception of its own responsibilities for teaching health-related concepts and awareness to its students. In relatively wealthy metropolitan areas, the one-child policy has led families to lavish attention on their only child; in so doing, they have taught that child most of the basics of health education. However, in the relatively poor and remote countryside, parents are generally unable to shoulder the burden of responsibilities relating to health education, and teachers in the local schools usually have limited training in this area. Health education therefore tends to receive minimal attention both at home and at school.

The third challenge is the general omission in Chinese schools of content relating to mental or psychological wellbeing, an omission that is particularly evident when this area of educational provision is compared to that in some developed Western countries, such as the United States. The lack in Chinese schools is apparent in several ways. For example, most schools in China do not have a staff member primarily responsible for students' psychosocial health, nor do they have school counselors. Topics relating to mental wellbeing are very rare in both the official K–12 curriculum and textbooks. During the nationwide curriculum reforms of the past 10 or so years, health education topics have been included as optional topics only, which means that children's access to this material depends on whether their school or teachers choose to include it.

Having become considerably more mindful of these constraints, the Ministry of Education has launched in recent years a number of nationwide initiatives aimed at promoting health and physical education. One such is the Sunshine Physical Education program, which the ministry implemented in 2007. This program "makes it obligatory for students to do one hour of physical activity each day in order to confront concerns about declining youth health" ("Students Required," 2006). The program also offers various household slogans, such as "Exercise one hour per day, live a healthy life,"[2] and it re-emphasizes the national standards for physical education that have been in place since 1990. However, it does not specify incorporation of the standards in the school curriculum, and it gives no guidance on who, within the school, should take responsibility for implementing the program. Although the program has certainly raised awareness of health care and education, its full effectiveness within schools continues to be compromised by the lack of a systematic enactment of health education nationwide.

Smoking prevention and education directed toward reducing smoking-related diseases are another challenging issue in China. In line with the stipulations of the World Health Organization's (WHO) Framework Convention on Tobacco Control, which China signed on 9 January 2006, China promised to ban smoking in all indoor public places from January 2011. However, only a few cities (among them Shanghai) have given legal effect to this initiative. But even in these places, "without a national law, it is difficult to control smoking" ("China Still Smoking," 2011).

China has over 350 million smokers, which constitutes over a quarter of its entire population (Chinese Central Government, 2011). According to National Health Service Survey data, "approximately one-third to one-half of current male smokers in China … [will be] likely to have died from smoking-related diseases by 2030 if they do not quit" (Qian, Cai, Tang, Xu, & Critchely, 2010, ¶ 2). As part of efforts to curb smoking, the Ministries of Health and Education decreed that smoking would be banned from 21 June 2010 in all Chinese K–12 schools. The ruling applies to both teachers and students. In addition, teachers are also prohibited from smoking in front of their students off campus, as part of the requirement that teachers provide positive role models for their students (Chinese Central Government, 2011).

> The Chinese government sees schools as important sites in many cities for anti-smoking activities, and they are using posters and graphics posted on school walls to promote the anti-smoking message. By July 2010, the Ministry of Education had certified all schools in Beijing as smoke-free campuses, while many other major cities in China had exceeded 85% compliance with the regulation within the six months following its enactment ("All Primary and Secondary Schools in Beijing," 2010).

A number of health education activities have also taken place in informal education settings over the past two decades. For example, in 2008, the Ministry of Health, having identified more than 20 million Chinese with diabetes and about 200 million more who were overweight ("200 Million Chinese Overweight," 2004), launched a nationwide campaign that attempted to raise awareness of youth diabetes. However, sustaining the impact of this type of event-specific campaign is difficult in China. Another example relates to recent global epidemics, such as SARS (severe acute respiratory syndrome) in 2005, and H1N1 (swine flu) in 2009. These considerably raised public consciousness about the need for health education. Because of the SARS crisis, schools in both rural and urban areas are now required to disseminate informational pamphlets to students and their families and to put up posters about how to avoid epidemic diseases such as SARS. Since that time, schools have also been encouraged to equip each student with basic hygiene knowledge and to limit the spread of germs by teaching students not to engage in unhygienic practices.

At the post-secondary school level, institutions of higher learning offer health education as selective course or lectures as requested (Chinese Research and Education Network, n. d.). Efforts to prevent common diseases in schoolchildren, such as short-sightedness, trachoma, tooth decay, malnutrition, and anemia, align with a program called Comprehensive Prevention and Treatment of Common Diseases among Students (China Education and Research Network, n. d.). Other topics related to non-epidemic diseases and health education covered in general higher education institutions[3] are those associated with sex education and AIDS prevention.

Sex education—and even sex-related topics—were prohibited in the curricula at all levels of the education system in China before 1977, a ban that was largely influenced by the ideologies of the Cultural Revolution, which deemed sex a taboo (Liu, 2008). However, during China's reform era, which began in 1978, people became more aware of the need for sex education in order to reduce high rates of teenage pregnancy and of sexually-transmitted diseases such as HIV/AIDS.

Although constraints on discussing sex in schools have loosened, sex education is still conducted primarily within informal education or as extracurricular events and activities. These include special lectures in universities and the practice of setting certain days aside to disseminate sex education-related materials, often through booths featuring posters and pamphlets. Some university-initiated events or activities that focus on raising awareness of AIDS prevention, and on caring for and reducing discrimination against people with HIV, have extended beyond the campuses to their surrounding communities. This kind of university–community collaborative effort has had a very positive impact in several major cities in China, such as Beijing and Shanghai.

Although there are only a few academic programs for training health education specialists in colleges and teacher education institutions, the country gives significant emphasis to health education research. There is also considerable concern among the academic community about the state of health education in China. *Zhongguo Jiankang Jiaoyu* (the *Chinese Journal of Health Education*), a monthly periodical subsidized by the Ministry of Health in China, is specifically dedicated to health education-related research, communication, and advocacy. However, the journal, which was founded as early as 1985, focuses more on health and medicine than on education. While it promotes increasing health awareness about specific health issues, it rarely focuses on health education in formal education settings.

The fact that the official authority responsible for China's health education is the Ministry of Health and not the Ministry of Education contributes to the situation whereby health education in China is conducted primarily through informal education avenues, rather than being explicitly included in the formal curriculum. However, educators in China are increasingly realizing the importance and necessity of formal lessons dedicated to health education in both primary and secondary schools.

China has become generally welcoming of international assistance in the area of health education. This assistance includes that from experts and academics in advanced Western countries and from international non-governmental organizations (NGOs). Alleviation of poverty, health improvement, and educational support are the three domains in which China most welcomes international assistance, in part because these areas are ones that are seen, in relative terms, as not so politically sensitive.

Among the projects attracting international support are those relating to AIDS prevention education in China's more remote areas. This work is being undertaken by the Chinese government in collaboration with international NGOs. Representative initiatives include the China–Gates AIDS and the Global Fund projects, both of which are specifically devoted to AIDS awareness and prevention. China also has in place its own NGOs, whose programs include health education and welfare-based health care. For example, the Beijing Association, an NGO founded in 1993, has, amongst other initiatives, conducted training courses, counseling, public information hotlines, and health education for migrants who move from the countryside to the city. As Liu and Fang (2000, p. 1) point out, NGOs such as the Beijing Association help "the government mobilize the whole society to be involved" with movements such as AIDS prevention.

Another area of international academic cooperation and assistance is exemplified by several research projects that have been collecting empirical data from within a variety of domains, including psychosocial development and physical health. The data are being used to inform solutions to health-related problems. One such project is the Gansu Survey of Children and Families (GSCF). This longitudinal, multi-level study of rural children's welfare outcomes, including those relating to education, health, and psychosocial development, has been running since the year 2000 (Population Studies Center, University of Philadelphia, n. d.). This project is being funded by the World Bank, the Spencer Foundation, the United States National Institutes of Health, and other institutions. Its research findings have attracted the attention of the media, as well as of local academics and policymakers (especially those at the provincial level), who have picked up the need for further localized research and health-related policy reform. The marked attention given to this project makes it one of the most important examples of international research work contributing to local health education in China.

Other examples of international collaborations and exchanges include the Harvard School of Public Health's Harvard–China Health Research Group. Established in 2010, the group aims to inform researchers, scholars, and educators in health-related fields about key issues and challenges facing health and health education in China. The group hopes to work toward more collaborative effort designed to prevent the chronic diseases that prevail in both China and the United States.

DISCUSSION AND CONCLUSION

For more than three decades, health education has been one of the main areas of focus of educational reform and development both in the public school systems and in informal educational settings in China. However, because of regional gaps in economic and educational development, health education reform has been uneven, which is why more concentrated strategic efforts are necessary in the country's less developed areas in general and its rural schools in particular. Improved implementation of health education also requires strategies directed at curriculum development and teacher training.

Theories and studies of human capital suggest, or even explicitly identify, that sound health *and* good education programs have positive, significant effects on economic growth. There is clear empirical evidence in China that "the interaction of health and education stock will not reduce their impact on growth and there is perhaps a trade-off between two forms of human capital investment" (Li & Huang, 2009, p. 374). Policymakers in China, particularly those within the Ministry of Health, are well aware of these academic findings and have acted accordingly. For instance, in 2005, the ministry initiated a multi-year, nationwide public health education program, the goal of which was to "curb the fast increase of non-communicable diseases in the country" ("China Launches Health Education Program," 2005, p. 1). During the ceremony to launch the program, ministry representatives were quoted in the media as saying, "Health education is a long-term process, but also a basic measure to prevent chronic diseases … It needs joint efforts of the government, the public and the private sectors" ("China Launches Health Education Program," 2005, p. 7).

The sustainable development of health education in informal school settings also requires systematic, unified effort by educators and policymakers. In 2005, China began to advocate the need to build a harmonious society able to work toward sustainable development of the economy and of the human population. The rationale underpinning the need for health education is thus no longer restricted to the domain of human capital development (i.e., nurturing a healthy and educated labor force). Today, those involved with the promotion and practice of health education are endeavoring to ensure all individuals are able to develop their capabilities and lead a fulfilling life. However, the social inequality, especially between the rural and urban regions of China, that adversely influences basic education, health care, and convergent areas, such as health education, continues to thwart government efforts to promote health care and health education for each individual in China.

The need for quality health education in China will likely continue to gain prominence because of the government's agenda of building a harmonious society that emphasizes sustainable development, not only in terms of economic development but also in terms of human capability and wellbeing (Ross, 2006). Because of health education's clear focus on a fit and healthy populace, this area of educational provision is slowly becoming more prominent in policy reform at the government level and in curriculum reform among educators. China's *Blueprint for Medium and Long-term National Educational Reform and Development (2010–2020)*, a document that was officially published in late July 2010, makes clear this growing trend. It positions health education as "… working towards the goals of strengthening students' physical health, scientifically arranging the time for studying, daily life and physical exercises … [ensuring] students … have one hour's time for physical exercises, and continuously improv[ing] the level of students' physical health" (Ministry of Education, 2010, p. 14).

In striving to ensure health education for all students nationwide, China is giving recognition to the need not only to improve the health of its students and their awareness of health care but also to ensure that the people around them and the larger communities of which they are a part live healthy, fulfilled lives. This is the ultimate goal of health education in China, especially at the K–12 level.

NOTES

[1] Homeroom teachers are the teachers who serve a pastoral role for a specified class. These teachers are also responsible for teaching one of the core subjects, such as Chinese or English.
[2] This slogan in Chinese Pinyin is "Meitian Duanlian yi Xiaoshi, Jiankang Shenghuo Yi beizi." More information about this program is available at jyb.co.cn, 2010.
[3] This provision is separate from education specifically related to the medical professions.

REFERENCES

All primary and secondary schools in Beijing achieved the standards for smoking-free campus. (2010, July 17). *Beijing Daily*. Retrieved from http://xiaoxue.eol.cn/yao_wen_9108/ 20100716/t20100716_ 497095.shtml.

China Education and Research Network. (n. d.). *Physical education in China*. Retrieved from http://www.edu.cn/20010101/21914.shtml.

China launches health education program to reduce chronic diseases. (2005, January 24). *Xinhua News Agency*. Retrieved from http://english.peopledaily.com.cn/200501/24/eng20050124_ 171656. html

China still smoking as WHO's deadline arrives. (2011, January 10). *Shanghai Daily*. Retrieved from http://www.china.org.cn/china/2011-01/10/content_21704023.htm.

Chinese Central Government. (2011). *The Central People's Government of the People's Republic of China* [website]: http://www.gov.cn/gzdt/2010-07/13/content_1653147.htm.

Li, H., & Huang, L. (2009). Health, education and economic growth in China: Empirical findings and implications. *China Economic Review, 20*, 374–387.

Liu, G. Z., & Zhang, W. (2008). School library support of health education in China: A preliminary study. *International Electronic Journal of Health Education, 11*, 13–31.

Liu, W. (2008). 1988–2007: Woguo qingshaonian xing jiaoyu yanjiu zongshu [1988–2007: A summary of the research on sex education for adolescents in China]. *Zhongguo Qingnian Yanjiu, 3*, 50–57.

Liu, Y., & Fang, S. (2000). *The efforts of an NGO in China on AIDS prevention and control*. Paper presented at the International Conference on AIDS, July 9–14, 2000.

Ministry of Education. (2010). *The blueprint for medium and long-term national educational reform and development (2010–2020)*. Retrieved from http://www.gov.cn/jrzg/2010-07/29/content_ 1667143.htm.

Population Studies Center, University of Philadelphia. (n. d.). *Gansu Survey of Children and Families* (n. d.). *Introduction*. Philadelphia, PA: Author. Retrieved from http://china.pop.upenn.edu/Gansu/ intro.htm

Qian, J., Cai, M., Tang, S., Xu, Li., L., & Critchely, J. A. (2010). Trends in smoking and quitting in China from 1993 to 2003: National Health Service Survey data. *Bulletin of the World Health Organization, 88*, 769–776. Retrieved from http://www.who.int/bulletin/volumes/88/10/09-064709/en/.

Ross, H. (2006). Challenging the gendered dimensions of schooling: The state, NGOs, and transnational alliances. In G.A. Postiglione (Ed.), *Education and social change in China: Inequality in a market economy* (pp. 25–52). Armonk, NY: M. E. Sharpe.

Students required to do 1 hour physical activity a day. (2006, December 26). *Xinhua News Agency*. Retrieved from http://china.org.cn/english/education/193876.htm.

200 million Chinese overweight, obesity expected to rise sharply. (2004, October 13). *People's Daily Online*. Retrieved from http://english.peopledaily.com.cn/200410/13/eng20041013 _160102.html.

Yimin Wang
Indiana University
Bloomington, Indiana
USA
email: yimwang@indiana.edu

NEIL TAYLOR, FRANCES QUINN, MICHAEL LITTLEDYKE AND
RICHARD K. COLL

28. THE INFLUENCE OF CONTEXT ON HEALTH EDUCATION

Observations, Conclusions and Recommendations

INTRODUCTION

This book follows two previous publications put out by Sense Publishers—
Science Education in Context and *Environmental Education in Context*, each of
which offered ideas and viewpoints from authors in mainly non-Western
countries. Given our interests and experience, it was perhaps a logical
progression for us to conceptualize a book about *health education* and to again
focus largely on non-Western contexts. Three of us have been involved in
teaching health education and three of us have lived and worked in non-Western
countries and experienced a range of health systems and health education
regimes at first hand. All of us have a background in science and environmental
education. Certainly, the links between the three aspects of education, that is,
science, the environment, and health, are strong. Science underpins many aspects
of health and health education, and the state of the environment can have a
marked effect on the health of individuals and communities. For example, air and
water quality are crucial environmental factors that can significantly affect
respiratory and digestive health respectively.

Furthermore, health education, like environmental education, is concerned, to a
large extent, with behavioral change. As such, it lends itself to *action orientation*.
It can be argued that health education, again like environmental education, is a
government, community, and individual responsibility. But key to effecting change
and improving health is an informed citizenry. However, as Carvalho points out in
Chapter 5 of this book, "Changing to healthier behaviors is a relatively complex
process that depends, among other factors, on each individual's personal attitudes
toward general health, health risks, and health-related topics (nutrition, sexuality,
etc.)."

As we explained in the introductory chapter, the theoretical basis to this book
is derived from sociocultural theories of learning. We agree that concepts of
health, particularly those of young people, are shaped by many factors—peers,
school, family, and various media, to name but a few. While many of these
beliefs are in keeping with those of the medical and health communities, children
in particular may construct views at odds with these communities. To appreciate
this problem, we only have to consider the "misinformation" associated with
sexual health, such as erroneous accounts about the ways in which sexually

N. Taylor, F. Quinn, M. Littledyke and R.K. Coll (eds.), Health Education in Context, 261–270.

transmitted diseases are passed on (see, for example, Taylor & Brierley, 1992). While misinformation is not always harmful, it can, in certain situations, be damaging.

The role of health education is clearly vital in developing an informed citizenry. However, providing this form of education in the most effective way tends to be difficult. In most curricula, health education is not a discrete subject in its own right but is integrated into other subject areas. Furthermore, it can be treated formally in the school system of a country and non-formally through projects in the community. Even within the school system, health education can be taught as part of the core curriculum or through less formal avenues. All of these issues have come to light in the chapters in this book.

The sections that follow draw out some of the key, and in many cases common, observations from the chapters. We then use these to develop a number of tentative recommendations for health education.

COORDINATION OF HEALTH EDUCATION INITIATIVES

The first observation is the very positive one that all of the governments across the diverse group of countries featured in this book are involved in promoting health education, often in conjunction with local and international non-governmental organizations (NGOs).

However, many countries report a *lack of coordination and effective cooperation* between key government sectors, in particular the Ministries of Health and Education. Tagivakatini and Waqanivalu argue that in the island nations of the Pacific region (Chapter 2), partnerships between these ministries are the exception rather than the rule; in general, health education initiatives tend to remain almost exclusively with the health sector. The authors from Namibia (Chapter 15) report a "clear gap" between what is happening in the Ministry of Health and in the Ministry of Education, while in Ethiopia (Chapter 14) informants interviewed by the authors unanimously described a lack of inter-ministerial collaboration between various sectors, such as the Ministries of Health, Education, and Agriculture. This apparent lack of cooperation is an unfortunate situation because these ministries doubtless have expertise that, used together, should assist in communicating the best information in the most effective way to individuals.

HEALTH IN CHANGING CONTEXTS

Societal and environmental changes in a number of countries are affecting health in different ways, but some general patterns are apparent.

First, there appears to have been a significant increase in *lifestyle diseases* globally. These diseases, as the name suggests, have for a long time been associated with Western countries and the "Western" lifestyle. However, a number of authors from non-Western countries report a rapid increase in potentially life-threatening conditions associated with obesity, in particular heart disease and diabetes. Yahya and Ali report (Chapter 21) a 250% increase in Malaysia in diabetes over the past 20 years. In China (Chapter 27), the Health Ministry has identified more than 20 million people with diabetes and a further 200 million potentially at risk from this condition because they are overweight. This increasing trend is also reported for Brunei (Chapter 24), Hong Kong (Chapter 23), Hungary (Chapter 6), and Thailand (Chapter 22). As countries continue to develop, their middle classes grow, and lifestyles become more sedentary, obesity and its associated health issues are likely to become an increasing challenge for health educators and a major strain on health systems.

Vietnam (Chapter 26) provides an example of the second social pattern evident in the country reports. There, economic reform has produced considerable economic benefits but, according to authors Dang and Weiss, this has come at a social cost. In response to increased economic opportunity, parents often work long hours, with many young children left alone for substantial periods of time without adult supervision. This change appears to be taking a toll on the *mental health* of some students. Recent research in Vietnam indicates that up to 20% of students had, according to professional judgments, experienced significant mental illness.

Families are also becoming smaller in Thailand (Chapter 22), with extended families increasingly being replaced by nuclear families. In nuclear family settings, parents tend to spend less time with their children, a situation that appears to be leading to mental-health-related problems in some adolescents, often manifesting as substance abuse and aggressive behavior. In some developing countries, such as Thailand, health issues are often perceived as belonging to Western societies, but rapid economic development and the decline in support provided by extended families suggests these problems will become much more prevalent in non-Western contexts.

A third aspect of health being affected by societal change is *ageing*. For example, Holmes and Joseph, writing within the context of Sri Lanka (Chapter 17), argue that rapidly ageing populations bring an urgent need to re-orient primary health care and health promotion toward healthy ageing. In particular, the authors consider that preparation for healthy ageing is an important concept, and that health education efforts should also aim to reach those in middle age before they retire. Holmes and Joseph point out that older people make significant social, cultural, and economic contributions to their families and communities. They often undertake childcare, domestic and agricultural work, guide young people, and influence reproductive, maternal, and child health choices. However, their ability to contribute is often undermined by chronic health conditions, poor nutrition, and preventable disability. To facilitate healthy ageing in Sri Lanka, various communities throughout the country have established Elders' Clubs, which promote good physical and mental health practices amongst the elderly.

Finally, the predicted impacts of climate change on many of the countries represented in this volume are an emerging aspect of changing health contexts. Mani, Banerjee, Pant, Porwal, and Godura outline the role of education in India (Chapter 18) as an adaptation to the potential health impacts of climate change.

SEXUAL HEALTH

The area of *sexual health* continues to be a very sensitive one in a number of countries. Writing about India, and specifically the state of Maharashtra (Chapter 20), Sharda and Watts argue that the increasing incidence of AIDS, sexual abuse, and teenage pregnancies signals an urgent need for effective sex education in India. However, attempts to introduce such education have been enormously contentious and have met with strong opposition, often based on the argument that sex education is at odds with the country's social and cultural ethos. Thus, despite young people accounting for almost one quarter of the population of India, and the authors contending that the reproductive health needs of youth are generally poorly understood and are ill-served, the state government of Maharashtra has been forced to withdraw its sex education program.

In Thailand (Chapter 22), cultural sensitivity is also a major barrier to effective sex education. According to the chapter's authors, Kruatong and Dahsah, open discussions about sex between parents and youth or in the classroom are generally taboo. In addition, sex education is taught in very academic terms in Thai schools, focusing on the biology of sexual reproduction and not sexual practice in a social context. Thus, it is unlikely to help address young people's questions and concerns in this area.

Similarly, Phiri (Chapter 10) describes the "denial syndrome" evident in Malawi, where government routinely denies the incidence of HIV/AIDS in the country and, more recently and overtly, of homosexual practices in Malawi. Here, a range of community groups are educating the population about HIV/AIDS, which is particularly important in a context where many of the country's youth do not attend school. In contrast, Conradie (Chapter 11) makes evident the important role that education plays in dealing with the challenges surrounding ethical conduct of clinical trials of HIV/AIDS treatments being conducted in South Africa.

FORMAL HEALTH EDUCATION SETTINGS AND PEDAGOGY

The importance of formal health education in schools is highlighted by many authors. One such is Moronkola, who points out that in Nigeria (Chapter 12) health education interventions by NGOs, although very valuable, are often short term and focused on specific health issues. However, marginalization of health education in some formal education settings, resulting in particular from the focus on *high-stakes examinations*, impedes its practical integration even when it is formally included in curricula. In Turkey (Chapter 7), for example, a high-stakes national examination system appears to create the impression that health education is "trivial" because it is not included in the national examination regime.

This also appears to be the case in China (Chapter 27). Wang reports that Chinese education, especially at the primary and secondary school levels, is generally an examination-oriented educational system. She says that while this situation is slowly changing, the examination culture is still dominant in most Chinese schools. Wang also points out that health education is predominantly concerned with the wellbeing of individuals and of the community, making measurement of associated learning outcomes difficult in the short term. The situation in China is further exacerbated by the fact that health education is not a mandated component of the curricula of teacher-education programs at the tertiary level. This situation creates tension within the teaching force, especially because there is no shared understanding of the most effective strategies for implementing health education.

Perhaps not surprisingly, given observations made by Coll and Taylor (2008) on science education and by Taylor, Littledyke, Eames, and Coll (2009) on environmental education, a number of chapter authors also regard *formalistic didactic teaching* as a major impediment to effective health education. Once again, this situation is often driven by the competitive examination systems outlined above. Bhutta, for example, reports that in Pakistan (Chapter 19) didactic teaching approaches at primary level hinder the implementation of the health curriculum and thereby limit promotion of good health for children and their communities. Bhutta goes on to argue for teaching health education interactively so that children learn more than just facts about health. Health education, she claims, must contribute to the development of appropriate health behaviors, positive attitudes, and the promotion of community-wide health and wellbeing. This point was also made by Ambusaidi and Al-Balushi, who argues for more learner-centered strategies in health education in Oman (Chapter 3). Examples of interactive and engaging learner-centered approaches are provided by Ajiboye and Afolabi in their description of "enter-education" (entertainment education) in Nigeria (Chapter 16), and by Wanyama and O-Saki in their account of the child-to-child curriculum in East Africa (Chapter 13).

The issue of implementing health education effectively at the school level is clearly difficult, given some of the issues outlined above and the range of additional concerns. As Platje and Słodczyk point out in relation to Poland (Chapter 9), various socioeconomic factors are rarely addressed in health education programs and so affect its success. In this respect, Ishak and Omar's (Chapter 25) description of the concept of sustainable school development in Sabah shows how health issues can be more broadly incorporated into education for sustainable development. The need to harness schools as a hub and a catalyst for broader family and community health education is also recognized by many of this book's authors, including Gvozdeva and Kirilina from Russia (Chapter 8).

One project that appears to take account of these issues, at least to some extent, is the *World Health Organization's* (WHO) *Health Promoting Schools Program*. This program, or an adaptation of it, appears to have been taken up by a good number of countries. Pakistan (Chapter 19), for example, used the program as a model for its national Health Action Schools project. According to the chapter's author, Bhutta, this initiative has contributed to improving children's health knowledge and self-esteem in the target schools. Lebanon (Chapter 4) has also embraced the health promoting schools concept, using it as the basis for establishing a network of health clubs.

The health promoting schools initiative has been widely taken up in the Pacific region (Chapter 2), with 17 small island nations adopting it. Their doing so appears to have resulted in a number of benefits. In several countries (e.g., Fiji, Palau, and the Cook Islands), adoption of the program has resulted in collaboration between the Ministries of Health and Education, often accompanied by the signing of memoranda of understanding. Health promoting schools has also resulted in the development of regional and local networks and the sharing of ideas.

The program appears flexible enough to allow individual countries to address their own particular health issues and to engage with a broad range of NGOs. However, perhaps the most important aspect of this initiative has been the shift in approach from health education to health promotion—a shift that should place greater responsibility on teachers, schools, and administrators to create environments, relationships, and policies that support the program. If implemented effectively, it should, as Tagivakatini and Waqanivalu (the authors of Chapter 2) contend, ensure that schools become places where all members of the school community work together to promote and protect the health of students, staff, families, and community members. As WHO (1998) emphasizes, a health promoting school is one that is constantly strengthening its capacity as a healthy setting for living, learning, and working.

Health promoting schools seems to align with the competency-building, action-oriented approach to health advocated by Carvalho in Chapter 5. Carvalho argues that schools should extend their purview beyond health risks and diseases to a focus on developing the experiences and skills that give children and young people the agency to improve their own health and wellbeing and that of others in their community. This situation, Carvalho reminds us, is one that enhances students' learning outcomes. Carvalho also argues against an exhaustive topic-by-topic approach to health education. She suggests that a more effective approach is to develop children's and young people's life skills and competencies so that they can consider the different health topics within the reality of the social and environmental contexts of their lives. However, such an approach, although commendable, may be difficult to implement, given the status of health education in some of the national curricula outlined above.

Finally, advances in *technology* may offer ways of better communicating health education. In Thailand (Chapter 22), PATH, an international nonprofit organization committed to solving health problems, has employed websites and interactive computer technology offering, for example, role-play games, to promote sexual health. Even in very poor countries such as Ethiopia (Chapter 14), effective electronic resources are available. UNESCO has developed two electronic, interactive resources on HIV/AIDS. These are available for free and can be used with any computer that has a CD-ROM drive, in any school. As computers become more widely available, such resources may offer a more cost-effective way than traditional paper-based media of disseminating health information.

RECOMMENDATIONS

The above observations lead us to suggest several ways in which many of the contexts reported here could strengthen health education.

Certainly, it seems appropriate for Ministries of Health and Education to work collaboratively in the area of health education. Given that one of the normal roles of health ministries is to monitor health conditions and identify issues of concern, they should be able to provide the most appropriate and current information on health issues in any particular country. Because addressing health problems or potential problems, such as rising rates of obesity, requires effective education, ministries of education should be the agencies best placed to communicate information from health ministries to large sectors of the population. That communication, in most instances, can most effectively be channeled through schools, which, particularly in developing countries, are often central to community life. If these key government ministries can work effectively together, then this collaboration should bring synergy to health education.

Recommendation 1: Those involved in any national health education initiative should ensure that appropriate ministries or departments are consulted and encouraged to work together.

A number of countries reported that health education within the formal education sector is presented in ways that fail to engage children. This situation is often due to formalistic teaching, a highly competitive examination system, the low status of health education, or some combination of these factors. This style of teaching prevents children from developing the sorts of competencies that might be anticipated in health education. However, the health promoting schools project (WHO, 1998), reported on very favorably by a number of authors from different contexts, offers a promising alternative. The whole school approach implicit in this initiative, and particularly the links that it forges with the community, appears to present health education in a more relevant manner than the type of health education that occurs in more formal classroom settings. Authors reported that implementation of the health promoting schools concept was effective in engaging children and developing their competence.

Recommendation 2: Where countries are already involved in the WHO health promoting schools project, governments should continue to support this. Those countries not already involved should consider joining the program, given the positive reports that it has received.

Some countries reported that societal changes, particularly the move from extended to nuclear families, was tending to have a detrimental impact on the mental health of young people. The extended family often offers a support network in contexts where government support for families may be minimal, so it is perhaps not surprising that abandoning this network may increase stress on families. Because this is a relatively recent phenomenon, albeit a rapid one, research may be required to determine not only its social impact but also its mental health impact, on children in particular.

Recommendation 3: In countries where there is evidence of a rapid transition from extended to nuclear family structures, research should be undertaken to determine the likely impact of this societal change on children's mental health and the measures that can be put in place to protect and promote children's mental health and wellbeing.

The issue of ageing populations is proving very challenging for a number of Western countries, in particular because of the strain this development is beginning to put on health systems. However, as Homes and Joseph point out in Chapter 17, some developing countries are also experiencing rapidly ageing populations. Again, societal change is having a mediating influence on this issue. The decline of the extended family has led to more old people becoming isolated, a situation that can adversely affect their health. The concept of preparation for healthy ageing in this context seems a very appropriate one, and the establishment of Elders' Clubs appears to have had significant success in addressing some of the health issues confronting older people in Sri Lanka.

> *Recommendation 4:* Governments and NGOs should explore the possibility of establishing networks of Elders' Clubs where they do not already exist. In establishing such clubs, a firm focus should be placed on educating older people in key aspects of health and wellbeing.

Finally, although information and communication technologies (ICT) are not available in all communities, access is increasing. Mobile phones can often be used in even quite remote communities in developing countries, and schools increasingly are being provided with computers. These technologies offer the opportunity to disseminate information about important health issues to large sectors of the population at a relatively low cost, particularly when that cost is compared to the costs associated with the more traditional distribution of paper-based media.

> *Recommendation 5:* Governments and NGOs should identify the extent to which ICT can be used to convey health education to both urban and rural populations and identify appropriate health-related packages for distribution. Trials could be carried out on the effectiveness of using ICT and social media to convey messages before full-scale employment is attempted.

SOME CONCLUDING THOUGHTS

Although this book can provide only a "snapshot" of what is occurring in health education internationally, it is encouraging to note the diversity of initiatives being undertaken across a wide range of countries. The book also illustrates just how context-dependent health can be. Each country has its own particular set of health issues and priorities, which means that education programs need to be contextualized to take account not only of these but also of different cultural and religious mores.

However, common themes have emerged from the chapter accounts, and the information provided gives countries opportunity to learn from the experience of others. As with all forms of education, financial considerations play a part in the amount of support available. In purely financial terms, investing in effective health education ultimately may pay significant dividends. There appear to be some looming global health problems, perhaps the most notable being those associated with obesity. These problems have the potential to put health systems under major strain and to result in huge costs. Appropriate action-oriented education can help to change people's behaviors and significantly reduce the impact of these concerns. So, investment in health education in the short term may result in significant savings in the longer term.

Despite the political support for improving health in developing countries articulated in the Millennium Development Goals (WHO, 2005), and despite significant associated financial commitments, it appears that there has been very slow progress in achieving these health goals in some of the world's poorest countries. We hope that the stories and commentary in this book will illuminate some of the impediments to progress as well as make apparent successful initiatives from insiders' perspectives, and thereby highlight the role that education potentially has to contribute to the better health and wellbeing of people across a diverse range of contexts.

REFERENCES

Coll R. K., & Taylor, N. (Eds.). (2008). *Science education in context: An international perspective of the influence of context on science curriculum development, implementation and the student-experienced curriculum*. Rotterdam, the Netherlands: Sense Publishers.

Taylor, N., & Brierley, D. (1992). The impact of the law on the development of a sex education program at a Leicestershire comprehensive school. *Journal for Pastoral Care and Personal and Social Education, 10*(1), 23–29.

Taylor, N., Littledyke, M., Eames, C., & Coll, R. K. (Eds.). (2009). *Environmental education in context: An international perspective on the development of environmental education*. Rotterdam, the Netherlands: Sense Publishers.

World Health Organization (WHO). (1998). *WHO's global school health initiative: Health promoting schools*. Geneva, Switzerland: Author.

World Health Organization (WHO). (2005). *Health and the Millennium Development Goals*. Geneva Switzerland, Author.

Neil Taylor, Frances Quinn and Michael Littledyke
School of Education
University of New England
Australia
email: ntaylor6@une.edu.au

Richard K. Coll
Faculty of Science and Engineering
University of Waikato
Hamilton
New Zealand